D1124572

After the Dance

MY LIFE *with* MARVIN GAYE

Jan Gaye

with David Ritz

Amistad

An Imprint of HarperCollins*Publishers*

The names and identifying characteristics of certain individuals have been changed to protect their privacy.

HarperCollins books may be purchased for educational, business, or sales promotional use. For information, please e-mail the Special Markets Department at SPsales@harpercollins.com.

FIRST EDITION

Designed by Suet Yee Chong

Library of Congress Cataloging-in-Publication Data has been applied for.

ISBN: 978-0-06-213551-3

15 16 17 18 19   OV/RRD   10 9 8 7 6 5 4 3 2 1

This book is dedicated to my children, Nona and Frankie; and my grandson, Nolan Pentz. We grew up together. We were three, and thankfully now we are four. There is a certain sadness that comes with accepting that Marvin did not live to see our children grow up and that his grandson will never know him in this life. His spirit stays close to us all, often through his music. His message to all of us is never forgotten. Save the children. They are the future. Seek peace and love through understanding and compassion.

"If you cannot find peace within yourself,
you will never find it anywhere else."

"I sing about life."
—Marvin Gaye 1939–1984

Contents

After the Dance

Distant Lover

The love story started in 1964 when I was eight.

On this May afternoon, approximately six months after the assassination of John F. Kennedy and three months after the arrival of the Beatles to the United States, I was seated in front of the black-and-white television that set atop Mama Ruth's Magnavox entertainment console. Louis McKay was seated next to me. When *American Bandstand* came on, we broke into smiles. Louis loved the opening act, Bobby Freeman singing "C'mon and Swim," an R&B novelty dance tune.

"He's cute," said Louis.

"Not as cute as Marvin," I said, my eyes fixed on the second performer, Marvin Gaye, singing "How Sweet It Is."

"He can't dance as good as Bobby," said Louis.

I didn't bother to argue. At that moment spoken words no longer mattered. My heart was speaking words that took me by surprise.

I had an instant crush.

"Janis!" Louis yelled. "You look like you're going crazy! You look like you've lost your mind."

I didn't hear Louis's screams. I was lost—lost in my little-girl love. I had a very rich imagination and was convinced that I would meet Marvin Gaye one day. I had all of his 45s and albums. I would study pictures of him. I would sing along, listening to him and Tammi Terrell on my phonograph, while imagining their romance. When I shared my love for Marvin, my friends told me I was crazy. I thought it was a crazy dream, too, but I still held on to it. I went to school with celebrities. I read stories about Elvis and Priscilla, Jerry Lee Lewis and Myra, and I felt like if I ever met Marvin, maybe I could be his girlfriend or wife. After all, my mother told me that she dreamed of my father before she actually met him. I just knew it could happen to me, too.

Dreaming of Marvin was a temporary escape from the foster home where I lived. Later I'd learn that it was, in fact, an unlicensed operation that flew under the radar. Social services had no knowledge of its existence. The woman who ran the place, Ruth Williams, known to the children as Mama Ruth, answered to no one.

Ruth was my primary caretaker from ages fourteen months to fourteen years. Ruth was both my guardian and tormentor. She renamed me Janis Williams, as though she were my biological mother. Because of my light complexion, freckled face, and curly locks, I was Ruth's golden child.

The rambling two-story house, built in the twenties and situated in central Los Angeles just off Pico Boulevard, housed some twelve children, two of whom were the stepsons of jazz singer Billie Holiday—Craig and Louis McKay. Because my dad was Slim Gaillard, a famous jazz singer himself, I felt a special bond with the McKay boys. In her mink wrap and fabulous wide-brimmed chapeau, Miss Holiday came to the home only once. She was a lady of ultrachic style and mysterious beauty. Slim was equally mysterious. A super-slick hipster who spoke his own brand of bebop lingo—he actually wrote an entire dictionary of a lexicon called Vout—Slim showed up no more than once a year to visit me, the sixteenth of his seventeen children. He always called me sweetheart.

Eight years later, sweet sixteen had come and gone.

I was no longer Janis Williams.

I had been reinvented as Janis Hunter, about to celebrate my seventeenth birthday. Three years had passed since I had left Mama Ruth's home. Since then, I had done all I could to suppress the long nightmare of sexual abuse.

My mother, Barbara, had taken me in. My mother's husband, Earl Hunter, had lovingly accepted me as his own child.

Mom was a white woman of Irish and French descent with dark hair and blue eyes. Although her first two husbands had been white, she was attracted to black men like Slim and Earl, hyper-hip characters with street style and extravagant swag. I saw the remote Slim as Father, but Earl—warm, loving, and protective—as Daddy.

Ed Townsend, a music producer, was part of Mom's circle of hipsters. He was forty-three, close to Mom's age, but to me he looked sixty-three. He spoke about a hit song he'd written long ago—"For Your Love"—and was not shy about his success in the music business. But none of this talk interested me until I heard Ed speak the two words that caused my heart to flutter:

Marvin Gaye.

"What about Marvin Gaye?" I asked.

"I'm producing his new album," said Ed.

"Oh, sure," I said, laughing. "I don't believe you."

"Ed's telling the truth," said Barbara.

"I still don't believe him."

"Would you believe me if I got Marvin Gaye to come over here to meet you and your mom?" he asked.

"Maybe," said Mom, "you could get him to come sing at the baby's seventeenth birthday party."

"I can do that," said Ed.

I thought about the possibility and wondered whether it would actually happen or if it was just a fantasy too good to come true. Despite my doubts, I told my friends that it *was* coming true. Marvin Gaye really was coming to serenade me on my birthday. My friends were skeptical, but ultimately they bought into my dream. No matter how improbable, they convinced themselves that Marvin was going to show up.

Mom decorated the cake and placed seventeen candles on top. At least twenty of my schoolmates came, including my close friends Destiny, Michelle, and Karen. To build up the excitement, we put on Marvin's records—*What's Going On* and *Trouble Man*. Months earlier, looking at the cover photo of *Trouble Man*, Destiny and I decided he was hands down the sexiest creature alive. Now that gorgeous creature would soon be walking through the door. We talked, we danced, but mainly we waited for the arrival of the superstar that all of us had heard on the radio and seen on television.

An hour passed. Then two. Then three.

Finally, I had to face facts: he wasn't coming. Some of my friends taunted me, saying, "I knew he'd never show." Others were sympathetic. Either way, I was humiliated. I felt like a fool. I never wanted to hear the name Marvin Gaye again.

But when I heard the name a week later, my heart changed my mind. My heart went wild. This time Marvin wasn't coming to me; I was going to him. Ed Townsend was taking me and Mom to the studio where Marvin was recording. I was going to get to meet the man who had danced through my dreams ever since I was eight, convincing me that, were we ever to meet, we would find each other irresistible.

Now fate was arranging that meeting.

Now fate was moving me in Marvin's direction.

Now fate was upon me—pressuring me to select an outfit that would seal a deal that had long lived in my imagination.

The outfit had to be perfect. The outfit had to be irresistible. I couldn't stop laughing to myself. It was all too good to be believed.

I chose a blue-and-ecru gingham shirt that tied at the waist. Being top-heavy, I chose a black leotard to wear underneath so I could unbutton the shirt and reveal the full form of my breasts. I chose skintight bell-bottom jeans and blue suede platforms. The only thing missing was a coat.

Mom, who lived an uninhibited life, had invited one of her more eccentric friends to stay with us. This was Pearline, a classy booster with taste. I especially loved her gray leather coat trimmed in fox with an oversize fox collar. To my starstruck eyes, this was the most fabulous fashion item the world had ever seen.

"Please, Pearline," I pleaded. "Can I wear it, just for this one evening?"

"You can," she said with a broad smile and easy laugh. "You better, girl."

I put my hair in braids, foolishly thinking that they'd make me look older.

The leather, the fox collar, the gold hoop earrings, the platforms—everything was snug, tight, and right. I put on minimal makeup, lip gloss, and blush.

"You need the right perfume," said Pearline, handing me a bottle of fragrance. Its heady musk of jasmine dew excited my skin. My neck tingled. The scent was outrageously sensuous.

Mom and I drove to the studio. Mom wanted to meet Marvin as much as I did. At forty-four, Mom was still a desirable woman with an alluring hippie-bohemian style.

But I had my youth. I had Pearline's fox-trimmed leather coat. I could not be outdone, not even by my captivating mother.

We arrived at MoWest, Motown's recording studio in West Hollywood, two women looking to reach a star. My curiosity had become an obsession. I had to know whether this Marvin Gaye character was real.

I heard his voice before I saw his face. His voice filled the studio. His voice filled my head and invaded my heart. Not a single voice, but many voices—the Marvin Gaye signature self-styled harmonies, Marvin singing in falsetto, moaning low and soaring high, Marvin shadowing himself, echoing sounds—sweet lush sounds—emanating from his darkest, deepest soul.

The sounds washed over me, sheets of silk and satin, notes soft as cashmere, come-hither strands spirit-filled and seductive, floating sounds that carried the promise of romance, the promise that all pain would vanish as long as the sound of his voice, effortless and ethereal, continued to call us into his world: a world of lightness, ease, and pleasure without end.

I had entered his world—a lush space that felt safe and soft and beautiful. It was a world apart, a world of pure sound. It felt like a world of pure love. It was also a world filled with the fragrance of pot.

Ed Townsend, in charge of the control booth, took over. He indicated that Mom and I should sit on a couch in front of the engineer at the sound board. Marvin was on the other side of the glass, singing into a microphone. His face matched his song. His face expressed a gentleness that carried the same promise as the song: that life, lifted into melody and framed by harmony, never has to be harsh. His sound eased all pain. There was distant pain in his voice, but pain transformed into beauty. His face was beautiful. The shape of his head appeared noble—his smiling eyes, the slight flare of his nostrils, the contour of his lips. His outfit—a faded army-green shirt, faded denim jeans snug at the crotch, a red wool skullcap, dusty work boots—was the essence of cool. He stood tall, regal, relaxed.

I thought of his image on the covers of his albums that I had studied for so long—*What's Going On* and *Trouble Man*. In those images he appeared distant. Here he was present.

I felt myself in the presence of a prince, impossibly handsome yet familiar and down-home funky.

As Marvin continued to sing, I stood. Before I removed Pearline's fabulous coat, I wanted Marvin to see it. Even more, I wanted him to see my body. When I caught his glance, I went to the restroom and unbraided my hair.

"Why did you do that?" asked my mom when I returned.

"The braids were too tight," I said. "They were irritating my scalp."

In truth, though, I thought my black wavy hair, dramatically cascading down my shoulders, would draw even more attention.

At the first break in singing, Marvin came to the control booth and headed in my direction. Ed came running to make the introduction.

"This is my girl Janis," Ed told Marvin. "The birthday girl."

Marvin spoke in a whisper-quiet voice that mirrored his music. His enunciation was perfect. His voice was so soft that I had to lean in to listen. His breath smelled like pot mixed with apples, fresh and sweet.

"Sorry I missed your party," he said. "I'm afraid I got caught up working late. Please accept my apologies."

"No problem," I managed to say. I was touched by his gentlemanly manners. I was touched by everything about him.

I was also afraid that, by calling me "his girl," Ed had given Marvin the impression that I was his daughter. But before I had a chance to set the record straight, Marvin had moved on to greet Mom. I could see that she was as excited to meet him as I was. I shot Mom a quick glance that said, *Don't even think about it!*

Marvin lit a joint and passed it around. The pot was strong, the high powerful. Mom and I had smoked pot together before. Having grown up in the drug culture of her and her friends, weed was nothing new. But this was Marvin Gaye weed, another essential element of his sensuous aura. The high went with the music, the music went with Marvin, and the intoxication was complete.

That night Mom and I were not alone among the guests. He had invited another mother-daughter team to watch him sing. The other mother, like mine, was also attractive. In fact, she wore a full-length gold-sequined gown. Her daughter, like me, was dressed provocatively. It was evident that, just as both Mom and I were deeply drawn to Marvin's seductive grace, so were our rivals.

What I didn't know—and would only later learn—was that Marvin reveled in rivalry. Berry Gordy, the founder of Motown, had taught him the art of pitting artist against artist, producer against producer, and woman against woman.

The gold-gown lady was all over Marvin, practically pawing him as she raved about her super-talented daughter, an aspiring singer.

All the while I sat back, noticing Marvin noticing me. We exchanged glances, not words. I saw that Gold Gown was coming on too strong. Gold Gown was wearing him out. I sensed that Marvin wanted to talk to me, but I also knew that silence was my friend. I knew to be cool.

Gold Gown was not reading Marvin right. He was too polite to say so, but he didn't want to be assaulted. He liked quiet. He liked shy. I heard that in his music. I heard that in his speech. Gentleness was the key. Grace was his style. He lived for subtlety. His way was nuanced, not aggressive. Aggression turned him off. Desperately, I wanted to turn him on.

If, as a child watching *American Bandstand*, I had fantasized about him looking at me, I now knew that fantasy was suddenly real. We exchanged a dozen glances. The glances said it all.

When his last song was sung and the session over, I could not leave without approaching him. Gathering up every ounce of courage, I softly tapped his shoulder and whispered, "May I just tell you one little thing, privately?"

"Of course."

Marvin and I walked away from the others.

"What is it?" he asked, scratching his beard and beginning to smile.

"I don't mean to bother you and I don't know if this makes a difference, Marvin, but I just wanted you to know that Ed is not really my father."

"Hmm, I see," he said as he stroked his beard. "That's interesting. I'm glad you told me that. And I'm also glad to have met you. I hope we meet again."

He took my hand in his. I felt the touch of his skin. I longed to kiss his lips as he told me good-bye. I longed to ask him if I could stay to hear more of his heavenly harmonies. I didn't want to leave his world, this cocoon of sweet, seductive sound.

In the car home, I yelled. I screamed. I bounced up and down. I shouted that I had met Marvin Gaye, the most gorgeous man in the world! Marvin Gaye had looked at me, spoken to me, given me his hand!

"Stop yelling!" said Mom. "Stop screaming! Stop jumping up and down!"

"I can't! I have to know if he's going to call me! I have to know if I'm ever going to see him again!"

"I have no idea."

"Tell me it's possible."

"Anything is possible, but not everything is right."

"What could be wrong?"

"He's much older, he's married. Ed says he has a seven-year-old son."

None of those words registered with me. I was convinced that on this night of nights my world had turned upside down. I had met the love of my life.

Sensitive People

Three years earlier, at age fourteen, I had left the unlicensed foster home of Ruth Williams—my part-time mother. I saw Ruth as a small birdlike woman with a knit hat on her head, tiny spectacles framing her intense brown eyes, and a fierce hold on the emotional and physical lives of the children she was paid to protect. She was the woman who shopped at the fashionable Bullocks Wilshire department store for cute little blouses and skirts for me, her favored daughter. Sears was good enough for the other children in her home. But I deserved a higher grade of clothing. I was made to feel special because my skin was not dark and my hair not kinky. I was told that I had "good hair."

Ruth was convinced that I had talent. That's why she made sure I was given piano lessons, ballet lessons with a world-famous dancer, and ice-skating lessons with a champion instructor. I was told—and I believed—that I could become a professional entertainer. Unfortunately, before any of those talents had time to develop, I stopped going to the lessons.

Starting at age six I was subjected to Ruth's "private examinations." The examinations, blatantly inappropriate, went on for years. When I protested, Ruth smacked me. When I asked my mother to take me out of the home, she refused. Mom could continue to take me on weekends, but during the week she needed her privacy as a functioning drug addict.

I called my mother Barbie until I was eight or nine. I had an obsession with Barbie dolls. Through those dolls, and Barbie's house and car, I could escape to a whole different world. My mom's life sort of represented this to me as a young girl—an escape from foster kid life. Ruth was the only woman whom I called Mama. Ruth looked down on my mother. Ironically, Ruth felt as if she was protecting me from a mother whose lifestyle was unsavory.

Mom was part of an informal group of white women drawn to black men. I liked these women. Their names were Leona and Lola and Bonnie and Sheila. In fact, my best friend and roommate at Mama Ruth's was Megan, Sheila's daughter.

As Barbara's daughter, I was confused by both the presence and the absence of a mother who lived a life apart from me. I was Mom's only child and, for all her wildness, she never abandoned me. Mom remained the most consistent presence in my life. The paradox, though, was this: while she never left me, she was always leaving me. Week after week, year after year, I was left in the care of Ruth.

"Barbie is taking me to Disneyland today," I told Ruth.

This happened when I was eight. I'd been waiting for this day all year.

"You're not going anywhere today," said Ruth.

"Why not?"

"I saw what you did at breakfast. You spilled your chocolate milk on the carpet. You tried to clean it up with your napkin, but the stain is still there."

"I'm sorry."

"You'll be a lot sorrier when I get through with you."

When Ruth went to the backyard to rip a thorny switch from a rosebush, I began to cry. I knew what was coming. I had suffered these beatings before. To escape, I ran to another part of the yard where Ruth's sister, Aunt Esther, lived in the back house. Esther had protected me in the past. But Esther wasn't home; her door was locked and there was no escaping. Ruth grabbed me by my arm and dragged me back into the big house.

"Complaining to your mother," said Ruth, "will only make it worse."

The beating left bright red marks on my back and bottom.

"Go to your room," Ruth demanded, "and stay there for the rest of the day."

Megan, who had suffered similar beatings, was waiting for me. Without saying a word, she applied ointment to my skin. In the past when Megan had been whipped, I did the same for her.

It took a long while for my tears to subside. Lying in bed, my only thought was that when Mom comes I'll get to go to Disneyland anyway. Mom had been promising me this trip for months. Mom could take me out whenever she wanted to. Ruth couldn't tell Mom what to do. Barbie was my real mom. I belonged to Barbie, not Ruth.

By lunchtime I was dressed and ready to go. I was sitting by the front door in the living room. When I heard the click-click-click of high heels on the sidewalk, my heart leaped. That was the sound of Mom walking. I hurried to the window and saw my mother approaching. Smoking a Tareyton cigarette, dressed in a green pencil skirt and bright yellow blouse, she looked beautiful. Her ruby-red lipstick matched the hue of her red hair. Her hair was dyed—I'll never forget the precise smell of that dye—and styled fashionably. There was an upbeat spirit to Mom's look that made me feel that everything would be all right.

I watched as my mom took a long drag off her Tareyton before dropping it to the pavement and crushing it with the toe of her right foot.

My mom will crush Ruth. My mom is taking me to Disneyland, happiest place on earth.

"There will be no Disneyland for Janis today," said Ruth, who had gotten to the door before I could even hug my mother.

"We're going!" I screamed. "We have to go! You promised me!"

"What happened?" Mom asked Ruth.

"Janis has been a very bad girl. Last week I bought her a beautiful new outfit for school. You'd think she'd be grateful, but instead she's been talking back to me . . ."

"No, I haven't!" I cried.

"Let Ruth get through," said Mom.

"Janis broke a cup and spilled her chocolate milk on my new carpet—and did so quite intentionally . . ."

"It was an accident," I protested.

"You don't want to reward such behavior, do you?" Ruth asked my mother.

"It's just that I promised to take her to Disneyland . . . ," Mom started to say.

Ruth stiffened up and looked Mom straight in the eye. "If you take her to Disneyland, you can also take her back to your apartment and keep her permanently. She needs discipline. Barbara, you know that I have my rules." I stood between these two women. I looked at Mom, then back at Ruth.

Surely Barbie will take me to Disneyland.

Mom leaned down and said to me, "Look, baby, there'll be lots of other times we can go. I promise I'll take you next month."

Heartbroken, I understood that the balance of power had tilted against me. Ruth had power over Mom. It came down to a single fact: Mom couldn't take care of me. She needed Ruth to do that. She paid Ruth to do that.

Ruth won.

Some six years later, I was fourteen and Ruth had finally been defeated. I had learned to stand my ground. I was full breasted—a perfect 36C—and, at five feet eight, had begun, in spite of my posture problems, to walk with a determined gait. Ruth no longer frightened me. The rage that had built up inside me was about to erupt. Ruth knew to get out of the way.

Mom knew that she could no longer force me to remain at a residence I so deeply loathed. She could no longer ignore my protests. She knew that Mama Ruth's house had caused grave emotional problems for me. She also knew that the Catholic school to which Mama Ruth had sent me employed a nun who had abused the students sexually. Craig McKay and I were among those students.

At fourteen, I'd had enough abuse to last a lifetime.

"I'm coming to live with you," I told Mom, "and that's it."

This was also the moment when the names changed.

I had already changed my name to Janis Hunter. I wanted to have the name of Earl Hunter, the man my mom had married and the warm and loving soul whom I adored.

True, Earl was a big-time coke dealer; and true, he once went to jail for killing a man. In fact, throughout my childhood I watched Earl move in and out of prison for various offenses. But that didn't keep me from loving the attention he lavished upon me. When Earl was around, which was often, he took me for long rides in his tricked-out Bonneville. Originally from Chillicothe, Texas, his speech was a seductive mix of southern drawl and the LA streets. Of all the men moving in and out of Mom's world—among them several celebrated athletes—Earl was by far the coolest. He and Mom fought like cats and dogs, but he always protected me. For most of my life my nuclear family would be fractured, but during these times when Earl was home from prison and Mom was working secretarial or waitressing jobs, I was comforted by a mother-father unity that, no matter how tenuous, afforded me some degree of security.

Mommy and Daddy were, in fact, living together when, at fourteen, I was liberated from Ruth. But life in their duplex on Cochran Avenue in Mid-City Los Angeles would never be *The Adventures of Ozzie and Harriet* or *Father Knows Best*. From the get-go, my life at home was as emotionally confusing as it had been with Ruth.

It was 1971 and the sound of Marvin Gaye's *What's Going On* filled the Hunter household. Earl and Mom played the album continuously. It was music that felt sad and sweet, joyful and jazzy, a new kind of rhythm and blues reflecting the troubled state of the nation.

For Earl and Mom, caught up in a campaign to free Black Panther George Jackson, *What's Going On* was the soundtrack for their growing political conscience. For me, it was simply more gorgeous music—more enchanting harmonies—from a singer whose soul seemed connected to mine. The album did not contain easy-to-digest hits like the songs from Marvin's earlier days—tunes like "How Sweet It Is" or "Pride and Joy." It did not feel forceful or angry or desperate like Marvin's "I Heard It Through the Grapevine." Some of the issues he sang about, like the deteriorating ecology in "Mercy Mercy Me" or the Christian ethos of "Wholy Holy," were above my head, but I never lost track of Marvin's plaintive voice. I was with him throughout the journey.

I studied the pictures on the 33⅓ LP—the photo of a forlorn Marvin singing in the rain; the montage of family members and musicians on the inside of the gatefold album. I realized that this was a very special project from a very special man. He had taken the time to include the lyrics on the sleeve. On a song he called "Right On," he sang about "those of us who got drowned in the sea of happiness." I wondered about that curious line.

How can you drown in happiness?

Is Marvin Gaye drowning?

Is Marvin Gaye happy?

"Marvin Gaye is a serious man," said my daddy Earl as he and Mom leaned back on the living room couch, lit up a joint, and listened to Marvin's "Flyin' High (in the Friendly Sky)."

"Marvin Gaye is a genius," Mom concurred.

Marijuana was a staple in the Hunter household. Mom indulged more frequently than Earl, who, as a highly successful dealer, exhibited more restraint. In their circle of friends, smoking dope and snorting blow were as common as drinking tea and coffee. I didn't think twice about it. I myself had begun to take little hits off half-smoked joints. I liked the feeling.

Listening to Marvin's album, Earl began to break down the meaning. He explained that *What's Going On* was the story of a black man who had returned from Vietnam to an American ghetto decimated by poverty and moral decay. Earl's words made sense, but I was mainly following Marvin's feelings. Even at fourteen, I felt inclined to follow wherever he led. Even at fourteen, I dreamt of entering his world.

This was also the year I lost my virginity to Bryant, the teenage boy who lived in the apartment on the first floor. It was Bryant, by the way, who loved *What's Going On* as much as Earl. Listening to it together, we wore out several copies. Bryant was a good guy, although the sexual experience that took place at a motel on La Cienega Boulevard was hardly earth-shattering. We both lacked experience.

This was also the year that Mom and Earl began their United Prisons Union, a storefront operation on Melrose Avenue designed to help men and women transitioning out of jail. My job was to paint the logo on the window. Feeling the political fervor, I was dying for an Afro, but with my curly hair that just wasn't happening.

The cause attracted the attention of Shirley Sutherland, wife of actor Donald Sutherland. When Shirley and Mom struck up a friendship, Mom urged Shirley to recruit me to babysit her adorable four-year-old twins, Kiefer and Rachel, at their luxurious Beverly Hills home. Bryant came along to help. Diana Ross lived around the corner and her brother Chico became my friend. So did Burt Lancaster's daughter Susan, who, in the midst of her rebellion against her bourgeois parents, actually came to live with Mom and me for a while. She took us to her father's luxurious house in Malibu to go swimming. But Susan seemed happier in our hood. She loved our inner-city alternative culture.

This was all heady stuff: me discovering this new and different Marvin Gaye singing about the mercy of Jesus in his "God Is Love" while moving between the worlds of my mom and dad and the super-rich Hollywood movie stars.

Mom had moved up a bit herself. She found a job in the office of a successful attorney I'll call Luke. As was often the case with Mom, boundaries were blurred between work and play. I never knew if Mom and Luke were lovers. But they were certainly friendly enough for Luke to invite Mom for an afternoon swim one Sunday. Mom was insistent that I come along.

"I want you to have a great time, sweetheart," said Mom as we drove into the rarefied atmosphere of Mulholland Drive. "But be polite. And if you do speak, don't be fresh."

"Don't worry," I said. "I'll be cool. I just wanna go swimming."

We pulled up to a grand estate at the top of a hill. In the driveway were statues of nymphs dancing around cascading fountains. A maid answered the door and led us through the house to the pool. There was a marble staircase, plush white carpeting, and enormous abstract paintings on the wall. Outside, the party was in full swing.

Twenty or so guests were milling about. Mom went over to say hello to two white men in bathing suits who were seated in lounge chairs. They immediately got up to greet us.

Luke, the host, was in his forties. Slight of build, he wore a black toupee and spoke with a thick New York accent. He kissed Barbara on the cheek before looking me over. He liked what he saw. So did his friend whom he introduced as Big Jack—not his real name—a potbellied man with dark eyes and a hairy chest. He stood over six feet and wore a gold Star of David around his neck.

"We have food and drink," said Luke, pointing to a serving table piled high with shrimp, lobster, and bottles of champagne. "We also have other refreshments."

"I'll take the other refreshments," said Mom as Luke handed her a joint.

"If you'd like to change into your swimming suit," Luke told me, "there's a cabana on the other side of the pool."

Walking to the cabana, I stopped to take in the view. A thick layer of brown smog covered the city below.

This is what it means to be rich, I thought. *You leave the dirt behind. You rise above the smog.*

I changed quickly. Putting on my two-piece cobalt-blue bikini, I was aware of the effect it was sure to have on Luke and Big Jack. I knew that my body would be carefully scrutinized. I knew that my physical attributes would be appreciated. I understood that, at least for a few minutes, I would be the focus of attention. I would be the star of this small party.

Walking back to where the adults had assembled, I saw that, after sharing a joint together, the trio had moved on to cocaine. A half dozen thick lines had been laid out on a glass table. As soon as I appeared, though, the snorting stopped. The men looked up at me and broke out into smiles. Mom smiled as well.

In a Lolita-like moment, I felt both shy and excited. I thought about taking off my top. Mom would have had no objections. She had always let me do whatever I wanted.

I recognized the power of my blooming sexuality. I wanted to feel that power even more fully. I wanted to thrill these men.

The longer the argument inside my head went on, the more the drama built, the more intensely the men scrutinized my body. I decided to seize the moment and give them what they wanted. I got in the pool and took off my top. Mom smiled with pride. The men were fixated.

The warm water felt good on my skin. I splashed around for several minutes, wondering if the men were going to join me. I worried that they would grope me. The thought disgusted me. Much to my relief, they were content to smoke, coke, and watch me swim around. At some point Mom and Big Jack got up and went into the house. When I decided to get out of the pool, Luke was there to hand me a large towel. I quickly wrapped it around my waist. Luke motioned for me to relax in a lounge chair next to him. Nervously I sat. A moment or two later Luke leaned in toward me. I noticed that his toupee was tilting to one side, making him look ludicrous. He reached out and took my hand. With his index finger, he gently but insistently rubbed my palm. This was the first time I had been given this signal. Any doubts I might have had about the meaning were dispelled as he moved toward me and pressed his lips against mine. The sensation of his tongue in my mouth was repulsive. I immediately withdrew and, still wrapped tight in the towel, got up from the chair and returned to the cabana, where I showered off the chlorine and changed into my clothes.

Mom was back poolside with Big Jack.

"Let's go," I whispered to my mother.

"What's wrong?"

"I just wanna go," I insisted.

"Luke's about to put some steaks on the grill."

"I don't care. I wanna go."

Seeing that I was dead serious, Mom told the guys that her daughter wasn't feeling well. They tried their best to convince us to stay, but I was insistent. We left.

No words were spoken on the drive home. The radio news reported that President Nixon was pledging to end the war in Vietnam. Muhammad Ali was cleared of draft dodging. Mom switched stations. Marvin Gaye was singing "Inner City Blues."

"Makes me wanna holler," he sang, "throw up both my hands."

The gentle groove helped me deal with the mess of emotions causing my head to throb.

Although the words he sang—"panic is spreading, God knows where we're heading"—were alarming, I was comforted by his voice. His voice eased my pain.

Mushrooms in the Desert

At seventeen, I was obsessed with a single question after meeting Marvin in the studio: *Will he call me?*

My desire to be ushered back into Marvin's magical world was fueled by my unhappiness at home. Since leaving Ruth's three years earlier, I had watched my mother struggle with sanity. Mom's breakdown was precipitated by Earl's infidelity.

It happened when I was fifteen and, on the spur of the moment, Mom hustled me into the car.

"Where are we going to, Mom?"

"Renee's."

Renee was Mom's best friend.

"What's happening at Renee's?" I asked.

"Maybe I'm crazy, but something tells me she's up to something."

Earl's yellow car was in Renee's driveway. That's all Mom needed to see. She raced back home and threw Earl's clothes out on the street. Less than a year later, Renee gave birth to Earl's child.

That was the year Mom retreated into inconsolable depression. Her only comfort came from her dog, Daisy, with whom she became obsessed. She could not stand to be without Daisy for a single second and lavished far more affection on the animal than she did on me, who, at the start of high school, had matured physically. Boys flocked to me, but they were just that—boys. I sought something more. When my teachers praised my intelligence, I began to understand that was the quality I sought in the opposite sex. When another teacher praised my sensitivity, I realized that was the very thing these boys lacked.

I made friends with some of the boys in the Fairfax High crowd, the Jackson brothers—Jackie, Jermaine, and Tito—and a few of their future wives. I also knew Veronica Porsche, who would later marry Muhammad Ali.

That was when I was fifteen.

At seventeen, the day after meeting Marvin, I was waiting for my phone to ring.

A million thoughts raced through my mind. I remembered how, only a week before meeting Marvin, I had encountered Don Cornelius of *Soul Train* fame. I had gone to a Lakers game at the Forum with my friend Destiny, and a couple of the players had invited us to an after-party at the Continental Hyatt House on the Sunset Strip. In a crowded room filled with people who—at least to our impressionable minds—appeared super sophisticated, we tried to be cool. When someone offered me a line, I presumed it was cocaine. Cocaine was hardly anything new to me, and I ingested it quickly. Within minutes, though, I felt sick. I heard someone say that the white powder was heroin, not cocaine. The next thing I knew I was in the bathroom, my head in the toilet, regurgitating like a child with the flu. But being young and healthy, I recovered quickly. I cleaned up and rejoined the party.

Destiny and I were hardly loose girls. We simply wanted to step out on the edge and see what a real after-party was all about. After becoming sick, though, the fascination ended and we decided to call it a night.

On the street in front of the hotel, we were looking to hail a cab, but none were available. That's when Don Cornelius pulled up in a big sedan.

"Be happy to give you ladies a ride," he offered.

Recognizing him immediately, we figured it would be safe. Don was the perfect gentleman.

On the night I had met Marvin, he too had been the perfect gentleman. That was well and good, but had he forgotten me?

The call came the next day. Mom picked up the receiver.

"Hi, Ed," she said. "What's happening?"

I ran over and tried to hear what Ed Townsend was telling my mom. I couldn't make out his words, but I didn't have to. Mom's smile said everything.

When the call was over, Mom said, "Marvin wants to see you again."

"When?"

"Tonight."

"Wow."

"And without me."

My first reaction was that I wanted my mother to come along. I wanted the security of her company. My second reaction, though, was that I didn't want her there. I was thrilled by the thought that Marvin wanted to see me alone.

"Is it okay for me to go alone?" I asked.

"Ed's coming by to pick you up tonight. Ed will be there the whole time. It's perfectly fine."

During lunch, I asked a buddy of Bryant's to sell me weed.

"I need a lid," I said, "but a lid of your best stuff."

Handing me a package wrapped in tinfoil, he assured me that the smoke was top grade. Showing up at the studio with my own dope would show Marvin that I was not a naïve schoolgirl. I was a sophisticated woman.

After school, I hurried home. I took a long time picking out my outfit. The last time I'd started off wearing braids. No braids tonight. Tonight I was letting my hair down.

"Don't forget that Marvin's a married man," said Mom, a half hour before Ed arrived.

"Please, Mom. Am I supposed to believe that you never dated a married man? Besides, Ed told us that Marvin and his wife are separated."

"I'm just looking out for you, sweetheart. I just don't want you to get hurt."

I ignored my mother's words and waited by the window. The minute Ed pulled up, I was out the door and in his car.

As soon as we walked through the doors of the studio, I felt myself safely and blissfully back in Marvin's world. That world was about sound and beauty. He was making beautiful sounds with his voice, singing a chillingly pleading song in which he begged his baby to stay. *Without you in bed beside me*, he implored, *sleep will never come.*

As he sang, his eyes were closed. When he opened them, he looked directly at me, seated on a leather couch in the control room. Marvin was standing on the other side of the glass. His eyes were smiling. He sang for another twenty minutes; I didn't move. It was just me, Ed, the engineer, and Marvin. Unlike last night, there were no other guests, no other mothers or young chicks looking to get next to Marvin.

When he finally took a break and came into the control room, he walked directly to me.

"I'm so happy you came," he said. "I really wanted to see you again."

"I brought you a gift."

I handed him the lid.

"That's really sweet of you," he said. "Why don't you roll us a jay?"

An experienced roller, I twisted up a joint in a few seconds and passed it to Marvin. He lit it up and exhaled. The smell was horrendous.

"Fuckin' elephant weed!" the engineer yelled.

I was humiliated. I wanted to die. I wanted the floor to open up so I could disappear.

"Not so fast, gentlemen," said Marvin, super sensitive to my feelings. "The fragrance might be a little funky, but the dope itself is pretty mellow."

I knew Marvin was lying. The dope was shit. He was just saying that to protect me from the scorn of the others. He *was* sensitive! He *did* care about my feelings!

My emotions soared as he sang for the next several hours. He sang another tender ballad, pleading with a woman not to leave him in the cold. He begged her to stay. The pattern was set: when he sang, his eyes were closed. When his eyes were open, they stared directly at me.

The connection was real.

At about ten P.M., he came back to me and said, "It's getting late and I know you have school tomorrow. Maybe I should run you home. Is it far?"

With my heart hammering, I said, "Not far at all. Olympic and Ogden. But I don't want to be a bother."

"It's not a bother," he said. "It's a distinct pleasure."

I couldn't get over the closeness between Marvin's speaking voice and singing voice. When he spoke, it was as though he was singing. And when he was singing, it was as though he was speaking directly to me. Both voices were painfully tender. Even more than the softness of his tone, I responded to the beauty of his enunciation. Each word came out whole. Each word seemed exactly right. There was a lyricism to his speech—a haunting and lilting quality—unlike any speech I had heard before. His elocution had an easygoing tone; he was down-to-earth, but he was also otherworldly. He spoke with the quiet confidence of a prince.

He spoke very little on the way to my house. I struggled to make small talk but feared that I'd sound young or naïve or foolish. He asked what I thought of his new music.

"I love it," I was quick to say. "I love all your music."

"Well, thank you. That means a great deal to me. When I record, I'm also wondering whether these songs will mean anything to anyone else besides myself."

"I'm sure they will," I said shyly.

He smiled.

I wondered whether I was coming on too strong with all this praise. Shouldn't I be coy? Shouldn't I be cool? I wasn't sure what to say. All I knew was that I loved being in his presence. He made me feel warm and wanted.

When we arrived at the duplex I shared with my mother, I couldn't help but invite him up.

"I don't want to upset your mum," he said, using the British expression. "Besides, I better get back to the studio. I'm terribly late delivering this record."

He walked me to the door and stopped at the bottom of the staircase. That's when my heart stopped.

"I want you to know that it's beautiful being with you," he said. "I hope I can get you to come visit me again."

"I'd love to."

It was then that he placed the palms of his hands on either side of my head. Standing over me, he leaned down and gently kissed my forehead.

"Goodnight, Jan. Sweet dreams."

I thought I'd faint.

The next morning, when I described my evening to my mother, she said, "I'm glad you like him, sweetheart, and I'm glad he likes you. I'm glad you got to hear him sing in the studio again. It's wonderful that he called. But if he doesn't call again, don't take it personally. Sexy singers are a different breed. Believe me, I know. Your father is one of those singers."

Rather than reply to Mom, I groaned.

That night, while I dreamt of Marvin, Mom must have thought of how she had once dreamt of my father, Slim Gaillard. The dream began when, in 1942, fourteen-year-old Barbara listened to the sounds of a romantic and seductively syncopated bebop ballad called "Anytime, Anyplace, Anywhere." She swore to her best friend Cathy that, come hell or high water, one day she'd marry Slim and have his baby. Mom yearned to escape the oppression of the white working-class confines of her Boston family. On the radio and in music magazines, she followed the fortunes of Gaillard and his partner Slam Stewart. The duo managed to combine dance music with the avant-garde jazz of the day. The romantic rhythms spoke of rebellion.

Mom sensed that Slim was a rebel. She read articles that talked about the competitive heat between Slim and Cab Calloway, another entertainer with a thin pencil moustache and gleaming slicked-back hair. Cab represented an older generation of the swing-time music of Duke Ellington and Count Basie. To Barbara, Cab was cornball. Slim was slick. Cab was yesterday. Slim was tomorrow. Slim symbolized adventure, the unknown, daring, dangerous world of dark nightclubs where black men played the mysterious blue music that spoke to Mom's heart.

Even as she grew up, even as she suffered through two unhappy marriages to white men, she never forgot the mysterious blue music of Slim Gaillard. She never gave up the dream of meeting Slim. And then, in 1955, in the middle of the first term of the bland white-bread presidency of Dwight Eisenhower, her dream came true. Mom went to a nightclub where Slim Gaillard was playing.

Mom dressed to look like Lana Turner: low-cut black dress, white-brimmed hat, white gloves. Her brother Don accompanied her. They sat at a table near the stage. The club was dark, the air thick with smoke. Most of the patrons were black. Don was uncomfortable. Mom wasn't. Mom felt at home. Mom drank in the ambience. She sipped a glass of cheap champagne. She was thrilled by the jazz music: she recognized the sounds of Charlie Parker and Billie Holiday, Miles Davis and Sarah Vaughan. Mom's taste was cultivated. She spoke the language of jazz. For years she yearned to share that language with a man of mystery: a musician.

That man was Bulee "Slim" Gaillard. When he walked onto the small stage and started singing in that language of his own—the scat-singing coded language he named Vout—his eyes immediately found Mom. He sang to her. He saw her mouthing the words not only to the lush romantic ballads but to the novelty bop of "Flat Foot Floogie," "Slim Slam Boogie," and "Atomic Cocktail." She was the hippest chick in the club—and he wanted her.

After the first set, he came to her table.

"I've been digging on your white gloves, madam," he said.

"Call me Barbara," she said. "And I've been digging on your music since I was . . . well, quite young."

"You're still quite young, Barbara. And, if I might be bold enough to say so, quite beautiful. Quite enchanting. I just hope I'm not intruding on your date."

"No date," she said. "This is my brother."

"Then this is my lucky night. If your brother has no objections, I have big eyes to take you to dinner after the show."

Before Don could speak, Mom said, "Don't worry about Don. He has to leave early anyway."

The first night was bliss. So was the second. On the third, Slim had to leave for LA.

"Of all the things I've read about you," Mom said before Slim left for the airport, "I still don't know where you come from. You told one writer you're Cuban but another wrote you were born in deep Alabama."

"I'm a citizen of the world, dear Barbara," said Slim. "I come from nowhere and I come from everywhere. Cats catch me if they can. And you, my sweet, have caught me in your Venus flytrap. I'd like to stay, baby, but this brother has to fly away."

"And if I fly after you?" asked Mom.

"I'd flip, flop, and fly. You don't gotta chase me down, sugar, 'cause when it comes to you, I'm down already. You dig?"

"I do."

A week after Slim had flown back to California, Mom scraped up enough bread for a ticket and flew the coop herself. She beat it out to LA and hooked up with Slim for another week of bliss. Didn't matter that he was married. Didn't matter that he had a gang of kids—something like fifteen at the last count. All that mattered was that she had her dream come true. Slim was hers. And then he wasn't.

Slim had to run out on the road where other women were waiting. He couldn't be burdened with Mom. Mom was fun, Mom was wild in bed, Mom was a hip kitty, but Slim was a tomcat looking for other alleys to prowl.

Mom went back to Boston, where she learned she was pregnant with Slim's child. Rather than face the disapproval, she never told her mother. Instead she decided to leave Boston once and for all. She liked what she had seen of LA—the mild weather, the tall palm trees, the highway that hugged the coast going up to Malibu. Besides, Slim was in LA. If she was going to have his child, why not stay in his city? Surely he'd come around to visit.

After I was born in 1956, those visits were few and far between. Slim never denied fatherhood, but neither did he take fatherhood seriously. Money was never forthcoming. Mom knew better than to count on Slim for support. Carrying me in a basket, she went to work as a phone operator. She had affairs with all sorts of men—from blues singer Joe Williams to big-time jocks like basketball's Ray Felix and football's Dick Bass. Some of her guys were less than stellar. They included a few notorious junkies, one of whom stole my coin collection. Early on I understood that Mom needed these men's money to pay the light bill and avoid eviction.

In 1973, though, Mom was hung up on one man and one only—Earl Hunter. Despite his betrayal, Mom never stopped loving him. And neither did I. It didn't matter that Mom and Earl had broken up. He remained an integral part of our lives. He never failed to come over to the house to check on me.

It was five days after Marvin Gaye gently kissed me on my forehead, and I hadn't heard from him. Earl came by to comfort me.

Mom was tired of my lamentations. She had already warned me about the uncertainty surrounding men like Marvin. Yet I remained convinced that what had transpired between us was real. I didn't simply feel that; I *knew* that.

Earl understood.

"All right, honey," he said, "I know you're upset, but what's really happening? Do you really know what's going on in the life of a guy like Marvin Gaye? He's got to be a busy man."

"But I know he wants to see me again. He said he did."

"Remember *Trouble Man*?" asked Earl, referring to the movie score Marvin wrote the previous year.

"I loved *Trouble Man*. And that picture of him on the cover!"

"You love everything Marvin does. But do you remember the story? Do you remember when he said, 'There's only three things for sure—taxes, death, and trouble'?"

"What are you saying, Daddy?"

"I'm not saying nothing, baby, except that Marvin Gaye is calling himself 'Trouble Man.'"

"He didn't look like trouble to me. He looked beautiful. He looked like he didn't have a care in the world. He said he was gonna call. So why hasn't he called?"

"He's working. He's singing. He's got a record to make."

"But I could see that he likes to have people around when he's recording."

"I'm sure he'll call you, baby."

"I'll get Mom to call Ed again."

"Ed is just another hustler looking to make money off Marvin."

"Ed's a songwriter," I said.

"Songwriters are the biggest hustlers of all. Ed wants to keep Marvin happy. If it makes Marvin happy to see you, Ed will arrange it. You don't have to remind him. You don't have to do nothing."

That night I got my mother to call Ed again. The news was not good.

"Marvin's having his doubts about Jan," said Ed.

"What are those doubts?" asked Mom.

"He's crazy about her but thinks she's too young. She's a high school girl, for God's sake."

"You knew that, Ed, before you asked us over to the studio. You knew that when you were going to get him to sing at her seventeenth birthday party."

"Look, I'm the man in the middle here. I got no agenda. I'm just saying that your daughter has really messed up his mind. Matter of fact, he's gone out to the desert somewhere beyond Palm Springs."

"What's in the desert?"

"Mushrooms," said Ed. "The cat likes to trip and read Carlos Castaneda."

The news broke my heart.

What difference did my age make? According to my English teacher, Shakespeare's *Romeo and Juliet* was the greatest love story ever written. In the play, Juliet was fourteen, three years younger than me. The teacher said that Shakespeare, with his uncanny insights into the human mind, understood that teenage passion and love was as legitimate as any passion and love. Age doesn't matter. In truth, love lives in the hearts of youth with its own special energy. I felt that energy. I felt love leading me back to Marvin. Love would surely lead him back to me.

And yet he was not calling. He was in the desert. Ed said he'd be gone for months.

That night I dreamt of tripping in the desert with Marvin. It was a crazy dream in which Marvin and I were running through fields of wildflowers. It wasn't clear whether he was chasing me or I was chasing him. Either way, we lost track of each other. We couldn't find our way back. The dream was exciting and bewildering. I awoke feeling frightened and frustrated.

Two days later, frustration turned to joy. It was late in the afternoon. I'd just returned home from school. The phone rang. Mom picked it up. Every time the phone rang, I prayed it was Ed. This time it was. I tried to listen, but I couldn't make out Ed's words. When the short conversation was complete, Mom smiled.

"He wants to see you," she said.

"When?" I asked.

"Tonight."

"What time will Ed pick me up?"

"Ed isn't coming by. Marvin is."

Come Get to This

I was excited beyond words.

Mom helped me put together what we both considered a sophisticated outfit—a low-cut, form-fitting black dress, matching high heels, gold hoop earrings. I was still troubled by the idea that Marvin thought I might be too young. So tonight I wanted to look older. I wanted to look right.

When the doorbell rang and Marvin Gaye was actually standing there, I was relieved. I'd been worried that he might not show. But not only did he appear, he was absolutely glowing. His outfit was casual—a dark tweed sport coat over blue jeans, a small diamond stud in his right ear, a fresh pair of high-top white sneakers. The trademark wool skullcap that he wore in the studio had been removed. His hair, a close-cropped natural, was gleaming. He had trimmed his beard. The cologne he had splashed on his face had a fresh lime fragrance. In his own Marvin Gaye way, he had dressed up for the date. His demeanor said that he cared.

He opened the door of his maroon Lincoln sedan for me. I slipped into the passenger seat, apprehensive about the evening ahead. Would I be able to keep up my side of the conversation? Would he find me too juvenile? Would he discover that we lived in two distinct worlds with little in common?

Within a few minutes, my fears disappeared. Marvin put me at ease. Everything about him was easy. Words fell easily out of his mouth. The words were gentle, never harsh. He was genuinely curious about my life. How was my day? What did I like and not like about school? In what subjects did I excel? Freely, he offered memories of his time in school—some good, some bad.

I asked about his trip to the desert. "What were you doing all that time out in the desert? Ed said something about mushrooms."

Marvin broke into a smile. His eyes were smiling when he said, "Shrooms are fascinating. Tripping is really something else. Reality takes another turn. You must be ready for that turn, though. You must be ready to step out of your ego and look back at yourself. There's a book called *A Separate Reality* by a man named Carlos Castaneda. If I gave it to you, would you read it?"

"Of course. I love to read."

"He says reality is what we make it. Your energy changes my reality, for example, just as my mind changes yours. He talks about how we have to learn to open the doors to our dreams."

"How do we do that?" I asked.

"It's already happening. We just have to wake up and accept the fact that we're inside our dreams. We're actually living those dreams."

I was in a dreamlike state as we arrived at an old-school Italian restaurant in Hollywood. We were seated in a dark, secluded corner. The decor was far from fabulous, but the place was quiet and comfortable. I noticed Mama Cass Elliot at a nearby table and asked Marvin if he'd introduce me. Like most girls my age—like most everyone, for that matter—I'd always been fascinated by stars.

He walked over to chat with Mama Cass. After a few seconds, he motioned me over. She was extremely sweet.

"Your date is a doll," she told Marvin.

A year later, when she died a tragic death, I thought of our encounter.

Back at our table, Marvin said, "I'm going to be a little naughty."

"What do you mean?" I asked.

"Watch."

He ordered an apricot sour for each of us. The waiter scrutinized me and was about to question my age when Marvin slipped him a twenty. The waiter nodded and returned with the drinks.

"It's my favorite," said Marvin.

"I want to try it."

"It tastes like apricot juice. You won't taste the liquor, but it will help you relax."

"I don't seem relaxed?" I asked.

"You're fine. Just have a taste."

"Do you believe in fate?"

"I believe in Jesus. I believe in doing his will. If his will is done, we find love in great abundance."

"But how do we know if we're doing his will?"

"We know when we're not—that's for sure."

"I like this apricot sour."

"You'll like the chicken cacciatore, too. Is it okay if I order for you?"

"Please."

The subject changed to music. "Do you like the new stuff you've been hearing in the studio?"

"Yes. Definitely."

"If you didn't like it, would you tell me?"

"I can't imagine not liking your music."

"I can't believe my good fortune in meeting you. I'm feeling something with you. Something strong."

Marvin took my hand. My heart melted.

The dinner conversation turned to the subject of searching. Marvin explained that the search never stops. I wanted clarity. *What search was he talking about?* The search for the truth. *How do you recognize the truth?* When something is pure. Marvin said that he viewed me as pure. A second apricot sour emboldened me to be candid. "Not quite," I admitted. "Pure of heart," he said. He complimented my complexion. He said that he loved my freckles. I said that I loved his dark brown eyes. "They always look like they're searching for something or someone," I said.

He said he'd been searching for his muse. Every artist needs a muse.

"What does the muse do for an artist," I asked, "that an artist can't do for himself?"

Surprised at the maturity of my question, Marvin leaned back, closed his eyes, and said, "She inspires. Her job is to inspire."

I wanted to ask, "Do I inspire?" but the question felt too needy. Instead I asked, "Is the muse always a lady?"

"A beautiful young lady with freckles on her face."

The chicken cacciatore arrived. It was tender. Marvin began opening up. I saw how he was searching to escape a marriage that had broken his heart. I also began to speak about my own difficult domestic situation. I was the product of a sadly broken family. His childhood was as nightmarishly confusing as mine. Sadness surrounded us both. Beauty surrounded us both. He said that the sheer beauty of my delicate facial features enthralled him. I was similarly enthralled by the fact that he was not simply fine, but stunningly so. For the moment, physical beauty erased the memories of old pain. Over potent apricot sours and tender chicken cacciatore, something spiritual was happening.

The spirit lived in our hearts even as it excited our bodies. In the car on the way home, Marvin reached over to take my hand.

"I have a tape from a session I did yesterday," he said. "Would you like to hear it?"

"Yes, please."

Riding in Marvin's Lincoln, listening to Marvin singing, I could not help but be transported. How could I not be tripping? His voice was velvet, but it was also unspeakably sad. He was singing about death—his own death. The lyrics said that were he to die tonight, it would be before his time. But that wouldn't matter. He wouldn't die sad because he had known "you." He had found true love.

It was an elegy, a plaintive melody that stirred my heart. I wanted to ask if I was the "you." Was I the muse?

"I wrote this after I met you," said Marvin.

He pulled up to the duplex where I lived with Mom and turned off the engine. That's when he reached over and brought me to him. I did not resist. He kissed me deeply. He kissed me again. The kisses lingered. The heat built.

"Would you like to come upstairs?" I asked.

"I would," he answered.

In her bedroom with the door closed, Mom was asleep and lost in a dream of her own. Marvin and I went into a small TV room where there was a couch and an easy chair. I sat on the sofa, wanting Marvin to join me. Instead he sat in the easy chair, leaned back, and motioned for me to sit on the floor between his legs that were spread apart.

I understood what this man—who was great, famous, richly talented, and beautiful—was asking.

He took his time, stroking my hair, holding my head in his hands, pressing it down into his lap. I could feel his excitement. I felt panicky and cool at the same time. Bryant and I had engaged in oral sex, so I knew what he wanted. But Marvin had his own way of building up the drama. He liked to tease. First he offered himself to me, but then withdrew. All the while he spoke softly, praising my mouth and my lips. Finally he allowed me to pleasure him. I looked up to see how much he enjoyed watching.

Afterward, he was in no hurry to leave.

"May I ask you one favor?"

"Of course," I said.

"I know your name is Janis, but I see you more as a Jan. Would you mind if I called you Jan?"

My heart beating wildly, I could barely say the word *yes*.

I was christened with a new name. Marvin was turning me into a new person. "That was beautiful, Jan. You're beautiful. Thank you for a beautiful evening."

When I got with Marvin I felt like it was meant to be, that this was my authentic life. I wanted to keep it. I wanted to have Marvin forever and in every way. I believed the best way to go about this was to be everything he needed me to be. I wanted to please him in every way. I wanted to be the woman with the most engaging and unforgettable conversation. I wanted to please him in bed with my passion and adventurous nature. I wanted to be that girl who was everything to him. In his long list of women, I wanted to be remembered. I wanted to be the exception, the woman who said yes to almost anything. I wanted to be the personification of the dream girl he sang about in his songs or had in his head. He was moving out of a relationship with a much older woman. I was young. I wanted to make him feel special and that he deserved all the goodness the world had to offer.

In the morning, Mom had questions about my date with Marvin, but I had few answers. I didn't want to talk about it. Thinking back to the night before, I realized that Marvin must have relished the fact that, while I was on my knees, my mom was asleep in the next room, only a few feet away. He could have suggested that we go to his place, or a hotel, or even in his car. Why did he want me to pleasure him with Mom so close by?

I decided that it didn't matter. The sex was far from what I had wanted, but it was a start. He was testing my willingness to follow his lead. And yes, I was more than willing to follow.

"As long as he was a gentleman," Mom told me at the kitchen table.

"He was."

"And you think you'll actually hear from him again?"

"I know I will."

When he came to fetch me two days later, it was not to take me to the studio or a restaurant, but to his apartment.

"I thought we could hang out here, just the two of us. What do you think?"

"I'd love it."

I expected that Marvin, separated from his wife, would have lived in a luxurious pad somewhere high in the Hollywood Hills. Although I didn't know the details of Marvin's separation, Ed Townsend, a Motown insider, had filled me in.

Marvin's wife, Anna Gordy Gaye, was fifty-one, eighteen years older than Marvin and seven years older than my mother. By all accounts she was a formidable woman. Some claimed that she, along with her sisters Gwen and Esther, represented the power behind Berry's throne.

"Berry has entrepreneurial energy," Ed told me a few days after I met Marvin, "but nothing like his sisters. Those gals really know how to hustle. Anna and Gwen ran the photography concession at the Twenty Grand, the hot nightspot in Detroit. They were in the middle of all the action. Not only were they savvy in business, they were glamour girls. You know how Marvin met Anna, don't you?"

"No," I said.

"He was a doo-wop singer in Harvey Fuqua's Moonglows. Harvey was the master doo-wopper, and also a slick music hustler. Doo-wop was a beautiful style of singing, but doo-wop was dying and Harvey had to bust a move. In the early sixties Motown was jumping off, so Harvey disbanded the Moonglows and took Marvin, his best singer, and went to Detroit. First thing Harvey did was start his own label, Harvey Records, and sign his first singer—Mr. Marvin

Gaye. He signed him for life. Before you knew it, though, Harvey Records was absorbed by Anna Records, which already had big-time talent like the Spinners and Joe Tex. By then Anna Records was run by Gwen Gordy, who soon became Mrs. Harvey Fuqua. And while Gwen hooked up with Harvey, Anna hooked up with Marvin. Remember—Marvin hadn't even turned twenty-one and Miss Anna was pushing forty. Marvin started out as a studio drummer, a part-time session man playing behind the Miracles. Didn't take Anna long to see that the boy was not only a great singer and a fabulous writer, but a flat-out genius. She was the one who brought him to Berry's attention. One thing about Berry—he knows his sisters are smart and he listens to every goddamn word they say. So even though Harvey had signed Marvin for life, Berry paid off Harvey, and Marvin was his."

"And Anna?" I added.

"Hell, yes. Anna was the one who molded him. You could say Anna made him. She knew he had to reinvent himself. She didn't want to know about his low-class upbringing in Washington, DC, with his weird-ass father, a preacher man who liked running around the house in his wife's clothing. Oh, no, Anna and them were a solid middle-class black family ascending to the upper class. The Gordys were tight-knit, and Marvin knew that by marrying into the family he'd have a leg up on the competition. And at Motown, it was all about competition. His first idea, though, was to avoid the cats competing for R&B hits and to sing straight-ahead ballads like Sinatra. He used to talk about how he was gonna have his own TV show like Nat King Cole. He saw himself wearing a cardigan sweater or a tux, sitting on a stool and crooning 'A Foggy Day in London Town.' Your boy wasn't a dancer. He didn't wanna get up there and shimmy and shake. Because Anna had so much sway with Berry, she talked her brother into letting Marvin record these ballads and hoped he'd sell millions of records like Tony Bennett or Andy Williams. Problem was, his records didn't sell shit. So while Marvin was messin' around singing his version of 'My Funny Valentine' that no one wanted to hear, Mary Wells was singing Smokey Robinson's 'My Guy' that *everyone* wanted to hear. Everywhere Marvin looked—whether it was the Miracles or the Marvelettes or the Contours—he saw the other acts cutting hits. Now, Marvin is stubborn, and he sticks to his guns longer than most men, but Marvin also saw himself as a winner. When that Motown assembly line got to turning out one hot-selling product after another, he sure as shit didn't wanna be left behind. So guess what he did?"

"I don't know," I said.

"Well, I do," said Ed. "He turned his attitude into a hit song. He wrote about a 'Stubborn Kind of Fellow.' That was his first hit. After that, he was off to the races."

"And all those other songs that he sang in the sixties—he wrote them as well?"

"Some he did, others he didn't. He did write 'Dancing in the Streets' for Martha and the Vandellas. And he did write 'Hitch Hike,' where he actually had to do a little 'Hitch Hike' dance."

"I saw him do it on *American Bandstand*."

"It was like he had two left feet."

"Shut up, Ed," I said, laughing. "I thought he was graceful. I thought he was gorgeous."

"The beautiful thing about Marvin is that as a writer, he's a collaborator. Hardly wrote anything alone. He needs to be sparked by a guitar lick, a piano line, a groove, or a lyric. Then he does the rest. It's like the record we're doing now. The one you been hearing over at the studio. Did I tell you he's calling it *Let's Get It On*?"

"It's the sexiest song on the record."

"You telling me. I gave him the groove and he did the rest. Same thing back in the early sixties when he wrote 'Pride and Joy' with Mickey Stevenson and Norman Whitfield. That's his ode to Anna."

"Did he love her? Does he still love her?"

"You can't go asking me questions like that."

"Why not?"

"'Cause I don't have the answers. You see, those two people have put each other through hell. Lord only knows the damage they've done to each other."

"In what ways?"

"In all ways."

"So what took him so long to move out?"

"Truth is, Anna got Marvin to work when no one else could. Marvin's a dreamer. Marvin's a philosopher. The boy's a poet. He really should be living on some island in Tahiti, eating coconuts and singing songs to the birds. I don't think Marvin was made for this world. He's too sensitive. Show business is about the grind. Show business is cold. Show business says, 'You ain't no better than your last hit.' Knowing that, Anna was always yelling at Marvin to get back in the studio and cut another hit. 'Stop dreaming, baby,' she'd say, 'and start working.' Part of Marvin is lazy, but part of him is ambitious. She lit the fire under his ambition."

"Sounds like she was in charge," I said.

"No doubt she mothered him. But Anna was also a sexy woman. She was a sexy mother. She was a lot worldlier than Marvin. When it came to sex, I believe she schooled him. And because he was so fine—with all these young chicks chasing after him—I believe he tortured her. I believe they tortured each other, 'cause I know that Anna had affairs of her own. Norman Whitfield wrote 'I Heard It Through the Grapevine,' but when Marvin sang it I know goddamn well he was thinking about Anna."

"What about those duets, Ed? When he was singing with Mary Wells and Kim Weston and Tammi Terrell, were they also his girl-friends?"

"I don't think so. They were beautiful ladies but they were aggressive women. Marvin doesn't go for the aggressive type. He likes 'em shy. He likes 'em demure. That's why he likes you."

"When he sang with them, though, he made you believe that something real was happening between the two of them."

"That's because he's a great singer, and great singers are great actors. Marvin could sing any song with any producer. That's another reason why he had that long string of hits in the sixties. He could take tunes written by, say, Holland-Dozier-Holland, the hottest of the Motown producers, and reshape 'em to fit his style. That's what happened with 'How Sweet It Is.' Same thing with Smokey Robinson. Smokey wrote 'Ain't That Peculiar,' but he'll be the first to tell you that Marvin made it his own. Marvin knew how to work with that Motown machine."

"But I've heard him say how much he hates the business. He's always talking about Motown's heavy hand in dealing with their artists."

"Marvin's a rebel, Jan. You got to understand that. He's Aries the ram. A hardheaded motherfucker. Hates authority. Hates being told what to do. Natural-born contrarian. So on one hand, you got a cat who wants to make it, a cat who sees the hit factory working overtime and isn't about to miss out on his share of the good shit coming off the assembly line. And on the other hand, you got a man who's been fighting father figures his whole life. He told me how he defied his own daddy, only to get these bad-ass whippings. He also told me how he got thrown out of the air force 'cause he wouldn't obey orders. So here comes Berry Gordy, father figure supreme. Berry's a controller. He's got to be. He's got to herd all these stray cats running around Motown. He's the fuckin' boss. But please, do not try and boss Marvin Gaye. It might work for a little while, but then it'll blow up in your fuckin' face. That's what happened when Marvin did *What's Going On.*"

"What happened?" I asked.

"All hell broke loose. It was the end of the sixties and Marvin was fed up being produced by Holland-Dozier-Holland and Norman Whitfield. He was gonna produce himself. He wanted to do more than turn out hit singles. He wanted to do a whole concept album. That meant turning the whole system upside down. It caused a revolution. You see, Berry—the dictator who actually put a portrait of himself as Napoleon over his fireplace—is essentially a producer, and so the company was a reflection of him. Producers ran the show. Producers wrote the songs and then decided which artists would sing 'em. Then the producers ran the sessions in the studio. Marvin saw that as ass-backwards. He felt like the artist, not the producer, was king. When he did *What's Going On*, it was a palace revolution."

"It was so different from anything else he'd done."

"He wanted to paint on a bigger canvas. He had a concept. The idea came from his brother Frankie, who'd been over in Vietnam where he wrote Marvin letters about the horrors of the war. That broke Marvin's heart. He looked around the country and saw all this devastation. So he took out his musical brushes and started painting the picture. He was creating a landscape. He wasn't thinking about hit songs. He was just thinking about telling it like it is. Berry didn't get it. When he heard it, he said it'd never sell. This was coming after Marvin had all those big hits with Tammi Terrell. More than ever, Marvin was looked on as the love man. That was all about romance. But *What's Going On* was all about reality. Berry said, 'I ain't putting it out.' Then Marvin said, 'Fine, but I'll never sing another fuckin' note for you again.' Berry had no choice. He released it, and the world went crazy. The world finally saw Marvin for the genius that he is. Berry had to eat his words. The producer was no longer king. Marvin the artist was king. You probably already know this, Jan, but after Marvin made his Declaration of Independence, Stevie Wonder joined the revolution. He followed Marvin down that same road—first with *Where I'm Coming From*, and last year with *Music of My Mind*. Stevie said, 'I'm producing myself, singing my own songs, doing it my own way.'"

"And everything you're doing in the studio now," I said, "all these songs about love and sex—where are they coming from?"

"You don't have to ask me that, Jan. You already know the answer. The man's in love."

8850 Cattaraugus

arvin's place was a $160-a-month furnished one-bedroom apartment on Cattaraugus Avenue, an anonymous-looking street in the lower-middle-class neighborhood of Culver City, a quarter mile away from Hamilton, the high school that I attended. It was shockingly plain. Apartment 1010.

"This is my place," Marvin explained. "Anna lives with little Marvin at her sister Gwen's place in Beverly Hills."

Little Marvin, age seven, was Marvin III, the son that he and Anna were raising.

The apartment was in a plain low-rise complex just off the Santa Monica Freeway. Not a hint of luxury. The living room had a hideous gold couch and a couple of worn easy chairs. The bedroom had a record player and a king-size bed facing a television. The decor didn't disappoint me. I couldn't have cared less. In fact, I was impressed that a superstar was content to live in such an unimpressive flat. I loved that he lived so close to my school. But mostly I loved that he had brought me to his domicile. To someone else it might have seemed dreary. I saw it as Marvin's secret hideaway. Even if he lived in a cave, it would be Marvin's cave. It would be a wonderful cave.

I knew it would be a fabulous evening: I saw that Marvin was in a playful mood. There was no doubt that he had brought me there to make love. That was what I wanted. There was no part of my mind, body, or soul that did not want to please him. I wanted to excite him. He had already excited me—just by choosing me. I was prepared to do what I'd done the other night, but I was hoping for more.

We relaxed in the living room. We kissed on the couch. The kisses aroused me, stirred him. We moved to the bedroom. Marvin handed me a huge wooden box that contained several ounces of pot.

"Could you roll us a jay, babycakes?" he asked politely.

"Sure," I said, seizing the opportunity to demonstrate my sophistication. Separating seed from stem, I worked quickly. I rolled a fat, tight joint and handed it to him.

"Beautiful," he said, lighting up and sucking in the smoke before passing it back to me. I inhaled deeply. The rush came fast.

Marvin loved his pot, and so did I.

Marijuana is an aphrodisiac. Marijuana is a buzz. Marijuana is a giggle-producing intoxicant. Marijuana puts a sensuous filter between you and the rest of the world.

Marijuana was a day-and-night part of Marvin's life. He lived high. I saw nothing wrong with this. My mom lived high on pills. My dad Earl lived high. Good weed was seen in the same light as good coffee. It was the fuel that kept us going, kept us mellow. Good weed seemed harmless. Because it heightened the senses, good weed was welcomed.

We got good and stoned. I lost some of my self-consciousness about my body. I'd been told Marvin liked women with big behinds. That left me out. But at least I had a full bosom. The more I smoked, the better I felt about myself.

We were laughing at a funny cartoon flickering across the television screen. We were embracing. We were disrobing. Slowly. His shirt. My blouse. His lips on the nape of my neck. The soft hair on his chest against my bare breasts.

I wanted him to want me, to enter me, to consume me.

When he did, for the first time in my life I knew what it meant to make love.

We pressed against each other as though this would be our last time, even though it was just the beginning.

I don't know why, but the lovemaking made me cry. The deep pleasures, the thrilling satisfaction, the look of love in his eyes.

The world was made new.

"You're my girl," he whispered in my ear.

There was nothing I could say.

The world was wonderful.

The world was less perfect when, a few hours later, I walked into the living room to discover a man sleeping on the gold couch. I rushed back to the bedroom to tell Marvin.

"Don't worry, sugar," he said, "that's only Abe."

"Who is he?"

"My man."

That designation meant that Abe was a glorified assistant whose only job was to cater to Marvin's every whim. Later, sometimes he'd call him "my servant" or "my butler," names that would crack me up.

Abe ran Marvin's errands that included, most importantly, maintaining his weed stash. Occasionally Marvin would send him out for a gram or two of cocaine. Heroin was never on Marvin's menu, although heroin was Abe's thing. He was, in fact, a junkie. Learning this put me on alert. I remembered Mom's junkie friends, many of whom were thieves.

Despite his habit, Abe was accommodating and personable. Yet his presence bothered me.

"How long is he going to be here?" I asked Marvin.

"He lives here."

What! My heart sank. Sensing my discomfort, Marvin reassured me that Abe would not be a nuisance. His job was to make Marvin's life easier. He promised that, in his words, "Abe will be like a ghost."

On every level, my life became more intense. It was all about Marvin, Marvin, Marvin.

The explosive power of our sexual union was incredible. We made love at every opportunity, night and day. We knew every inch of each other's bodies. We never used birth control. It was clear that Marvin wanted me pregnant—and I did nothing to prevent that.

Beyond the sex, there was a pervasive spiritual component. The spiritual component changed everything.

Two weeks before meeting Marvin, I was a bored high school junior, bothered by an increasingly depressive atmosphere at home.

Two weeks before meeting me, Marvin had been struggling to complete an album on which he'd been working for nearly three years. Estranged from his mother-figure-mentor-wife, he'd been living the life of a bachelor.

Now I had never been less bored or depressed; now Marvin had never been more motivated to work. For both of us, the darkness had unexpectedly lifted.

People around us were skeptical. People were saying that the difference in age would do us in. For a thirty-three-year-old married man to start up with a girl barely seventeen was scandalous. But scandal excited Marvin's rebellious spirit. Besides, there were no practical barriers to get in our way.

If I had come from a conventional family, there could well have been a problem. But Mom was hardly a conventional woman. Earl Hunter was hardly a conventional dad. And my biological father, Slim Gaillard, the rogue bebopper, was the least conventional character of all. In short, I was free to do whatever I wanted to do. And there was nothing I wanted to do more than be with Marvin Gaye every second of every day.

I was hardly the only one who harbored this feeling. Marvin projected the kind of übercool calm that made everyone want to be with him. He loved to laugh. He had a wild and sometimes corny sense of humor, especially after smoking a good joint. If he was in the studio, you wanted to run over and catch a little of his mellow—whether he was singing or just hanging. You didn't mind if he told the same joke over and over. You wanted to kick back with him and hear him, in his easygoing way, talk about the parables of Jesus or the foibles of Berry Gordy or his own foibles when, back in Detroit, he decided to quit singing to try out for the Detroit Lions football squad. Marvin took himself very seriously but, then again, he didn't take himself seriously at all. He talked about his regard for Bing Crosby and Perry Como, singers who were relaxed beyond reason. Marvin moved at a slow but steady pace that made it easy for you to scale down your all-too-nervous rhythms.

Between Marvin and myself, the rhythm of romance quickened. I was in the studio all the time, watching Marvin work his magic. He needed to see me, needed to touch me, needed to sing to me. He said that my presence awakened his spirit. He said that my beauty brought out his beast.

I found beauty and excitement in his sexual beast. I experienced it as a gentle and patient beast, even as his passion for making love quickened my own desire. We couldn't stay away from each other. Every night he fetched me in either his maroon Lincoln or his moss-green Cadillac. When he couldn't wait till nighttime, he began picking me up in the afternoon at school.

One day he arrived at Hamilton High behind the wheel of a snow-white Bentley. When I spotted him in the car, I ran to greet him. We embraced.

"Let's just take a drive," he said.

"Fine," I agreed.

I could feel that he was in a reflective mood. After we'd gone a few blocks, he began talking about his recent past and his decision to abandon Detroit. It took a while. He told me that after Berry Gordy, Diana Ross, Smokey Robinson, and all the others had made the move west, he was the last to leave. The least likely man to follow the pack, Marvin resisted Anna's argument that he needed to stay close to Motown. He described how last year Berry Gordy had turned Diana Ross into a movie star, casting her as Billie Holiday in *Lady Sings the Blues*. The movie was a triumph; Diana was nominated for an Academy Award. With Anna's prodding, Berry could do the same for Marvin. But none of that was going to happen in Detroit. Hollywood was the place.

Marvin said that he knew, though, that he could never have written *What's Going On* in Hollywood. Those songs carried the feel of hardcore urban Detroit. He had great affection for the Motor City. Yet fighting the freezing Michigan winters and facing the snowdrifts covering his front door, Marvin had to face another fact: he was, after all, concerned about his career. He cared deeply about increasing his visibility and popularity. In spite of his inherent shyness, his deep insecurities, and an almost crippling fear of performing, he was a fierce competitor. He had always wanted to be more than a star. He'd wanted to be the biggest star of all.

That drive was what brought him out to LA, where, as Anna predicted, he found success in the movies. He explained that it wasn't in a starring role—that could well come later—but as a composer in his brilliant score to *Trouble Man*. Soon after arriving in Hollywood, he was asked to record a duet album with Diana Ross. Marvin had conflicted feelings about the project.

He said that he and Diana had always been friendly, but this particular partnership was problematic. In the aftermath of *What's Going On*—with no less than three top-ten singles—Marvin's stock had dramatically risen. He was finally recognized as an independent artist, not just another cog in the Motown machine. He neither needed nor wanted an outside producer. He also freely admitted that he was jealous of the attention that Berry Gordy lavished on Diana Ross. Initially, Marvin refused to do the record.

He explained how Anna's bond to her baby brother, Berry, was ironclad. She wanted to help Berry realize a project that would help Diana. At the same time, Anna was convinced that a Marvin-Diana duet album made artistic and commercial sense for her husband. In the sixties, her singular ability to coax Marvin into the studio—especially during those times when depression had him down and reluctant to work—had proven effective. Like no one else, Anna could motivate Marvin. It took time, but she finally persuaded him to do this Diana Ross album. Marvin caved, but he carried his resentments to the sessions. He came in puffing on an outsize joint. A pregnant Diana refused to sing around the smoke. The vocals were ultimately done on separate dates. The production itself was old-school Motown—Berry Gordy and Hal Davis were the producers. Marvin made two demands—that he receive producer royalties and that his name appear before Diana's. Both were summarily rejected. His job was to simply come to the studio and sing. Ultimately that's what he did. To his ears, the results sounded dated—a sixties-style record out of step with the seventies, and sales of *Diana and Marvin* would be less than spectacular. Marvin would never do another album like it again.

He told me how the incident further fueled the tension between him and Anna. It was Anna and Berry who had connected Marvin with the William Morris Agency in the hopes of landing film roles. He was cast in two small films—*The Ballad of Andy Crocker* and *Chrome and Hot Leather*—but the parts were insubstantial and led to nothing bigger.

Now I could understand why Marvin saw his connection to Anna—and, in turn, her connection to Berry—as an impediment to his freedom.

"This Bentley is Anna's car, not mine," Marvin told me during the drive. "She loans it to me to remind me of her elegance and her power."

I felt a knot of fear forming in my stomach. As Marvin drove in the direction of the studio, I stayed silent.

"What's wrong?" he finally asked.

"You've never picked me up in this car before. I'm just not comfortable being driven around in Anna's car."

"Why?"

I was afraid of displeasing Marvin, but at the same time, I needed to speak my mind.

"It's strange," I said. "And also a little creepy. What's the point of picking me up in a car that belongs to your wife? What are you trying to say? What are you trying to prove?"

Marvin offered only the slightest of smiles.

For the first time I saw how he derived some perverse pleasure in creating discomfort, for himself as well as for others.

The relief was always the music.

When we finally arrived at the Motown studio in West Hollywood, it was Marvin's music that softened my discomfort. In Marvin's world, his music made everyone and everything all right. His music consisted of many voices. Overdubbing those voices—stacking the vocals—was a technique he mastered while recording *What's Going On*. He called it a spiritual exercise in harmony. Each of these voices was unique—a sweet falsetto, a tender midrange, a sexual growl, a bottommost plea. Each emanated from his heart, yet each represented a different part of his one-of-a-kind musical mind. Each contained pain. Each contained hope. If he could blend these different voices with such ease and grace in his music, surely he could blend the differences in his own personality.

"You look happy," Ed Townsend told me when Marvin had left the studio to take a phone call in the office. "I see he's in a good place. I hope he stays there."

"He will," I said.

"You're doing a good job of making him happy."

"Thanks a lot, *Dad*," I said with heavy sarcasm. "Anything to keep him satisfied."

"Some people can't handle happiness, so they find a way to fuck it up."

"Maybe he just hasn't found the right person to make him happy," I said.

"Maybe you're right, baby. I hope so. If anyone can keep him satisfied, I know it's you."

I thought about that word, *satisfied*. It came up in the title of the song that Marvin was tweaking that day: "Just to Keep You Satisfied," the final cut on the album *Let's Get It On*. As beautiful as it was, the song didn't feel like it belonged on the record. It pointed to another story, another time, and another character.

"Just to Keep You Satisfied" was about Marvin and Anna. The lyrics were explicit: Anna was his wife; she represented his hopes and dreams; he endured her jealousy even as he cherished their lovemaking; his deepest desire was to satisfy her; but it wasn't meant to be. Mental strain tore them apart. Differences could not be reconciled. They tried over and over again, but it was too late. Much too late. The marriage was doomed. The marriage was over.

I had never heard Marvin sing more beautifully or with such profound sadness. I was comforted by his acknowledgment that his relationship with Anna was obviously finished. I wanted it finished. I wanted Marvin for myself. But I also couldn't help but feel the strength of the emotional bond revealed in this song. I couldn't help but feel how much Anna meant to Marvin. And I couldn't help but fear the power that this woman still held over him. There could be no doubt: Anna was my adversary.

As a result, I made a concerted effort to please Marvin in every way. When he described Anna as being dominant, I knew I had to be more submissive. When he told me the story of how, during a brutal argument, Anna had stuck the stiletto heel of her shoe into his forehead, I swore that violence would have no place in our relationship.

On her side, Anna had a long history with Marvin. She had money, power, and influence. She was one of the few people on the planet who could make him work. On my side, I had youth and sex and a free-love hippie attitude that Marvin found alluring.

Either way, it was clear that the longer I was with Marvin, the more Anna would do to make his life miserable.

Anna was a hard act to follow. But, she represented structure. In Marvin's world, Anna came first, then Berry, and then himself. I represented freedom. I was the one who put his happiness first. Marvin bragged to others about it, claiming that I was incredible because I worshipped the ground he walked on. I enjoyed hearing that but after a while I saw the flaws in my thinking. It showed that I wasn't making myself happy, and in many ways, I began to take it out on myself and Marvin.

Another week went by of beautiful lovemaking at the apartment and beautiful music at the studio. Another week when, from time to time, Marvin wandered off to Hamilton High to shoot hoops on the outdoor basketball court.

For me, the only problem was Marvin's man Abe. He was still living at Cattaraugus, where he slept on the hideous gold couch. Marvin knew that I was uncomfortable in his presence but wouldn't deny himself the convenience of having his personal assistant close at hand. Compared to other superstars, Marvin was living a super-spartan lifestyle, but he was also spoiled.

Marvin's contradictions became more evident with every passing day. He was adamant on separating himself from Motown. When the Motown execs called, wanting to hear the new record in progress and wondering when it would be ready for release, he ignored them. He had no interest in their input and blatantly disregarded their deadlines. But late at night, when he and I were alone driving through the city, he'd turn to me and say, "I wonder what Berry will think of this record. I wonder if he'll like it."

I saw that Marvin's confidence and insecurity were in constant conflict. One day he was certain that the new album was brilliant. The next day he worried how, after the political consciousness of *What's Going On*, the world would regard the carnal intensity of *Let's Get It On*. He kept vacillating. The record would be a huge hit. The record would be a huge flop. He'd be rewarded or he'd be ridiculed. He didn't need Motown to tell him how much they loved the album. But he did need everyone in the studio to reassure him that it was great.

On this particular night, after spending another three or four days sweetening the vocals, Marvin was still reluctant to let Motown hear what he had done. He was behind the wheel of the green Caddie. I was by his side. I was still amazed that the man of my dreams had let me into his world. He kept saying that, like a dream, I had stepped into his life. A midnight mist covered the Sunset Strip. Tourists lined up outside the neon nightclubs. Working girls stood in the shadows of the streetlights. Some were long-legged beauties. Others looked tired and sad.

"Would you roll us a jay, dear?" Marvin quietly asked me. He loved calling me dear. I loved how the word fell so easily from his lips.

We shared a joint. It wasn't a fresh high—we had been smoking off and on since early afternoon—but it was a good late-night high, a high that let us cruise through Hollywood with the sweet anticipation of heading home and making love. It was a trouble-free high that had us especially mellow . . . until we heard the siren and saw the flashing police light.

Marvin pulled over. Two cops stepped up to the car. Marvin had no choice but to roll down the window. The smell of pot was pervasive.

"Please get out of the car," said the first cop.

"Aren't you Marvin Gaye?" asked the second.

Marvin was upset, but he hid it well. He knew the police would search the car and find a bag of weed in the glove compartment.

"Officer, if I could use your car phone to make a single call," he said, "I'd be most grateful." Instant charm!

They obliged him.

It took only ten minutes for a tall, beautiful light-skinned black woman to pull up beside us. This was Suzanne de Passe, high-ranking Motown exec and Berry Gordy's closest aide. She was no-nonsense. She gave me a look as if to say, *Wow, two stoned idiots.* She was friendly but stern with Marvin before moving quickly to address the police. I couldn't hear what Suzanne was saying, but she was obviously effective, because within minutes the cops were leaving the scene. There were no tickets, no repercussions. Marvin got off scot-free.

On the way back to Cattaraugus, Marvin was silent. I knew that he was relieved, but I also knew that he was unhappy that I had witnessed his dependence on Motown. Like a child in trouble at school, he needed his lifeline—Motown—to rescue him, even though Motown was the authority against which he rebelled. This incident had made him feel less like a man and more like a boy.

There was no lovemaking that night. In the morning, there was the awkward presence of Abe.

"You're not comfortable when Abe is around, are you?" Marvin asked me.

"You know I'm not."

"And if I asked him to move out and invited you to move in— how would that make you feel?"

The question took my breath away. I had been wishing for this very thing. It hadn't been two months since that night I'd first come to the studio.

"Yes! Yes! Yes!"

"And what if your mother objects?" asked Marvin.

"My mother? No problem. How soon can Abe go?"

"Be patient, dear."

Patience didn't come easily. I was afraid that Marvin would change his mind and never ask Abe to leave. He'd never allow me to move in.

As my love for Marvin grew, so did my own fears and insecurities.

I started to grow up as our relationship grew. Even though I was seventeen and under the influence of drugs, I was beginning to realize that I, too, needed someone to make me feel special, to want to make me happy. I wanted to give him the children that he asked for. I wanted to let him have his flings, even if I had to bite my lip later and cry when he was away. I gave in when I probably shouldn't have. I danced along that dangerous line of being accommodating but not giving in too much, and I was often left alone and hurting.

In Love with the Night

My mother and I awaited the arrival of Marvin, who was on his way to gather up all my worldly possessions and move them into his simple, unimpressive one-bedroom apartment. Abe was gone.

"Are you sure you know what you're doing?" my mother asked me.

I was sure of one thing: my connection to Marvin was the strongest emotion I'd ever felt.

"I'll be fine," I told Mom.

"I don't want you to get hurt."

"I won't. He loves me, I love him."

"You haven't even known him a couple of months."

"You've married men you've known for less time than that."

"He's already married."

"He's separated."

"But still married."

"The marriage is over. He's even written a song about how it died."

"A song isn't a divorce."

"He's getting a divorce."

"I want to trust him," said Mom. "But I know these singers. I know them all too well."

When Marvin arrived, it was as though he had heard that remark. He was barely polite to Mom. He resented whatever authority, no matter how tenuous, my mother held over me. In his mind, I now belonged to him, not Mom.

He swept me away.

My possessions weren't any more than a hope chest from Pier 1 and clown-shaped salt-and-pepper shakers.

The minute I arrived in the apartment, I felt a huge difference. Before, I was a visitor. Now I belonged. In the following weeks, Marvin and I fell deeper in love. Late at night, when Marvin couldn't sleep, he sat in front of a little keyboard and fashioned melodies with such astonishing ease that I could only watch and marvel. As he pressed the keys, the wordless sounds he sang carried a lush beauty that was otherworldly. It was as though he was lost in prayer or meditation. After a while, he reached over and picked up a paperback book, dog-eared to a particular page. He stopped playing and began to read out loud. As he recited the lines, his eyes were lit with love, alive with a glow I had never seen before. He kept looking at me. I held his gaze.

> O, speak again, bright angel! for thou art
> As glorious to this night, being o'er my head
> As is a winged messenger of heaven
> Unto the white-upturned wondering eyes
> Of mortals that fall back to gaze on him
> When he bestrides the lazy-pacing clouds
> And sails upon the bosom of the air.

"What are you reading?" I asked.

"I found this in one of your books."

I walked over to where Marvin was seated and saw that he was reading from my copy of *Romeo and Juliet*.

"It's when Romeo is looking at Juliet up on the balcony," said Marvin. "I won't be able to say it as well as Romeo. No matter what words I use, I'll never be able to explain how much I love you."

"I've always loved you, dear."

"That was before you knew me. But what about now—now that you know me?"

"I love you even more now."

"I need to hear you say that. I'll never tire of hearing that."

"I'll never tire of saying it," I said.

His eyes filled with tears. I was weeping as well. We embraced, holding each other tight, elongating the moment in which our world consisted only of this embrace. No coldness, no cruelty, no pain, no problems, no heartaches, no hardships—just this closeness, this union, this love.

Later that night he turned back to the keyboard in search of a song that had eluded him. I fell asleep on the couch. The sound of his voice informed my dreams. When I awoke, he was still playing. Day was breaking.

The next morning, I rolled the first joint of the day and started dressing for school. Still in bed, Marvin accepted the joint and begged me to stay.

"What's the point?" he asked.

"To learn."

"I can teach you everything you need to know," he said only half jokingly. "We're reading Shakespeare together, aren't we?"

"Literature is one thing, driver's education is another. I'm learning to drive."

"I'll teach you. I'll be a far more loving and patient teacher than whomever the school provides. I think it's time for you to leave school."

"To do what?"

"To do what you've said you've always wanted to do—live your life with me."

The offer was undoubtedly tempting. Much of school was boring, but I wasn't ready to leave. Ever since I'd been a little girl I had been told that I was bright. Quitting school didn't feel right. Wasn't a diploma the key to the future? At the same time, I couldn't imagine a greater future than being with Marvin. And, truth be told, I did harbor a secret ambition to be in show business. I knew I could sing. I could dance. And yet I did want my degree.

"Why should you care if I stay in school?" I asked.

"I care about us being together—every hour of every day. I don't want to share you. There are all those strapping young high school football players looking to love on you."

"They're boys, Marvin, not men."

"Nonetheless, they're my competitors. They're young and horny and I'd not be surprised if more than a few broad-shouldered jocks have caught your eye."

"They bore me."

"You say that now, but when you're still young and fine and I'm old and gray, you'll say that same thing about me."

"Never."

"So say you'll leave school and stay by my side. I want to be with you every hour of every day."

"Marvin . . ."

He reached out and brought me back to bed, where we made love until we were exhausted. I arrived at school two hours late.

At the end of the school day, Marvin drove up to Hamilton High in the white Bentley. I was happy to see him, but not the car.

"Did you tell them you're leaving?" was the first question he asked.

"Whoa," I said. "You just brought it up this morning. Won't you give me a little time to think about it?"

"Long ago and far away a poet once wrote, 'At my back I always hear time's winged chariot hurrying near.' Time is rushing, rushing, rushing."

"Well, I really do need time to think it over. But it's hard for me to do any serious thinking in this car. You told me you weren't going to drive it anymore."

"I'm returning it now. I'm bringing it back to Anna. She and little Marvin are at her sister Gwen's."

"We're going over there now?"

"Does that bother you?"

"Of course. You know it does. How could it not?"

"I just need to switch cars and pick up my son. It'll take just a minute. Be cool, dear."

We drove up to Gwen Gordy's house, where Marvin parked the Bentley and had me wait in his maroon Lincoln in the driveway.

Waiting for Marvin to emerge from the house, I was nervous. I didn't want to be there. I hated that he had forced me into this position. I wondered whether he was putting me on display. Had he driven me here so that Anna could get a glimpse of the Other Woman, the young chick with whom he was having a torrid affair?

When the door to the house opened and Marvin emerged, followed by his seven-year-old son and then Anna, my heart sank. Anna was scary—a strong woman in her fifties who, with a determined gait, walked to where I was seated on the passenger side of the Lincoln. She was heavily made-up, a not-unattractive matriarch with a round face and fair skin. She wore a purple crushed-velvet pantsuit, diamond earrings, and a heavy gold chain around her neck. Her hair had been softened and styled. Her eyes burned with anger. She was focused on me.

"Look here, Anna," said Marvin, "don't go and start trouble."

Paying no attention to her husband, Anna ordered me to roll

down my window. Filled with fright, I lowered the electric window only an inch. I was afraid Anna might haul off and sock me.

"I just want to see what someone like you looks like," Anna said with undisguised disgust.

A few seconds passed. I was speechless, but Anna was not. She added, "Now that I've seen it, don't ever bring it back here again."

The words haunted me for the rest of the day: *Now that I've seen it, don't ever bring it back here again.*

I wasn't a person. I was an "it." I felt like shit.

Marvin drove off with me in the passenger seat and little Marvin in the back. He said we were having lunch at Roscoe's Chicken and Waffles restaurant on Gower Street. Marvin's arrival caused a commotion. Fans ran over to ask for an autograph. Everyone wanted their picture taken with him. Polite to a fault, he accommodated nearly everyone. But seeing that his son was not happy sharing his dad with the world, Marvin gently cut off contact with his fans, explaining that this was a family moment and would they do him the courtesy of affording him a bit of privacy. His request was expressed so solicitously that the people quickly backed off.

I considered his remark about this being "a family moment." In truth, Marvin's nuclear family was shattered. His relationship with Anna was damaged beyond repair. He said little about his biological family. His mother and father were back in Washington, DC. Marvin spoke of his mother in saintly terms. He adored her. He rarely mentioned his father at all, but when he did a look of consternation passed over his face. Clearly he held no affection for the man. When I asked more about Father Gaye, Marvin said only, "He's very strange." Then there was the "happy Motown family" that Marvin called a myth. Gordy's strategy of exciting competition between his artists and producers had led to vicious sibling rivalries.

Within that family, though, certain people treated both Marvin and me with extreme kindness. Clarence Paul, for example, was wonderful. He was a writer-producer who had acted as Stevie Wonder's surrogate father during Stevie's early years at Motown. He also acted as a surrogate big brother to Marvin.

Marvin was looking for a surrogate family—a wise uncle figure like Harvey Fuqua, an understanding surrogate sister like Gwen or Esther Gordy, Anna's siblings. He found it impossible to come to terms with his own biological family.

These fractured families—both Marvin's and mine—were huge obstacles to overcome. And yet, given the power of our love, I believed we had the potential to create a strong and wholesome family of our own.

I wondered if Marvin felt the same.

Two weeks later I found out when I brought him news that gave me both trepidation and joy:

I was pregnant.

Impatient for Your Love

I'm touched," said Marvin. "I'm joyful. I'm grateful to God. I couldn't be happier, dear."

He took me in his arms and held me to his chest. My heart beat wildly. I was deeply relieved. He had proven to be the man I knew he was.

"A son," he whispered in my ear. "We will have a son."

His statement took me aback.

"And what if it's a girl, Marvin?"

"I think you're having a boy."

I didn't like that thought. I didn't like the pressure.

"We'll see," I said, forcing a smile.

We dropped the subject of boy versus girl, but his attitude continued to bother me. At the same time, I wanted to please Marvin. In the early years of our relationship that single mantra—*I must please Marvin, I must please Marvin*—never faded. If I didn't please him, I was afraid he'd discard me.

The news of my pregnancy came at a great time. Marvin's long-overdue record was complete. I had been to the studio countless times where I had heard the songs over and over again. I never tired of listening to that strangely erotic-romantic suite of songs. Even though Marvin contemplated his death in "If I Should Die Tonight," even though he was pining for a woman lost in a faraway landscape in "Distant Lover," even though he was drenched in sorrow and regret in the marriage-ending "Just to Keep You Satisfied," the album's dominant theme was sex, sex, and more sex. He wasn't simply pleading "Let's Get It On" once, he was pleading twice with "Keep Getting It On" and reinforcing the act of love a third time with "You Sure Love to Ball."

At the moment it had been decided that "Let's Get It On" would be the first single—the very night he finally played the album for the Motown executive who flipped out and called it an across-the-board smash—Marvin and I went back to our little cave on Cattaraugus. He slipped the single into the cassette player and together we slowly slipped out of our clothes. Our naked dance of love gradually moved to the bedroom, where the song of love repeated endlessly as the act of love was the most intense in our still-young relationship. I had never been more inside his music, inside his life, inside his heart. That night the world was beautiful, blissful, passionate, and peaceful. Nothing could go wrong.

And then everything did.

I thought it was the result of being too sexually active. Turned on about being parents, Marvin and I had intense, athletic lovemaking sessions. With *Let's Get It On* playing in the background, we tried to get as close to each other as was physically possible.

It was only days later when I began hemorrhaging. The blood was sudden and startling. I called my mother, then Marvin, then the doctor. Marvin met me at the hospital, where the doctor used the one word I did not want to hear: *miscarriage.*

The impact on both of us was enormous. We felt a great sense of loss.

"Dear," said Marvin, "these things happen. God gives and God takes away. We praise him for his goodness and trust that next time he will bless us with a healthy boy. I have no doubt, darling, that there *will* be a next time."

I wished he wouldn't have restated his insistence on having a boy, but no matter—I was greatly relieved that he was comforting and loving and still committed to our relationship. As crazy as it might sound, I was afraid of disappointing him. I even feared that the miscarriage might chase him away. Fears of losing Marvin—fears of being undermined by those around him, fears of being banished from his world—were never far from my consciousness.

For years to come, love and fear shared the same chambers of my heart.

On certain nights the anxiety subsided. On one such night, the moon was full and the world was at peace. Marvin and I were driving up Highway 1 past Malibu. In the backseat were the actor Richard Lawson and his future wife Denise Gordy, the niece of Berry and Anna.

There seemed to be no hidden tension. Marvin and I had socialized with Richard and Denise before. We all got along splendidly. We loved to get high and laugh like little kids. The weed we had been smoking intensified the happy mood. The stars glittered. Moonlight danced off the Pacific. The ocean breeze was cool and refreshing. The universe was a friendly place. On the way up the coast, switching radio stations, we heard "Let's Get It On" three different times. The song was soaring up the charts. Marvin couldn't have been more delighted.

A few miles north of Malibu at Trancas Beach, the car sputtered to a halt. Without losing his customary cool, Marvin announced, "I'm afraid we've exhausted all our resources."

"What do you mean?" I asked.

"No gas," said Marvin.

"No problem," said Richard. "The men will go get gas while the women wait behind."

Marvin and Richard were gone for a good hour. When they returned, they were empty-handed.

"The gas station was closed," said Richard.

"But all is not lost," Marvin added. "Our resources are, in fact, not completely exhausted." He reached into his shirt pocket and pulled out a joint. Denise and I applauded. Smoking added to the wild and woozy nature of the night.

"What now?" Richard asked Marvin.

"Now we explore," said Marvin. "Look at that beach!"

Not concerned about a thing, Marvin was the first to throw off his shoes and step onto the sand. Denise followed by removing her top. I was a little hesitant.

"What about you, Jan?" asked Marvin. "Surely you have nothing to hide. Reveal yourself, dear. Reveal yourself proudly."

For a second, I flashed on that awful day in Bel Air when, at age fourteen, my mother had allowed me to strip for Luke and Big Jack. But that was different. Those guys were creeps. Marvin was my man. He was proud that I had perfect breasts. I exposed them.

As we all made our way down the beach, Richard, not to be out-done by the women, decided to remove his pants. It took Marvin less than a minute to do the same. Our ridiculousness only added to our pleasure. Where were we going? We didn't know, didn't care. We cavorted as though we didn't have a concern in the world.

Not fifteen minutes passed before we saw a woman coming in our direction. Marvin and Richard stepped back into their pants. Denise and I didn't bother to put on our tops but covered our breasts with our hands. The woman stopped in her tracks.

"My God," she said, "you're Marvin Gaye. You're absolutely beautiful!"

Before Marvin had a chance to reply, I whispered, "That's Margot Kidder?"

"I am," said the movie actress. "And I'd love for you guys to come to a party. I'm on my way there myself."

"We've no good reason to refuse your kind invitation," said Marvin. "Lead the way."

Boldly, Margot planted herself next to Marvin. I thought that she might have the hots for my man. A few minutes later, the five of us reached a well-lit beachfront house where a party was in progress.

"Look who I brought," announced Margot as we entered the living room. "It's marvelous Marvin Gaye! Can you believe it?"

The host was the well-known actor Peter Boyle, thrilled that his friend Margot had somehow found Marvin wandering the beach outside his home. By mere chance, someone at the party had brought a copy of *Let's Get It On*. Within minutes the song was blaring. All eyes were on Marvin, basking in the attention.

The party people freely shared their goodies. There was plenty of pot, coke, and acid. There was wild hippy dancing, arms flopping around with hips swerving. There was incense burning and candles lit everywhere. It was a laid back atmosphere. A few of the couples wandered off into the bedrooms. Margot stuck close to Marvin. Given the free-flowing sexual vibe, I wondered whether she would actually make a move on him. Before Margot had a chance, though, Peter Boyle made a bizarre move of his own. He took off the music to announce a surprise.

"Gather around, everyone," he said. "It's time for me to offer up something I've been waiting to show you all night. With our surprise guest of honor now in attendance, I will not keep you waiting."

The next thing I saw was Boyle pulling down his pants and revealing his pale, hairy backside. It was quite a sight. That's when Marvin decided that it was time to split. Against the protests of Peter and Margot, the four of us bade the party people good night and headed back to the car. Peter gave us a can of gas, and we were on our way home. There was a full moon out that night.

"How'd you like the evening?" Marvin asked me when we were back on Cattaraugus.

"Interesting."

"Interesting good or interesting bad?"

"It was a little crazy," I said. "I still can't believe what we saw, but I'm glad we went."

He kissed my forehead and slowly undressed me.

"It was exciting seeing you on the beach," he said. "It's exciting seeing you on the bed."

That night we made beautiful love. In one another's arms, we slept until early afternoon.

When I awoke, Marvin was staring into my eyes.

"I want us to go away," he said.

"Where to?"

"Away from everyone, where it's only you and me and Mother Nature. No city smog or crime or sirens in the middle of the night. No sounds except the chirping of birds and the rustling of leaves. Fresh air. Blue skies. At night, looking at the stars. Let's just get away from it all. Escape. Hide."

"But your record's out and it's a hit. They want you to promote it."

"Even a better reason to get away. What do you say, dear? Will you come with me? Can you run away with me into the woods?"

"Where?" I asked again.

"It doesn't matter. As long as it's in the middle of nowhere and no one can find us."

"And why is it so important that no one finds us?"

"Because I want you all to myself. I want *us* all to *ourselves*. I want nothing interfering with our love. I want nothing between us and God and nature."

"Are you really serious about moving out of the city?"

"Serious as sin. And it will be a sin if we don't make our escape from the madness that's about to unfold. What do you say, dear? Will you run away with me?"

"You know I will."

Topanga

From his perch on top of the world, Marvin was tired of seeking. He wanted to be sought. And though there were times when he loved the spotlight, this was a time when he assiduously avoided it. After the triumph of *What's Going On*, he had worked for years to develop a follow-up that would create as great a furor. He had accomplished just that with *Let's Get It On*. Yet rather than welcome the accompanying acclaim, he ran from it.

I couldn't help but wonder if he was running from himself. Even though I remained in awe of his talent, I had seen that his insecurities, hidden under a veneer of cool, were potent. Those insecurities alarmed me. While Marvin was gratified that his new album was an immediate hit, he worried that it might soon stop selling. Because Anna was furious with him—and because Anna had such influence with Berry—he worried that Motown might work against him and cut off promotion. He worried that his fans would lose interest in him. He also worried that, in order to bolster sales, he would have to tour. Performing in public was something he dreaded. He had long suffered from stage fright.

I didn't like seeing Marvin scared. I didn't like seeing him as anything but perfect. Yet every day his imperfections, in tandem with his seductive charms, became more obvious. This was especially true when we escaped to the rural retreat he called our romantic paradise.

Topanga Canyon, across Highway 1 from the Pacific Ocean, was less than an hour's drive from Mid-City LA, but a world away. It was that part of the Santa Monica mountain range that, only a few years earlier, had been home to a large colony of hippies, including the Charles Manson family. Marvin's rustic mountaintop A-frame home was built on three levels. It was all pinewood and glass. It smelled fresh and clean. Its remote location didn't bother me in the least. In fact, it excited me. I'd have Marvin all to myself.

"Is it too hippie for you out here?" he asked.

"You forget that I grew up with hippies. My mom's a hippie. I'm a hippie. We're all hippies. Groovy! Peace! Far out!"

"I hope you won't be offering any invitations to your mom to visit us anytime soon."

"I won't be offering invitations to anyone. I just wanna be with you."

"And the dogs, of course."

Marvin had bought two handsome Great Danes, Shad and Caesar, to safeguard us from any outside intruders. He loved them a little more than I did. Uninvited guests and curiosity seekers would not be able to find the house. There was no paved street or address. The only way to reach the place was to call from a gas station on Highway 1 and have either Marvin or me drive one of his two jeeps or his green pickup truck down the mountainside. The visitor must then follow the jeep through a series of twisting roads. Thank God, I reflected, that Marvin had taught me to drive. Before long he bought me a black Porsche 911 that zoomed through the canyon like a rocket.

Marvin had also taught me to make his favorite dish: mashed

potatoes, hamburger patties, gravy, and mustard cabbage cooked according to a special recipe from Marvin's mom. There were frequent trips to the little health-food market. There were blissful evenings by the wood-burning stove with Marvin at his little portable keyboard. There were long and languorous lovemaking sessions in every part of the house—on the living room rug, in the loft, in the kitchen, outside on the balcony, under the stars above. In the morning he and I awoke to a chorus of birds. At night the coyotes howled. Time stood still. Love deepened. The real world was remote, but the real world never stopped calling.

For weeks Marvin kept the outside world away. For our protection he had an AK–47 assault rifle and a shotgun. We hunkered down, but that didn't stop Motown from knocking at our door. Requests poured in. As *Let's Get It On* became the sensation of the summer and one of the fastest-selling hits in history, every DJ in the country wanted Marvin on his show. Motown execs were telling him that if he toured, sales of the record would quadruple. But Marvin said no. No interviews, no tours. Leave him alone. Let him sing to me. Let him sing to the birds. Let him enjoy this respite from the crazy world of show business.

"I'm an artist," he told me over and over again. "I'm not made for show business. Show business views artists as products. I am a highly sensitive person and you, dear, are all I need to be happy—not the fawning crowds or the mad demands of money-hungry Motown."

I cherished his words. I wanted this time to last forever. I wanted to believe that we would, in fact, live out our lives in Topanga Canyon, free of the world's worries and pressures. That belief, though, couldn't last for long. The world offered prizes that Marvin's ego couldn't resist. One was the promise of a *Rolling Stone* cover story.

Observing Marvin at close range, I saw that his insecurity was the flip side of his egomania. There were days when he swore he would no longer perform again because he doubted his ability to sing before a live audience. On other days he unhesitatingly said that he wanted to be remembered as the greatest singer in the world. A *Rolling Stone* cover excited that part of him that sought glory and reveled in his own talent. His grand plan was to have *Rolling Stone* seek him out here in the wilds of Topanga. If they put him on the cover, it would have to be on his terms—no studio shot, but Marvin photographed in his rustic hideaway, communing with nature.

When the magazine met his terms, he was satisfied. He was doubly gratified because precious few black artists had graced the cover of *Rolling Stone*, a publication primarily devoted to white rock 'n' roll.

Marvin drove the jeep down the mountain to fetch the reporter, Tim Cahill, and the photographer Annie Leibovitz. When they returned, he introduced me as "his friend." Then we all got stoned. Marvin had never been more charming. He began speaking of the mysterious nature of his father's esoteric Christian church. He described what it means to speak in tongues and to tarry—to repeat "Thank you, Jesus" over and over until the Holy Ghost has entered your spirit and cleansed your soul. He talked about being able to sense the spirit in the song of a bird, an ocean breeze, even a raindrop or snowflake. When asked to speak more about his father, Marvin's eyes glazed over. He paused for a very long while. His answer was a song. "My father has a magnificent voice," he said, "and when he sings about Jesus, his is the sweetest sound you can imagine." Then he sang his father's song. Tim and Annie were mesmerized. I was mesmerized. The sun sank behind the mountains. The dusk was golden. Photos were taken.

"I used to be afraid seventy percent of the time," Marvin confessed. "Now I'm only afraid ten percent of the time."

Another joint was rolled. The subject switched to sex. I wondered what he would say.

On the inside of the *Let's Get It On* album, he had written, "I contend that SEX IS SEX and LOVE IS LOVE. When combined, they work well together, if two people are of about the same mind. But, they are really two discrete needs and should be treated as such . . .

I don't believe in overly moralistic philosophies. Have your sex, it can be very exciting, if you're lucky."

He looked at me and said yes, very lucky. He admitted that when it came to sex he was a fantasy person. When asked if all his fantasies had come true, he turned coy. He wondered about the thin line between an exciting fantasy and an exciting perversity. He wondered if sex, given willing participants, should ever be considered perverse. He concluded by saying that we Americans needed to loosen up and be free.

When the long interview was over and the *Rolling Stone* people were gone, I considered all that had been said. I was particularly intrigued by Marvin's remarks about sex. The sex between us, while always exciting, had started to take a different turn. Marvin had become more oral, which, of course, pleased me. Even though I began our physical relationship in his lap, he had increasingly become more willing to reciprocate the favor—a breakthrough for him. At the same time, he had introduced into the mix a certain kinkiness that, although not exactly my style, was something I was willing to entertain. Not to do so would only anger Marvin. I went along with his program, which, from time to time, involved fantasies of me with other women.

These variations did, in fact, bring me new pleasures. The omnipresence of pot and the increasing use of cocaine facilitated my willingness and widened my enjoyment. At times I feared that I was falling down a slippery slope but quickly dismissed such anxieties.

"No need to be uptight," Marvin urged. "If it feels good, that means it *is* good."

I didn't have to justify my willingness to be led down the path. I felt privileged to be on the path. I still couldn't believe that somehow this extraordinary man had chosen to live his life with me by his side.

Nestled inside a woodsy canyon, looking down from the mountain, I watched time move slowly. An entire day might be devoted to nothing more than an unhurried walk along the beach to watch the sun slip into the ocean. We sat on the sand and stayed silent as the waves crashed to the shore. Flocks of birds staged whirling formations and flew off into the distance. I took his hand; he kissed my face.

Back up at the house, I was not surprised to see that Frankie Gaye, Marvin's brother, had arrived. Family members were always showing up. Three years younger than Marvin, Frankie bore a striking resemblance to his older sibling. Frankie had Marvin's quiet demeanor. Like Marvin, he spoke in a whisper. Like Marvin, he was a gentle soul. He harbored ambitions to sing but, unlike Marvin, lacked the drive to break into show business. He was also a Vietnam vet—the returning soldier at the center of *What's Going On*—and a man who had been deeply traumatized by the war. On the surface, though, Frankie was an easygoing character. Only his heavy drinking habit bothered Marvin, who had little taste for alcohol.

"He'll be hanging out with us for only a few days," Marvin told me. "You don't have a problem with that, do you, dear?"

"Of course not. He's family." I loved Frankie, who had the same lighthearted sense of humor as Marvin.

I soon learned, though, that family—especially the Gaye family—could be as much a burden as a blessing. When Frankie's stay extended beyond a few days to a few weeks and then months, I despaired. The love nest was crowded.

On another front, another invasion threatened our domesticity. Motown never stopped calling with the same messages: Your album's a smash; you're more popular than ever; your fans are dying to see you, hear you, show you their devotion. How can you resist their love? How can you resist their money? How long can you hide out?

Promoters found their way through the canyon to Marvin's door with extravagant offers.

"You'll be returning to the stage a conquering hero," they promised him.

He lit a joint, he smiled, he pondered, and then he refused. But they refused his refusals and ultimately came back with more money, more perks, more ways to flatter his ego. Finally he succumbed. He set a date for one concert and one concert only. During the late summer of 1973, he committed to playing the Oakland Coliseum in November. The decision came after weeks of mental turmoil.

"At least you've made up your mind," I offered in the way of comfort. "Maybe you'll even like getting back in the ring."

"If you really knew me," he snapped, "you wouldn't say that. I'm just not ready."

"Then why did you agree?"

"To make you happy."

"To make *me* happy? What!"

"Yes, dear. Don't you want to watch me onstage being adored by thousands of women and then come home with me?"

"Of course. And your show will be great."

"It'll be a nightmare. I've screwed up."

"Then cancel."

"I've given my word."

"It'll be fine, Marvin."

"Roll a jay, dear. I need a smoke."

"No problem," I said.

The smoke only increased his apprehension. When the first rehearsals came around, he skipped them. The promoter began to panic. Marvin hadn't appeared in public in over a year. He didn't have a regular band or a set show. There was an enormous amount of work to do. He needed to get started, yet he kept procrastinating.

Tickets were printed. Ads were placed. The Coliseum sold out within minutes. Orchestrations were written, musicians hired. If he didn't start rehearsing now, he'd be in deep trouble. Marvin was courting disaster.

"Marvin loves to cut it close," Frankie told me.

"Why?"

"He loves the drama."

"Drama or not, he's going to have to start rehearsing. He can't cancel now."

"Tell the promoter that it's off," Marvin said. "November is too soon. I'm not ready."

"But . . ."

"No buts about it. It's off."

A month later, it was on again. Marvin had rediscovered his courage. He was also motivated by a need for cash. Although *Let's Get It On* was a hit, royalties would not be forthcoming for a while. In the time since *What's Going On* and *Trouble Man*, Marvin had spent all the money he had made. When it came to finances and, for that matter, all practicalities, Marvin was defiantly irresponsible. He spent what he wanted to spend when he wanted to spend it. He never heeded the advice of accountants or managers.

"I'm simply unmanageable," he was quick to say.

He ignored all admonishments about saving money and, most alarmingly, paying taxes. Only when he was forced by dire consequences—like losing the house in Topanga—was he moved to action. Yet even then, action was not immediate.

The Oakland concert, canceled in November, was now rescheduled for the first week of the new year. The mechanism was set back in motion. He was due for the first rehearsal in Hollywood for a show that was only three weeks away.

When he missed the rehearsal everyone panicked—everyone except Marvin. Though anxiety was building up on the inside, on the outside Marvin was cool as a cucumber.

"I want to get an RV," he said. "I hate flying. I'd much rather drive up to Oakland in a big van."

He got the van.

"You're my copilot," he told me. "Are you ready for our big adventure?"

"Where are we going?" I asked.

"To the city. To ride out," he said, using his favorite term for cruising.

It was late when we arrived on Sunset Boulevard. During the trip down the coast into the city, Marvin mused about the mysteries of shamans and sorcerers.

The Hollywood night was abuzz. The neon was screaming. Marvin directed his attention to the working ladies who displayed their wares under the streetlamps and on the corners that he had obviously visited before.

At the same time, passing by a homeless man living out of a cardboard box, he said, "How I envy him! He's truly free. No responsibilities, no ties to the hellish conformity of this world."

He hungrily surveyed the women—the more salacious the better. The ones with outsize backsides interested him most.

"Stop here," said Marvin, spotting a hooker. "Please go out and get me that newspaper, dear."

"Sure," I replied. I was torn, but I went.

The newspaper rack held copies of the *LA Free Press* with its semi-pornographic ads for sexual assignations.

"Find anything interesting?" he asked.

"Not really."

"Would you be nice enough, dear, to go back out there and ask that lady if she'd like to join us for a smoke?"

I hesitated.

"Nothing to be afraid of, dear," he said.

I realized that there was no going back now. On this trip to the forbidden planet of illicit sex, I had become his partner. If I had been stronger—more sure of myself, less afraid of losing Marvin—I might have resisted, but I didn't.

I approached the working woman who, as Marvin anticipated, eagerly accepted the invitation. When the visitor stepped into the van, Marvin switched on the overhead light that illuminated his face. Expecting to be recognized, he was geared up to relish the moment.

The young lady, however, did not recognize him. Marvin was crestfallen. His interest waned. He gave her twenty dollars and sent her on her way.

On other neon nights there were times when Marvin wanted me to watch another woman service him. Conversely, Marvin began to speak of fantasies in which he watched me with other men. Over the next years, a few of these fantasies were realized.

I was led into a world that was entirely about him. I was lost in my obsession with making Marvin happy.

As I approached my eighteenth birthday, I'd been with Marvin for twelve months. More than ever, I felt lucky that he still wanted me around. I realized that a million other women would jump at the chance that I had been given.

It didn't matter that he was using me to fulfill his fantasies. I was willing to be led and fed whatever stimulants he offered.

I felt compelled to give him whatever he needed. If I didn't, another woman would. Maybe that woman would be his wife Anna.

I loved him and was willing to let him mold me.

Our love was growing. Every day we grew closer. As he slept, I watched him breathe. I imagined that, even in his dreams, we were together. When he awoke, he saw me by his side. He held me. He sang me a morning song. He said, "I love you, dear."

He was all I needed. He was all that mattered.

"Jan"

The weeks leading up to the concert in Oakland were pure chaos. Marvin's normally mellow manner was undercut by his nervousness about the upcoming performance. He was a wreck.

"I shouldn't be doing this," he told me on our way to rehearsal.

"But you are doing it," I said.

"I was cajoled, I was manipulated, I was talked into going against my own good instincts. My fans will be let down."

"Your fans will be thrilled. You'll be fine."

Marvin's fear of performing—his vulnerability—made me love him more. It made him more human, more endearing.

"The music isn't right," he said. "The arrangements are off."

"You're the boss, dear. You'll change them and make them right."

"The clothes aren't right. I don't want to wear some ridiculous stage costume."

"Let me worry about the clothes," I said.

"Will you? Can you?"

"I think I can. I think I know what will make you happy."

He took my hand and brought it to his lips. "Bless you, dear. Bless you for keeping me sane."

My vision came to me quickly: I took the basic outfit Marvin wore in Topanga—the clothes that best suited his relaxed nature—and brought them to a clothier who tricked them out. His favorite super-comfy denim shirt was studded with rhinestones. His red watch cap was adorned with sequins. He wore his own worn-down work boots, but they were studded, painted silver, and customized with high platform heels.

"It's rural funk," said Marvin when I presented him with the clothes. "I love them! I love you!"

For the moment, his anxieties were chilled. But they returned after he missed the third straight rehearsal. His absence was alarming both the promoters and Motown, who had a great deal at stake. Nearly three years after the triumph of *What's Going On*, this was being hailed as Marvin's second coming. They wanted to know why he was avoiding rehearsals. Why was he cutting it so close? And now, days before the actual concert, he was threatening to once again cancel the whole thing.

"By now you have to know that he grooves on this," Frankie told me one night when Marvin was out of earshot.

"Do you really believe that?"

"I know that. He likes to see everyone worrying to death on his behalf. It gets him off. He loves chaos."

"Topanga isn't chaos. Topanga is calm."

"Topanga is beautiful," Frankie agreed, "but Topanga isn't real. You've already seen that Topanga won't last for long."

While Marvin was dreading the Oakland show, Frankie was looking forward to the date because Marvin had assured him that they'd be able to work together. Frankie, Marvin's brother, saw this as his big chance.

When the big day arrived—January 4, 1974, a day before my eighteenth birthday—the chaos had not subsided. If anything, it had grown. Marvin had not only missed the sound check, but the orchestra had not been able to rehearse onstage. The few rehearsals Marvin did attend back in LA were hardly sufficient.

Gene Page, the veteran musical director who reminded me of Uncle Albert, the ditzy upside-down character played by Ed Wynn in *Mary Poppins*, was running around in a panic. The Motown delegation, which included members of the Gordy family and Suzanne de Passe, was in a state of high anxiety. There was talk that Marvin might not show.

But Marvin was in the house. Marvin was in his dressing room. I was with him. I was helping him put on his studded denim attire. I was sharing several preconcert joints with him. I was holding his hand that had turned sweaty and cold. I was assuring him that the world still loved him.

Due to the presence of the Motown people, I was dealing with my own anxiety. They gave me dirty looks and regarded me as nothing more than a groupie. They had a long history with Marvin. I did not. They felt that he belonged to them, not to me. I feared that they would find a way to undermine my relationship with Marvin and cause him to cut me loose.

Meanwhile, amid all this emotional chaos, fifteen thousand screaming fans awaited Marvin's appearance.

I listened as the overture began. There were hints of Marvin's trademark motifs, melancholy refrains from past hits. The anticipation was overwhelming. The overture seemed to go on forever.

I had moved to the wings to watch the moment at which not

Marvin, but Frankie—with his uncanny resemblance to his brother—stepped into the spotlight. The crowd went wild. They thought they were seeing Marvin. Frankie simply stood there, relishing the moment, basking in the glory that was not really his.

"Now the man you've really been waiting to see," Frankie finally said, "Mr. Marvin Gaye!"

Frankie stepped out of the spotlight as Marvin stepped in.

The crowd went even wilder.

Now what?

Would the lack of rehearsals render the show a disaster?

Would Marvin's fears undercut his ability to sing?

He rose to the great occasion. It took a while, but soon he was soaring. Soon he was singing "Trouble Man." He *was* Trouble Man—sexy and dangerous, gentle and sweet. He was flying high in a friendly sky, he was whispering "Mercy, mercy me," warning us of the fate of our ecology, he was walking through the inner-city landscape of the blues. All this was fine. All this was cool. All this was well-mannered and mellow Marvin. But when the romantic Marvin emerged, and he broke into the opening strains of "Distant Lover," pandemonium broke out. Women lost their minds. Their piercing screams shattered the night.

Marvin loved being loved—and I loved watching him drink in the adoration. I was thrilled.

The thrills increased when I heard the first notes of a song that Marvin had written for me, simply titled "Jan." He had played me the song—a tribute to our enduring love—and hinted that he would perform it, but during several of the rehearsals he chose not to sing it. Until now, I wasn't certain that he would.

I listened closely to every word of his spoken introduction:

"Here's a new song I wrote," he said, "a song about a little girl, really a beautiful young lady. She asked me to write it, I promised her I would . . . it goes like this."

Suddenly my excitement took a nosedive. I had never asked him to write it. He offered. I was disappointed that he told the audience that I asked him to write it. It took away some of the pleasure and the romance of it all. However, it remains one of my favorite songs to this day.

I understood that the presence of the Motown execs had affected him. Everyone pretended to like the song and that he wrote it for me, but they typically didn't like reissues on any albums. They especially hated the fact that he had left Anna and was living with some young chick. So if he was going to write a song about the chick, it was only because the chick asked him to. No big deal.

But to me it was a huge deal. The fact that he was singing this song at a concert being recorded as a live album was confirmation of his commitment to me. This concert would become a historical document. But now that document would indicate that the song was my idea. I was completely humiliated. Yet the song was out there—and so were his feelings for me. At the same time, I hated being portrayed as an insecure teenage girl who had to beg her man to write a song for her. Of course I had wanted Marvin to compose such a song—what woman wouldn't?—but I'd never made that request. I knew him well enough to know how he resented such requests.

Thus it was with heavy equivocation that I heard him sing how Janis was his girl, how there was no one sweeter, how his life would be tragic without her, how she was unique and how he was her greatest fan.

The words got to me. His performance got to me. Throughout the show, my heart never stopped pounding. The longer he performed, the more confident he grew, the louder the response of his adoring fans. When it finally came time to do his current red-hot hit, just the opening guitar lick of "Let's Get It On" was enough to drive the fans into a complete frenzy.

Afterward, the dressing room was a madhouse. Everyone wanted to join in the celebration, get close to him, tell him how great he was, take a picture.

Hours later in the hotel suite, he and I were finally alone.

"It was beautiful," I said. "You were beautiful."

"I didn't forget to sing your song."

"Why did you tell the audience that I asked you to write it?"

"Well, dear, I didn't want to upset anyone."

I knew what he meant. As a superstar, you have to make all the ladies believe that they are special. If he wrote a song for me on his own, it would mean that they are not special to him. He was also afraid to upset the Motown execs, and surely, Anna.

I considered complaining about his inaccurate introduction to the song but didn't. "Thank you," was all I said.

"Did it make you feel special?"

"It did."

"And did it make you want to go back to Topanga so we could be alone again?"

"Yes, if we ever could really be alone."

"We can. We will. I'll tell Frankie to leave. It will all work out."

I agreed, but the calm never came.

Nestled back in the canyon, I saw that Marvin's usual cool had been undermined by the triumph in Oakland. His ego had been excited. The moments of quiet humility were noticeably fewer. When Motown delivered a million-dollar check reflecting royalties, Marvin made a copy and hung it above the fireplace.

"Why put it there?" I asked.

"To remind me," said Marvin.

"Of what?"

"That I've already made and spent three other fortunes."

"And you intend to squander this one?"

"No, I intend to ignore the demands of this cold world and stay here with you, dear."

"But what about this manager of yours who keeps talking about a world tour?"

That manager was Stephen Hill, a highly educated black Jamaican with green eyes and wavy hair who spoke in an aristocratic tone and had won Marvin's confidence.

"Stephen is brilliant—and also strong enough to take on the Gordys. He has no fear of anyone."

Do you? I wanted to ask Marvin, but stopped myself in time. I realized that in some ways the answer was yes. But I knew that Marvin didn't want to admit it. Marvin wanted to act as though he had no fears. There was the macho Marvin who did not want to remember the times he had gone to Berry, begging him to bail him out of one financial mess or another. The macho Marvin also did not want to recall the long years in Detroit when, according to those closest to him, Anna ruled the roost.

Those were the same years when, to prove himself, macho Marvin trained to be a boxer. When the attempt was unsuccessful, he began investing in boxers. His latest fighter had recently been knocked out in the second round in a prize fight in San Diego, leaving Marvin more deflated than the fighter himself. I saw that hiring a super-confident manager like Stephen Hill was Marvin's way of regaining his always-precarious confidence.

"Stephen keeps saying that you shouldn't be living in the canyon," I reminded Marvin. "He thinks you need to be in Los Angeles or New York."

"What he thinks and what I do are two separate matters, dear," said Marvin. "What I'm most interested in doing is loving you all day and night until we make a beautiful baby boy together."

When I failed to have my period at the end of January, I harbored hope that I was pregnant again. I kept the news to myself, though, for fear of disappointing Marvin.

Our lovemaking, while blissful, had a new edge of determination. I flashed back to the night after the Oakland show when, high on the success of his performance, he came inside me with a force I had never felt before. Had that been the magical moment of conception? Exactly nine months later I would learn that it was.

Against the backdrop of growing love there was the subtext of growing fear. Maybe it was being isolated in the canyon; maybe it was all the pot we consumed; maybe it was coming home one day to find that Shad and Caesar, our Great Danes, had been attacked and maimed by someone who also stole the AK–47 rifle that Marvin had hidden in the house.

Serenity soon turned to paranoia. We feared that the perpetrator of the crime would come back to kill us. Our security was compromised. We panicked and fled to the city for the weekend where in a hotel suite we turned on the television to watch reports of a brushfire raging through Topanga Canyon.

The day after the blaze we drove back to see if the house had survived the flames. It had, but our nerves had not.

Topanga was no longer an option. The tranquil retreat had transformed into a nightmare. Fires raging, killers on the loose.

"I don't think we should ever come back here," said Marvin.

I didn't argue.

We climbed back into the jeep and headed down the winding roads through the canyon for the last time. Looking back at the home we had once shared, I realized that we were running from our fears. We were also running from a period of our lives in which our love had been nourished. I regretted the run but, sharing Marvin's anxieties about the unexplained crime and the deadly blaze, I also welcomed it. Either way, I was glad that we were running together. Our relationship had strengthened. We had survived Cattaraugus; we had survived Topanga; we had survived the hysteria of Oakland.

I had every reason to be jubilant, if only for the fact that when we reached the ocean and followed the coast back to the city, I shared with Marvin the news that he had been hoping to hear.

A child was growing inside me.

Mother, Mother

I think of my mother, Barbara, and of Marvin's mother, Alberta.

I consider their struggles as mothers. And then I think of my own challenges.

Within days of turning eighteen, I had learned that I was to become a mother.

When, in 1974, the doctor confirmed in March a due date in September, I knew that nothing would ever be the same.

I felt new joy. I saw the gladness in Marvin's eyes when he heard the news.

"A boy," he said. "A son."

"Perhaps," I said.

"For certain," he confirmed.

I wished his hopes had been different. I wanted him to say that any healthy baby would be a great blessing, but this wasn't the time to confront his prejudice. The important thing was that I had made him happy. What's more, his positive reaction to the pregnancy was

further confirmation of the strength of our bond. Those cynics who
dismissed me as a temporary distraction would soon see that they
were wrong. Marvin didn't want out. He wanted in. He wanted to
start a family with me. That single fact helped ease my gnawing insecurities. I'd do everything in my power to maintain a high level of
health during my pregnancy. I vowed to protect my child and my
relationship with Marvin.

After we left Topanga and moved into a luxury apartment in Brent-
wood, there were wonderful times—quiet dinners at the Hungry
Tiger in Hollywood, intimate evenings at Harry's Bar in Century
City, where Marvin made me feel especially sophisticated.

There was a quick trip to Detroit where Marvin took the time
to show me the different homes where he and Anna had lived. He
introduced me to Esther Gordy, Berry's sister, who was sweet and
welcoming. We went to the 20 Grand, the famous Detroit nightclub where all the Motown acts had honed their skills. James Brown
was performing that night. Before the show, Marvin took me to the
dressing room to introduce me to James, who had rollers in his hair.
His false teeth sat in a jar. He mumbled in a manner that I couldn't
understand. It didn't matter. Marvin understood James and acted as
his translator.

One day at the office of his company, Right On Productions,
someone showed up with a pound of potent weed that looked like a
bagful of hops. Marvin called it Cheeba Cheeba. Everyone who came
through grabbed a handful. The supply was soon exhausted. Marvin
wanted more and asked Frankie to scout around for smoke of similar
quality. Frankie scored. When he brought in a pound of killer pot,
Marvin named the new supply Frankie Frankie.

There were road trips up the coast in his RV to Carmel and to
Ventana in Big Sur, an inn with a sweat lodge and super-healthy
food. Marvin loved being captain of his RV. He loved being out on

the land, in the woods, and on the beach. On one of those trips he bought a ranch in Round Mountain, an idyllic spot in Northern California. That was the time his mom, along with several nieces and nephews, came along. I was thrilled because after we arrived, Marvin gave me an adorable little kitten. Trouble arose, though, when his mother refused to ride in the same RV with the animal. I promised to keep the kitten out of her way, but Mother Gay wouldn't relent. (Marvin had added an "e" to the family name.) Marvin had to choose between his mom and me. He chose his mom. It broke my heart when I was forced to leave the kitten behind.

Off the road and back in LA, mounting professional demands put Marvin on edge. He was elated that *Let's Get It On* had turned into the biggest hit of his career. Never had he been offered this much money to tour. Yet he was also disappointed in himself for not resisting the lure of the limelight.

"I don't need to go out there," he told me. "I need to stay home with you, sing lullabies to the baby boy growing inside your womb."

"I would love that," I said.

"But there is the question of my public. I feel as though I owe my public—the same public that's dying to give *me* their hard-earned cash for the pleasure of hearing me sing. How can I let them down? How can I refuse their offering?"

"You don't have to."

"You won't think I'm greedy? You won't think that I'm abandoning all my artistic principles?"

"Don't artists want to be appreciated like everyone else in the world?"

"Of course. Adoration ain't so bad."

"You deserve it."

"But I still have no desire to go out there and make a spectacle of myself. Why should I shake my ass?"

"You don't have to shake it. Just show it a little."

He laughed, but he was still troubled by the prospect of touring.

Inside Marvin's mind, the arguments raged on. He wanted more money but didn't want to go on the road. He wanted more adoration but didn't want to do the demanding work of mounting a show.

Stephen Hill put the arguments to rest. He put together a multi-month schedule that would earn Marvin millions. The money was too big to reject. The coast-to-coast concerts would take place over the course of my pregnancy. Naturally, I wanted to accompany Marvin on the tour.

"The travel is too brutal for you to come along, dear," Marvin said. "I won't subject you to the stress and strain. You can fly out for a date here and there, and I'll be flying home to see you on many weekends, but you're better off situated in one place. I think the best place would be with my mom and family back in Washington."

I was mortified. When I expressed skepticism about that plan, Marvin had a surprise that had me smiling.

"Stephen has booked the first concert in Jamaica," he said. "It's his home country and a place I dearly love. I want you to come to Jamaica with me. It'll be a dream."

The dream was exotic, even if short-lived. The sky was sapphire blue, the beach sun-bleached white. Tropical breezes blew through the open windows of the suite in the fabulous resort overlooking Kingston Bay. Marvin stretched out in bed, me by his side. He gently stroked my stomach, which, in my second trimester, had started to swell.

"Put on a robe, dear," he said. "Stephen is on his way up."

Stephen arrived in the room like a commanding officer. He was firmly in control. He said that for this Jamaican concert Bob Marley had been booked as Marvin's opening act. When he began to explain Marley's importance, Marvin stopped him.

"I know all about Marley," said Marvin. "I love and respect him. You don't have to sell me on Bob Marley."

Stephen *did* have to sell Marvin on the post-Jamaica ten-state tour he had put together. Marvin was still resisting the ordeal. The demands on his time would be too much. The grind would wear him down. He didn't want to be away from me. He refused to back down.

"That's impractical, Marvin," said Stephen, "and, to be blunt, inconceivable. You will not back out. You will fulfill your commitments as you initially promised."

When Marvin remained adamant, Stephen used flattery to win him over. Doesn't Marvin want to enhance his already legendary status as an international artist? Why, right here in Jamaica the highest-ranking government officials, including the prime minister, Michael Manley, have been clamoring to meet him. He will be the guest of honor in stately mansions belonging to the most powerful people on the island. That will be true wherever he goes.

The flattery worked. Marvin recommitted to the tour. Stephen was relieved and reminded him that, at Marvin's own request, he had made arrangements to fly in the Gay family from Washington, DC.

The news surprised me. I thought it would be just the two of us. When Stephen left, I questioned Marvin.

"Why do you want your mother and father here?"

"Who said anything about my father? My father is certainly *not* coming. I don't want to discuss my father. Far as my mother goes, you know that she is my heart. I want her to see this glorious place. She has worked all her life so I could have opportunities like this. Why would I deny her this treat? Why would you ask me to?"

"I wouldn't. I'm glad she's coming . . ."

"Are you?"

"It's just that I love being alone with you, but I understand."

"Then you'll understand if my brother and sisters are coming too."

I didn't say a word.

"What's wrong, dear?" Marvin asked.

"Nothing. You want me to be surrounded by your family. I understand."

"But do you understand that all those years I was married to Anna . . ."

"*Was* married? You still are."

"For all those years I was together with Anna, my family felt shunned. She wanted nothing to do with the Gays. She looked down on them. They were never welcome in our home in Detroit, never welcome when we moved to Los Angeles."

"And you didn't say anything?" I asked.

"I left Anna. I'm with you. And I expect you to welcome and love my family as I expect them to welcome and love you."

I first met Marvin's mom, Alberta, some months back in Los Angeles. The encounter was not unfriendly. Mother Gay was a woman with a sweet disposition and quiet manner, much like her sons. She accepted the fact that Marvin had taken up with a young woman—what choice did she have?—but at the same time regarded me with unspoken skepticism. She was not cold to me, but neither was she embracing. I felt that Mother Gay had adopted a wait-and-see attitude: *My son is obviously infatuated with you, but let's see how long it lasts.*

When Mother Gay arrived along with Frankie, sister Zeola, and older sister Jeanne, there were hugs all around. For now, the mood was pleasant. As they lunched with us on the patio, they talked about how Marvin might help them relocate to LA. With Anna out of the picture, they felt empowered to reestablish their place in Marvin's life. They saw that I, unlike matriarchal Anna, had neither the power nor the inclination to exclude them. I wanted to please Marvin. And if ingratiating myself with his family brought him pleasure, I had no choice but to go along with the program.

The absence of Father Gay was profound. During those rare moments when he was in the mood to discuss his dad, Marvin had told me how the man never held down a job for long. His position as a minister in a charismatic church was his central work. But it didn't pay. Marvin's mom was forced to toil as a domestic to keep the family in food and shelter.

"My father fashioned himself as an important man in this somewhat bizarre congregation," Marvin once explained. "But as a kid, I didn't see it as bizarre. I saw it as beautiful. The women were all dressed in white. The women loved my father. They revered him as an exalted spiritual leader. They also loved me when they heard that I had inherited his gift for singing. His voice, praising God, rang out loud and true. I felt the spirit of God—the loving and living God—in that little church where I knew, even as a young boy, that I would one day take my father's place. All the elders said so. The women in white told me that I was highly favored. I felt blessed. I felt privileged to go with my father as he rode around Maryland and Virginia where he was asked to sing and preach at other holy churches belonging to our little sect. We were different from other Christians. I liked that feeling. It felt special to go to a church that celebrated the Sabbath on Saturday, not Sunday, and strictly followed all the rules of the Old Testament as well as the New.

"The strictness meant that you obeyed God. Since Father saw himself as God's chosen leader, he demanded strict obedience from everyone, including Mother and especially his children. My brother Frankie and my sisters Zeola and Jeanne were intimidated. They were compliant. They knew not to challenge his authority. But because I had been anointed and felt empowered by my own gifts, I was not compliant. I was defiant. My defiance brought out Father's brutality—or maybe it was vice versa. I don't know, and I can't tell you when it happened, but when it did, everything changed."

"How?" I asked.

"I went from idolizing Father to loathing him."

"That's a strong statement."

"Not strong enough. Not after what he did to me."

"What did he do?"

"You don't want to know."

"I do, I really do."

"I don't want to say."

"You don't have to."

I thought of the brutalities I had suffered as a child. Ruth. The nun. But at least at that moment, he was not ready to say any more. I wanted to share more of my past with Marvin, yet I didn't. I knew better.

To everyone around Marvin, including me, it was clear that his story was the only one that mattered. Not that I minded. I willingly suppressed my story for the privilege of being included in his. I identified with Marvin so closely that it was his concerns I worried over, not my own.

Here in Jamaica his focus was to re-form a family that had been lost to him for so long. At the same time, everyone in Marvin's family had an agenda. His mother wanted to be closer to her son the superstar. Frankie yearned to be a superstar himself and hoped Marvin could help him realize that dream. Zeola displayed an obsessive starstruck love for her brother reminiscent of the female fans who attended his shows. I had my own aspirations of being in those shows. Everyone wanted something from Marvin. And that's how he liked it.

I saw that Marvin needed to be needed and wanted to be wanted. He loved to be in the position of doling out favors, whether emotional or material. And like everyone else surrounding him, I needed and wanted the favor of his love.

The prime minister of Jamaica had requested the favor of Marvin's presence at an exclusive dinner party. Stephen Hill, wearing his managerial status like a badge, was certain that Marvin would be pleased to attend. Stephen Hill was wrong.

Instead Marvin and I fled the resort with Ras Daniel Hartman, our Rasta friend who had promised us a tour of the real island. No dinner gown for me, no tux for Marvin—just jeans and T-shirts and flip-flops and an escape to a picturesque beach where Marvin gratefully accepted a ganja-filled clay pipe and smoked the local greenery that eased his mind and mellowed his heart as he soaked in the overwhelming beauty of the people playing in the sand and splashing in the clear blue water.

"This is paradise," Marvin whispered as he kissed me behind the ear. "A beautiful day for my girl."

He touched my stomach and said, "Our baby is feeling this incredible vibe."

In an open-air jeep, we cruised up and down the hills of the island, stopping at a roadside stand to eat curried goat, beef pies, jackfruit, ackee, codfish, and red beans and rice—the island's best down-home food.

"You must show me Trenchtown," said Marvin.

"Hey, mon," said Ras, "it's funkier than you might imagine."

"Bring it on."

Walking through the slums of Kingston, Marvin was recognized and celebrated. He was surprised and moved when so many of the impoverished people of Jamaica reached out to touch his hand. He stopped to speak with the women, play with the children, smoke ganja with a gathering of older men. At times like these, Marvin appeared most content, most himself, a humble prince quoting Jesus about our moral obligation to serve the least among us. I admired how he shunned aristocratic Jamaica to spend time and explore the back alleys and stop in the makeshift studios where the reggae music was made.

Trenchtown is considered the ghetto in Jamaica. It is filled with people trudging through the mud with no shoes. They were people who didn't have anything. Going from his high life to this sharp contrast didn't bother Marvin. He moved easily among the wealthy and the impoverished; those who had money and those who had nothing at all. The have-nots that he sang about on *What's Going On*. He saw everyone as the same and treated them with the same dignity. He also believed, and taught me to do the same, to help whenever possible. On this day, there was a rousing. Everyone was excited about something. We didn't realize what it was until we came upon the dead cow. The locals were enthusiastically picking at it because it meant that they would have a solid meal. Adults and children alike were pulling at the animal's flesh. We both started crying, as Marvin tried to comfort me through his tears.

"Don't let it upset you, baby," he said, guiding me away from the disturbance. Ras Daniel took us into his hut. We smoked some weed that he offered and discussed the politics of the island.

I felt a little better. Marvin exposed me to so much through his music. And there I was in Technicolor real life witnessing the kind of human desperation that he sang about. He showed me that we had to offer more than compassion.

A few hours later, after we left Ras Daniel's hut and were on our way back to the hotel, we were shocked to find that the entire cow was gone. Many of the animal's bones were taken and there was barely a carcass.

The concerts Marvin was doing were fundraisers for these people of Trenchtown. Helping them out inspired him to do a great performance.

Two days later, that was the music I heard as Bob Marley and the Wailers opened the concert. Breaking practice, Marvin left his dressing room dressed in an outfit I had designed—white overalls and a white studded T-shirt. I had convinced him to lose his skull-cap, at least for this one night. He and I walked to the wings while Marley was onstage.

"This groove is spreading all over the world," Marvin whispered to me. "This is a man carrying an important message."

I noticed Marley looking over in our direction. Seeing that Marvin was watching him, he flashed a broad smile as he broke into "Get

Up, Stand Up." An hour later, when Marvin was onstage, it was Marley standing in the wings, one master acknowledging another.

During the sets of both singers, I was mesmerized. In those few hours, I was treated to both pure Marley and pure Marvin, two geniuses conveying much more than mere excitement with their music. I felt like I was living a dream.

On that starry night in Jamaica, with the crowd rocking back and forth to the rhythms of the isle and the far-off cities of America, the music of Bob Marley and Marvin Gaye blended into one. Their sounds commingled. Their spirits married. There was peace in Jamaica. Pregnant, I felt there was peace all over the world.

The Beast

When I'm touring," Marvin insisted, "I want you to go back to DC with Mother and the family."

"Why?" I asked, still reluctant to go.

"Because you'll be safe there. Mother will care for you. She'll make sure you eat right and get your rest."

"I don't like this plan, Marvin," I said.

"The tour is too much for you."

"I can deal with the tour. I'm stronger than you think I am."

"Please, dear, don't argue. I'm leaving you with my family. You'll love them and they'll love you."

The Gay home in Washington evoked the aura of the Addams Family. The minute I walked through the door, I was uncomfortable.

Mother was essentially a sweet lady but had little interest in me. I quickly saw that her main concern was the man who ruled over the household like a lord: Father.

Father Gay's presence—or absence—was always on Mother's mind. For long periods of time he remained in his upstairs bedroom,

separate from Mother's. When he wanted something—a cup of coffee, a sandwich, a freshly ironed shirt—he rang a bell attached to a
string. When he decided to make his grand appearance, it was always
an event.

The first time I saw him I was shocked. In that instant, I knew
why Marvin had been loathe to discuss him.

He came down the stairs with pink rollers in his hair. He wore a
form-fitting shirt unbuttoned to expose his upper torso. It was not a
pretty sight. The curlers were strange enough. But the white-toned
panty hose under his plaid Bermuda shorts and the fact that he was
wearing his wife's red flat sandals put him in a category all his own. I
didn't know the name of that category. All I knew was that this man
was beyond strange. Slight of build with undistinguished features,
he was imperiously vain. He strutted like a peacock. He spoke like a
trained actor. When he addressed me, he was courteous. But I was so
freaked out by his appearance, I hardly heard his words.

Mother Gay called him Doc. He called her Babe and kept a note-
book that critiqued her housekeeping. Surveying the house like a
drill sergeant, he jotted down, "Dishes: dirty . . . couch: dusty . . .
curtains: soiled." More disturbing than this, though, were the frequent female visitors who arrived at the house and, with Mother
Gay's knowledge, paraded up to his bedroom. They were typically
women from his church with big behinds.

"Father," Frankie told me, "is a booty man."

When Father wasn't around, Frankie was also telling me the
facts that Marvin had not been able to bring himself to describe—
the gruesome details of the beatings that Marvin suffered as a boy.

"My sisters and I obeyed him," said Frankie. "That was the easi-
est way out. Why make him mad? But Marvin isn't made that way.
You can't tell Marvin what to do. Mother spoiled Marvin early on,
made him feel like he was a little prince. Well, the king might be the
king, but the prince ain't listening to him. Making it even worse, the
king is dressing up like a queen. He's wearing frilly blouses that look

more suited for Mother than him. Sometimes we catch him wearing Mother's underwear. We hate that. We hate how he goes out in the streets with his hair in curlers. It's bad enough we can't go to any of the normal black churches where our friends go. We gotta go to his strange little church that tells us we can't dance or listen to rock 'n' roll. And we also gotta hear the taunts of our buddies calling him queer. We know that's not true. But we can't shout back and say, 'Hey, our dad likes women 'cause we see 'em coming through the house.' We just gotta shut up and take it. That's rough, especially since we're always reminded that our last name is Gay. There were times, though, when we didn't take it. There were times when both me and Marvin had to fight to defend our father's honor. After one nasty fight where Marvin got his nose bloodied and Father asked him why, Marvin just came out and said it. He told him that he looked like a homosexual and that he was bringing shame to all of us."

"How old was Marvin when this happened?" I asked.

"Nine or ten."

"What did your father do?"

"He beat the holy hell out of him. Only this time it was different. This time he locked him in our room and made him wait there for an hour. While Marvin waited, Father kept snapping his belt against the door so Marvin could think about what was about to happen. It was like torture.

" 'You got one chance to get outta this,' Father said. 'You gonna come out here and apologize to me and everyone else in this family, or I'm coming in after you.'

"Marvin shouted back, 'You're the one who should be apologizing! You're the one going round looking like a queer.'

"That did it. Father went in after him. But this beating was different. Not only did he give him a whipping, but he tore off all his clothes beforehand. It was a struggle. Marvin fought back, but he was only a kid. He couldn't fight off a grown man. Father overpowered him, he beat Marvin butt naked, not just with the leather belt but with the buckle as well. He tore into his skin and left these big welts. Then Father made him stay home from school for weeks 'cause he was scared the teachers at school might see the marks on Marvin's back and call social services. After that, you'd think Marvin would learn—as I did—not to answer back. But he never learned that. No matter how bad the beatings, Marvin never backed down.

"But it wasn't just Father. It was an uncle of ours who actually molested Marvin. When Marvin told Father about it, Father didn't believe him. But I knew Marvin was telling the truth. I saw it happen. I wanted to stick up for Marvin, but I was afraid of Father. We all were."

I got chills hearing these horror stories. They deepened my empathy for Marvin. They had a strange effect, causing me to minimize my own problems growing up. *If I had it bad, Marvin had it worse.* This was part of my pattern of magnifying the importance of his story while belittling my own.

The stories also further alienated me from Marvin's father. In fact, I could no longer see him as Father. I saw him as the Beast. I avoided him as much as I could. That was easy because he was usually hibernating in his bedroom. When I did encounter him at the dinner table, I had nothing to say. When he addressed me, it was only to remind me to take care because I was carrying his grandson. Always his grandson, never his granddaughter.

After a couple of months of living in DC, I didn't think I could take any more. I called my mother back in LA.

"What's wrong, baby?" asked Mom.

"I hate it here."

"Then leave."

"I don't want to leave."

"You don't want to leave a place that's driving you crazy?"

"I don't want to make Marvin mad."

"Well, I'm mad. I'm coming there."

"I wish you would."

Mom flew in to Washington. Mother Gay, Father Gay, and Marvin's siblings treated her with indifference. I was glad to see her. I wanted her comfort and reassurance. I needed relief from the oppressive vibes that permeated the Gay household.

Mom's presence provided a buffer between Marvin's family and myself. Compared to the Gays, Mom seemed absolutely sane. In her own way, she was a tough character. With her around, I felt protected.

On a few occasions Marvin took a break from the road to visit his family and me. I noticed how he and Father assiduously avoided each other. Father rarely left his room. When he did come downstairs, Marvin got up and left. Few words were exchanged. The atmosphere was ice cold. Not even the smallest hint of affection.

Meanwhile, the family continued to campaign for their move to LA. I saw the subtle ways that Mother Gay worked on Marvin.

"There isn't anything she wants that I wouldn't give her," Marvin told me when we were alone. "She is deserving. She is worthy. She is the most wonderful woman in the world. It will be amazing to have her close to me in LA."

"And your father?"

"We'll keep the house here. He'll stay behind. He likes it here."

"I hate it here," I couldn't help but tell Marvin.

"I'm sorry, dear, but this was the only way you could understand where I'm coming from. I love you even more for putting up with all this. It shows me how you truly love me."

I was happy to hear his words, but happier still when, seven months pregnant, the stay in DC ended. Finally, the prison sentence was over. Though I had been there for only three months, it felt like a lifetime.

Marvin and I flew back to LA, where he rented a beautiful two-bedroom apartment in Brentwood.

My final trimester was made bearable by the fact that I was no longer living in the same household as the Beast. And with the tour behind him, Marvin was loving and attentive.

One of the happiest—and strangest moments—of my pregnancy involved visiting Quincy Jones, then married to Peggy Lipton.

A few years earlier, when my boyfriend Bryant and I were tripping on LSD, I had hallucinated and, in my mind's eyes, seen Quincy and Billy Eckstine. It was as though they were standing before me. I had forgotten the incident until Marvin and I arrived at Quincy's house. Peggy, who could not have been sweeter, walked us to the backyard where they were grilling steaks. And right there, standing shoulder to shoulder, were Quincy and Billy Eckstine! It was surreal, an unexpected flashback to my acid vision. Fortunately, I was able to maintain my composure and enjoy the graciousness of Peggy, Quincy, and Billy.

Marvin's career continued to flourish. America was still grooving to "Let's Get It On." The live version of "Distant Lover," released from the concert album in Oakland, was another smash hit. Motown was understandably eager for Marvin to get back in the studio and cut another record. But Marvin was making no moves in that direction. The more Motown urged him to act, the more inactive he became.

"Maybe I'll leave Motown," he told me one afternoon.

"Are you serious?"

"Perhaps. But even if I don't, I like the idea of worrying them because, with their prodding, they never mind worrying me."

He brought me along to a meeting with Gil Friesen, an A&M Records executive who had contacted Marvin about switching labels. Friesen responded to Marvin's warm and winning personality. This super-hot label that recorded artists like Quincy Jones and the Carpenters would be honored to sign Marvin. Friesen considered him a genius, comparing him to Mozart and Picasso. He laid it on thick.

Marvin loved the lavish praise. As Friesen rattled on, Marvin squeezed my hand, as if to say, "This is it. This is our future. The end of all my old ties to Motown. The start of something new."

On the ride home after the meeting, I was excited. Marvin was leaving Motown. That meant leaving all the Motown people who wanted me out of Marvin's life.

"When will you tell Motown that it's over?" I asked.

"When it's over, dear."

"Isn't that going to be soon? This man offered you millions."

"At the end of my current contract, Motown will offer me millions as well."

"But the Motown people drive you crazy. They make you unhappy."

"But they also made my career."

"Your talent made your career, Marvin. You don't need Motown anymore."

"To up and leave is no simple task."

"Why not?"

"There's history there."

"History of misery and conflict."

"Well, dear," said Marvin, "perhaps misery and conflict make for great music. Perhaps without misery and conflict my well would run dry."

"That's a strange thing to say."

"The truth," said Marvin, "is always strange."

"I just want you to be happy. And I just don't think Motown makes you happy."

"You should know by now, Jan, that some people don't think they're worthy of happiness. Some people believe happiness is for fools. I believe that true artists have to suffer."

At this moment of Marvin's musing, we were driving down a Sunset Strip decorated with billboards for albums by the Captain and Tennille and Kiss. After smoking a joint, Marvin grew more philosophical.

"I have no argument with anyone's music," he added. "If it's superficial, that's fine. If its aim is to bring mild pleasure or some sensual delight to the ear, why, that's wonderful. But if I take my music seriously and do what God has asked me to do, I must use it to awaken the mind of man. I must let the world know that, when it comes to our journey through time, there is more than meets the eye. We must look beyond the veil. True artists lift that veil. And, dear Jan, if I am not a true artist, I am nothing."

When Marvin spoke this way, I didn't reply. I simply listened. He spoke with such passion and eloquence that it was impossible not to believe his every word.

The Beauty

I remember what all mothers remember about giving birth: the pain, exhilaration, fear, relief, joy—the whole extravagant mess of emotions that accompanies that miraculous moment.

It was September 4, 1974. Marvin was by my side. I saw in his eyes what could only be understood as disappointment. The infant was a girl.

When I went into labor, Marvin was so dear and sweet. We were at the house and I said, "It's time!" The moment he heard the words he started freaking out. He went into the bathroom and got a toothbrush, toothpaste, and a pair of underwear. I started laughing trying to figure out his line of thinking, especially since they were a pair of his underwear and the toothpaste did not have a cap on it. By the time we got to the hospital, there was toothpaste all over his underwear, as he was holding it so tightly.

"Dear, just throw it away," I told him laughing. I couldn't believe it, but I was comforting him, even though I was about to give birth to our first child.

It was beautiful. Marvin never left my side for two days, which meant he missed a concert. Anna was waiting for him on the other end, in Detroit. That interrupted our blissful couple of days.

I spent the following days a worried mess. I was concerned that Marvin was with Anna, and I feared they were plotting to take my child. I was relieved to see his smiling face when he returned from Motown, greeting me and his baby daughter, Nona.

My words were, "I'm sorry."

Marvin's words were, "That's all right, dear. She looks just like you. She's just beautiful."

Her name was Nona, and she was greatly loved by all. Marvin nicknamed her Pie.

Because Anna Gordy was raising Marvin III, Nona became the first grandchild to whom the Gays had access. Whatever reservations they may have had about me, they embraced Nona unconditionally. In the coming months, they—along with my mom, Barbara, and daddy Earl—would take turns holding and cuddling her.

Yet at the moment of her birth, I had pangs of remorse. I felt that I had disappointed Marvin.

"It's crazy to be sorry about something that you have no control over," Mom told me in the hospital room after Marvin had left. "When the sperm hits the egg, the result is up to God, not us."

"I know that," I said with tears running down my face. "I just wanted to make him happy."

"He *is* happy. He's deliriously happy. No one seeing this child could not be happy. She's all sunshine and sugar. So cheer up, baby. Get it together. It'll all be fine."

In my mind, it wasn't all fine. It turned out that two days after Nona's birth, Marvin had a gig in Detroit. While he was still at the hospital with me and Nona, Anna was calling him. She was waiting for him in Detroit. Marvin explained that at this point they were merely friends. But because I was vulnerable—after all, I had just given birth—and insecure, I didn't want Marvin to go. He went anyway. And I couldn't help but wonder whether if I had given birth to a boy Marvin would have stayed by my side.

My fears about Anna were misplaced. Their romantic relationship had died years before. Three weeks after Nona's birth, we all went on the road together. Marvin was thrilled with his baby daughter. Over and over again, he declared his undying devotion to his new family. He saw a chance to finally fulfill his dream—a loving woman, a loving child, simple domestic happiness. Yet while "simple happiness" was certainly something I longed for, it wasn't actually what Marvin wanted. Because when happiness arrived, he went about planting the seeds for future misery.

He knew that his fathering a child with a young woman would antagonize Anna, who was unable to conceive a child of her own. The battle with Anna, begun in the sixties and still raging in the seventies, was far from over. Nona's birth represented an escalation in the war.

I also witnessed Marvin insulating himself from sound advice. His accountants told him to put away part of his ever-increasing income to pay his ever-increasing back taxes. They formulated a generous budget for him and urged him to watch his impulsive spending. But I saw how he ignored them. He just wouldn't deal with his tax issues. He wouldn't stop buying whatever he wanted. He bought his mother a house in the LA area. He kept buying cars and all sorts of property. He threw all caution to the wind.

I didn't have a clear picture of Marvin's financial reality. But I did have firsthand knowledge of his unmanageability. A case in point was manager Stephen Hill. After the trip to Jamaica, his relationship with Marvin deteriorated. As a savvy businessman and astute student of human behavior, Hill was sure that he had Marvin's number. With all his sophistication and sensitivity, he was certain that he could get Marvin to behave. For a while, Marvin allowed Hill his illusion.

But when push came to shove, I saw how Marvin simply couldn't be moved. He wouldn't go back on tour. He wouldn't go back in the studio. He wouldn't meet with Motown officials to discuss his future. He wouldn't seriously consider moves outside music—acting opportunities in television or movies—to widen his audience.

"I am in love with Jan," I heard him tell Hill. "I am in love with my new life. Let me live life outside the madness of show business. Give me my peace."

Like many a manager before him, Hill's tenure with Marvin would eventually end in frustration.

With Nona beside us, Marvin and I grew closer.

"I want to be closer to you," he said. "Close to our daughter. Close to everything and everyone important to your life."

I was heartened to see Marvin cultivating relationships with both my daddy Earl and my father Slim. I saw it as another sign of his love for me.

The first time I took Marvin to Earl's house was memorable. I hadn't prepared him. I didn't say much about the man who had essentially raised me—only that he was cool. Marvin had no idea how cool. Earl had that dangerous street edge that Marvin found so alluring, not to mention the most potent cocaine in the city. Marvin had his whisper-quiet, lighthearted banter; Earl had his salty, kicked-back Texas drawl. The ladies adored Earl. In no time, he and Marvin were thick as thieves. Watching these men get high together—the two men I loved most in the world—brought me great satisfaction, especially since it was a mellow smile-and-laugh high, a high that bonded them. Each played his role beautifully—Earl the respected and confident gangster, Marvin the artist of sophisticated funk. Earl's hipness added to my credentials and, in my mind, made Marvin value me more.

Slim Gaillard was hip in a different way. When word came round that his little girl, whom he had ignored for most of her life, had hooked up with Marvin Gaye, Slim came running. One night he showed up at the studio when I was watching Marvin finish up a few overdubs. Slim's entrance was spectacular—dark glasses, crumpled hat, crumpled suit, socks around his ankles, scruffy shoes, and a Grizzly Adams beard.

He gave me a big bear hug before telling Marvin, "Hey man, you stole the prettiest flower from my garden. You robbed me, brother, robbed me blind. You do realize that you're the luckiest cat this side of bebop heaven, don't you?"

Marvin loved great characters, and Slim was one of the greatest. He regaled Marvin with stories of playing Central Avenue in LA and Minton's in Manhattan. Hanging with Bird. Scatting behind Dizzy. Laughing it up with Lady Day. Hanging at the track with Nat King Cole. Tracking musical changes with Miles and Monk. Clowning with Sinatra. There was no one Slim didn't know. There was nothing he hadn't done. His self-celebration was made palatable by the word pictures he painted: Blowing the blues on the beaches of Havana with Chano Pozo banging the bongos behind him. Slipping into the jazz cellars of Paris while the city's slickest musicians studied his licks and tricks.

"I've written some four hundred songs," Slim would say, "and had another four hundred stolen by the coldest cats from Nome, Alaska, to Pensacola, Florida."

Slim wouldn't shut up, but Marvin didn't mind. Neither did I. Marvin was seeing that, as a child of both Earl and Slim, I was the daughter of two very different street aristocrats, one more impressive than the other.

After the blessed birth of Nona, Marvin even extended his charm to my mom. When she came to visit Nona, he was welcoming and warm.

Later that night, though, he discovered me crying inconsolably. He took me in his arms and asked what was wrong. I hesitated to tell him. I myself didn't understand my reaction to the news conveyed by a childhood friend and confirmed by Mom.

"What is it, dear?"

"Mama Ruth."

Over these past months, Marvin had heard my horror stories, just as little by little he'd told me the horror stories from his own childhood.

"What about that awful woman?"

"She's dying."

Marvin closed his eyes. Several seconds of silence passed before he took my hand and asked me, "You want to see her, don't you?"

"How did you know that?"

"I can just feel it."

"Do you think it's stupid to want to say good-bye to someone who did what she did to me?"

"No, dear. I think it's good. It's closure. There are times when closure is necessary. If you want to see her, I'll go with you."

"I want to take Nona. I want to show Ruth that, despite everything, I have a beautiful man and a beautiful child."

"We'll take Nona. We'll let you say whatever you need to say to this woman."

"But why am I feeling that I need to see her?"

"She was a huge part of your life. Good or bad, in many ways she was your mother. Your relationship with her is incredibly deep. It's a good thing to see her, Jan. It really is."

During the ride to the nursing home in Pasadena, I was an emotional mess. I was certain I was doing the wrong thing by bringing Marvin and Nona; but I was still uncertain why I was doing it at all. I felt shaky and frightened.

"Let's turn around and go home," I told Marvin when we had practically arrived.

"You need to follow your instincts. You need to see this through, dear."

My fear mounted as Marvin parked the car, as I removed Pie from her baby seat and took her in my arms, as the three of us walked down a hallway in a nursing home reeking of musty carpeting.

We came to the room and knocked. A frail voice said, "Come in."

Marvin held my hand tightly as the door slowly opened. Inside, on a single bed, was a slight sparrowlike woman who, with some effort, looked up at me. It was Ruth. Her eyes were still sharp. It took her a few seconds to focus. When she did, her thin lips broke into an uneven smile.

"My baby," she said in a voice that was barely audible. "My golden girl. My Janis. I've been waiting for you. I knew you'd come."

I thought I'd know what to say. I had even rehearsed the lines: *You hurt me; you tortured me; you fucked up my childhood; you vicious horrible bitch; I just came for the satisfaction of watching you die.*

But these were not the words that came out of my mouth. I had no words, only tears streaming from my eyes.

"Show her Nona," Marvin finally said. "Show her Pie."

I walked closer to the bed to give Ruth a better look at our baby.

"Beautiful child," was all Ruth could say. "Beautiful mother. You know that I loved you. I loved all my children."

I still couldn't respond. All I could do was stand there with my baby in my arms.

Again Marvin spoke for me.

"Jan wanted to come and tell you good-bye," he said.

"Oh, where is she going?" asked Ruth.

Marvin hesitated to answer.

I finally had the words—*You're going to a place where you can no longer hurt anyone*—but the words remained unspoken.

Raw Soul

After the birth of Nona, I was alarmed by my weight gain. I had lost my perfect shape. My bodily imperfections had an enormous impact not only on my sense of self-worth, but also on my relationship with Marvin. My body had been my currency, my greatest asset. Marvin had loved to praise my physical beauty. When that praise stopped and criticism began, I fell into fear. He said that he loved me as the mother of his child but was no longer in love with me. Those words shocked and stung. Why this sudden change? Where was this coming from? I was too taken aback to reply.

"You need to lose some weight, dear," he said.

I panicked. *Lose the weight*, I thought, *or lose Marvin.*

I hit the gym and worked out religiously to get down to 126 pounds. The weight loss afforded me some comfort and seemed to please Marvin, but there was another body issue that caused me even more alarm.

One day when I was shopping with my mother and trying on clothes, I stood in front of a full-length mirror in a dressing room.

I took off my top and saw these pronounced red marks below my navel.

"Mom!" I cried. "What the hell are these?"

"Stretch marks."

"Will they go away?"

"Of course not. They're something to be proud of. Badges of motherhood."

"I hate them."

"All women hate them. That's only natural, baby. But you'll get used to them."

"I want to get rid of them."

"I've read that doctors are working on certain kinds of surgeries, but I'm not sure it's all been perfected yet. We can look into it if you want to, but it's easier just to accept them."

But would Marvin?

The answer was no, not entirely. My once-ideal form was blemished. The imperfections bothered him. The weight was gone, but the stretch marks remained.

"Surely there is a way to rid yourself of those things," he said one night.

His words were harsh, as though I appeared repugnant to him.

"My mother and I have looked into some possibilities, but there's no guarantee that they'll be effective. I'm not crazy about the idea of plastic surgery."

Marvin just smiled. The smile drove me a little mad. He wasn't insisting that I have surgery, but at the same time he was hardly supportive of my current condition.

Days passed. Then weeks. He touched me less even as I yearned for him more. I needed reassurance, affection, attention. I feared that my postpartum condition would permanently turn him off. Postpartum depression started to weigh me down.

When Marvin and I did sleep together, the sex was less satisfying. The bloom was off the rose.

"**Come up for the weekend**," said my sister Cass, who lived in the Bay Area. "There's a band I want you to hear."

Cass was five years older than me. She and I had different mothers but were both daughters of Slim Gaillard. We were thick as thieves.

Getting away for a minute sounded good. I thought it might lift my postpartum blues. Besides, Cass was fun. As Slim's child, it was no surprise that she liked to party.

I left Nona with Mom and got the okay from Marvin to spend the weekend with my sister. I flew up to San Francisco, where Cass picked me up and whisked me back to her place. A beauty with a stunning figure, Cass got dolled up for the evening. Not to be outdone, I put together a knockout outfit myself.

Party time.

"What's the band called?"

"Raw Soul."

"And they're that good?"

"Better than good. Dynamite. I'm in love with the lead singer," said Cass, not at all concerned with the fact that she was married.

I breathed in the night air. The hills of San Francisco were beautiful. The city felt alive.

"Feels good," I said. "I haven't been out in a while."

"You gotta get out more."

"It's hard to do. We had the Pie so quickly. And with my daughter came big responsibilities."

"I'm surprised he let you come up here."

"He's not my dad."

"He acts like it sometimes."

"Come on, Cass. You make it sound like I'm his hostage."

"Look, Sis, I'm thrilled for you, I really am. You won the heart of one of the world's most talented men. But I also know that guys like that are possessive as the devil."

"Marvin's different. He's basically spiritual."

"I think he's basically sexual."

"You hardly know him. You've only met him a couple of times."

"I knew it the first five minutes I was with him. I felt it. All women do. Why do you think he's so popular?" asked Cass.

"His voice."

"His looks."

I flashed back to the first time Marvin looked at Cass. There was no doubt that he was attracted—and vice versa. But they both had the good sense to leave it alone. I was grateful. The last thing I wanted was to compete with my sister. At the same time, I couldn't deny the sibling rivalry.

When it came to other women wanting Marvin, I had my guard up all the time. I was always asking myself: *Do I look as good as them? Do I dress as well?*

Cass and I arrived at the club, called the Scene. Raw Soul was already on the bandstand. The place was jam-packed. It was a young crowd. The vibe was casual, the ambience cool. Cass led me to a spot near the band. Men took note of the two super-sexy women sashaying through the club. I liked the attention. It'd been a long while since I'd been appreciated. I was back in form. I accepted a joint from Cass and took a hit.

Mellow high. Mellow crowd. And most mellow of all, the band. Their groove was kicked-back, tight-and-right R&B. A different sound.

The lead singer had soul to spare. Slender of build, short of stature, he was a cool brother. Short-cropped beard. Dark bedroom eyes. I couldn't help but notice him noticing me. Cass noticed the same thing.

"His name is Frankie Beverly," Cass told me. "He's already taken. He's mine."

"I wasn't even thinking . . ."

"You were looking."

"You're high," I said.

"Everyone here is high. They're funky, aren't they?"

"They're bad."

"Frankie wants to meet you," said Cass.

After the first set, we went back to the dressing room, where it was clear that Frankie Beverly wanted to meet Marvin.

"He's my hero," said the singer, his eye on both of us.

"I'm going to let him know how much I love the band," I said. "I'm gonna try and get him up here to see you."

"That would be in-in-in-incredible," said Frankie, who spoke with a slight stutter. "I don't know how to t-t-t-t-thank you."

"Thank *me*," said Cass, "for introducing you to my sister."

"She's a cool sista," said Beverly.

"We're outta here," said Cass, whisking me out of the dressing room, out of the club, into the car, and back into the San Francisco night.

The excursion helped my frame of mind. Hanging at the club, hearing the band, meeting the singer, being seen and desired by men had done wonders for my sinking spirit. And, to be honest, I found Mr. Beverly extremely sexy.

I returned to LA to find Marvin in a good mood. He was talking about buying a house far out in the country. While Motown was putting pressure on him to plan a new album, his only plan was to escape Hollywood.

"I need time between projects," he told me as we drove out to the foothills of the San Fernando Valley, some forty miles from Los Angeles, where a real estate agent was going to show us a home. "I need the well to fill back up."

"That's good, Marvin," I said. "Take your time."

"I will, dear. I'm not some music machine churning out hits. That's Berry's way—the assembly-line Motown method. I can't be pressured. I won't be. We need space between us and them."

I was gratified that he said *we* and not *I*. Nona and I were part of his plans. We were now his family. The home he envisioned was for the new and calm domestic life he yearned to live.

The home appeared perfect. It was in Hidden Hills, a small community of luxurious but tasteful suburban homes on enormous lots with paths for horses running through the community.

"I love the name," Marvin said softly. "Hidden Hills. It is here where we will hide and live happily ever after."

"I love the house," I said as we inspected the property, which sat on five acres on Long Valley Road. The ranch-style design was casual. There was a swimming pool, hot tubs, and horse stables. What caught Marvin's eye, though, was the regulation-size basketball court.

"We'll buy the house," he told the agent even before being told the price. "My management will be in touch."

Marvin was on a buying streak. There was property in Jamaica, a ranch in Round Mountain, a place in Lake Tahoe. There were all sorts of cars—a Cadillac, a Mercedes, a Rolls-Royce, a Jaguar, an Excalibur, not to mention a motor home and a van.

"The motor home is for us and the kids," he told me. "We need to have another baby."

I watched Marvin's moods swing from despondency to ebullience. When he was down, he sulked and spoke of the hopeless condition of the world. He claimed that the devil was winning the war with God. When he was up—like today—his spirit was bright and loving. God was in charge. All was good. Why not spend money on a better life for those he loved most?

On the ride back to the city, Marvin praised my beauty, expressed his love for me, and gave gratitude for the ways in which I had enhanced his life. We held hands. For the moment, he seemed to have forgotten that only days before he had said he was no longer in love with me. I saw no reason to remind him of that painful statement. I was thrilled to see that he had changed his mind.

"I want to know about your trip to see Cass," he said. "You said something about a band. You couldn't stop talking about them."

"That's because they were great," I said. "Great band. Great singer. He idolizes you. He wants you to hear him."

"And you think they're happenin'?"

"I know they are."

"Then maybe we'll make a quick trip up the coast to see them."

"You won't be sorry."

The trip happened in a hurry. The meeting between the soul men was magical. Frankie was enamored of Marvin's genius but professional enough not to be intimidated by his presence at the Scene. Frankie and his band performed flawlessly.

"Raw Soul isn't the right name," Marvin said afterward. "These cats are smooth as silk."

"That's what I said," I asserted, elated that Marvin loved the group as much as I did.

After the show, the smooth grooves of the music were reflected in the rhythm of the banter between Marvin and Frankie. I saw how the men were in sync. They both loved to lay back, enjoy a smoke, and engender a laugh. They were both quick to praise the other's creativity.

Marvin promised to help Frankie find a deal with a major label.

"Who are you going to take them to?" I asked Marvin when we were back in their hotel room.

"Not Motown. I have enough competition at Motown. Frankie's better off at another label. But don't fret, dear, I will help your boyfriend."

"He is not my boyfriend."

"I saw him looking at you. I saw you looking at him."

"I was only looking because Cass is in love with the guy. Cass is already sleeping with him. He's a cute little guy—that's all."

I tried to deny my attraction but didn't get far. Strangely, though, Marvin did not appear upset. He seemed excited by the prospect. It was the kind of potential drama on which his dark side fed.

That same night when we made love, he was aroused beyond his normal passion. I was thrilled to see that his desire had been restored.

"I love you so much," I whispered.

"I love you, dear, but can't help but wonder one small thing."

"Tell me."

"When we were in the throes of all this sweet ecstasy, were you really thinking of me . . . or were you fantasizing about him?"

"'Him'? Who?"

"Little man, of course."

Oh boy, I thought, *here we go*.

"I was only thinking of you, Marvin. I promise, I swear."

"I can't believe you're not haunted by that fantasy."

"Why not? He's fucking my sister and I'm with you. Hello!"

Our verbal wrestling match continued until we got tired of squabbling and went back to making sweet love.

Blessings and Burdens

We enjoyed the celebrity life. It was especially cool to meet Elliott Gould at an awards show. A huge Marvin fan, Elliott invited us to his home the following week. At the time he was married to Jennifer Bogart. Because Elliott was significantly older than Jennifer, I related to them as a couple and was eager to spend an evening with them. I dressed up for the occasion. Marvin put on a new brown sharkskin suit with matching brown shoes. He looked especially elegant. On the drive over, I was excited at the prospect of making new friends. But when we arrived at the Gould home, Marvin wouldn't park the car.

"What's wrong?" I asked.

"I don't feel like socializing," he said. "Let's go home."

My argument—that Elliott and Jennifer were expecting us—fell on deaf ears.

"Why are you doing this to me?" I asked. "Why are you disappointing me like this?"

Marvin didn't respond. He turned the car around and we never saw Elliott and Jennifer—not that evening, not ever.

At other times, Marvin could be especially sensitive and generous.

"I think you should go shopping, dear," Marvin said one day. "Buy something absolutely smashing. Buy whatever your heart desires. The sky's the limit."

"What's the occasion?"

"A surprise to end all surprises."

"Tell me, please," I whined.

"And ruin the surprise? I think not. Hurry off to Beverly Hills and get something nice. Hurry your ass. The limo will be here at seven."

Excitedly, I went off and returned a few hours later with what I considered a sensational outfit.

When I appeared before Marvin, he smiled approvingly.

"Just as I imagined," he said. "You will be the princess at the ball."

I was wearing a revealing two-piece halter dress, black satin heels, and pale pink glasses with rhinestone-covered frames.

"The princess is nothing without the prince," I said. "And the prince is looking pretty hot himself."

The prince was dressed in a black silk suit, an elegant white embroidered shirt, and patent-leather tuxedo shoes. He had splashed on Royall Lyme, his favorite fragrance.

Once inside the limousine, the prince remained secretive.

"You're really killing me," I said.

"Don't die on me, dear. At least not until you see what the gods of good fortune have in store for you."

The limo ride was long, fifteen miles down one freeway, fifteen miles down another. On the way, we shared a joint.

It was a hazy night. The smoke put us in an especially romantic frame of mind. I looked out the window and saw that we were approaching Long Beach Harbor. In the distance was the *Queen Mary*, the old luxury liner brought to port and turned into a hotel-museum. The limo pulled up to the entrance of the ship, all aglow with colorful lights. Music floated on air. Beautiful people milled about the decks. A great party was underway. My heart was racing.

Paparazzi were at the foot of the gangplank. Marvin and I stopped to pose for a few pictures.

"Who is the party for?" I asked.

"Shh . . . you'll see . . ."

I felt like I was stepping inside a dream. The ship was beyond elegant: the woodwork, the chandeliers, the promenades, the people. There was Gregory Peck, there was Kirk Douglas, there was Sidney Poitier, there was Elizabeth Taylor. And walking down the main staircase was Michael Jackson together with Paul McCartney.

The two men moved directly to Marvin and me.

I'd known Michael and his brothers since high school. Michael gave me a hug.

"It's so cool of you to invite us to your party, Paul," Marvin said. "Jan has been dreaming of this moment for many, many years."

Overwhelmed, I had no words except "So nice to meet you."

"Marvin," said Paul, "you have a lovely lady here."

With that, he took my hand, gently kissed it, and, along with Michael, moved on to greet the other guests.

Back in Hidden Hills, Marvin wanted reassurance that he had, in fact, made me happy.

"What do you think?" he asked. "Wasn't tonight a nice surprise?"

"Beautiful," I said. "I've been dreaming of meeting Paul ever since I saw him at Dodger Stadium with the Beatles in 1966. How can I ever thank you?"

"By giving us another child," Marvin said, before engaging me in passionate love.

Good news! Five months after giving birth to Nona, I discovered that I was pregnant again. These were the early months of 1975. I was now nineteen years old and had known Marvin for barely two years. I was elated. I was hopeful that the news would bring us closer together and bridge the gap that had opened when I became a mother and experienced bodily changes.

Marvin was equally elated, convinced that this time God would give him a son. He saw this as a great blessing.

At approximately the same time that Marvin and I learned of my pregnancy, Anna Gordy Gaye could no longer stand the embarrassment of her husband not only living with a teenage girl, but having children with her as well. She filed for divorce.

I understood. What woman wouldn't?

Marvin had publicly humiliated Anna. Their disagreements, which had been relatively tame in the past few months, suddenly exploded into full-out warfare.

I saw that warfare excited Marvin, even as Anna's legal procedures threatened his financial viability. While he was spending money recklessly, she was looking to wreck his monetary stability. She demanded heavy monthly payments for herself and their son. Beyond that, there were back payments due on repairs to the home owned by Marvin and Anna, not to mention legal and accounting fees.

Marvin's response—to throw the legal papers in the trash—alarmed me. I urged him to face the reality of what was happening.

"I can't deal with this stuff now," he said.

"Eventually you'll have to," said his lawyer. "Eventually you'll need to respond."

"You can respond now. Tell her that over the years she's gotten enough. Tell her to go to her brother. Berry has more money than God. Let him take care of her."

"I'm not sure you want to get Motown entangled in all this."

"When has Motown ever *not* been entangled? They're entangled in every part of my life."

Yet I did see how Motown and Berry diligently tried to separate Marvin the artist from Marvin the husband of Anna. Motown revered Marvin the artist. Moreover, Motown had a large investment in him and wanted nothing more than additional Marvin Gaye music.

But I was just beginning to understand that Marvin the man—the man who dreamt of playing for the Detroit Lions and becoming a professional boxer—had to prove his manhood. If cornered, he'd come out fighting. He perceived Anna's legal actions as threats. He saw them as tests of his strength. He told me that he had no choice but to take her on and prove his personal power.

It was clear to me that Anna's resources were greater than Marvin's. But that fact didn't make Marvin more cautious; it made him bolder. He actually liked assuming the role of the underdog—David versus Goliath. That heightened the drama. He was ready, even eager, to go to war.

Marvin would not yield to a single one of Anna's demands. Nor would he yield to Motown, which was imploring him to start recording new material. It made me think of the name of his first hit back in the sixties—"Stubborn Kind of Fellow."

Meanwhile, as I watched Marvin do battle with Anna and Motown, another precious life grew inside me. And on various nights I saw him leave his bitterness about his marriage and lose himself in a rare species of heavenly music that had nothing to do with any of the current vogue, the sounds of early disco that were beginning to flood the airwaves.

Because he didn't love to dance, dance music was last on Marvin's wish list of recordings. First on the list were the standards, the classic love songs from past eras, the deep-blue ballads that address love lost, love found, love remembered. I saw how these tear-stained melodies and heartbreaking messages spoke to his heart, just as they spoke to mine. They had nothing to do with commerce. They were not hit singles geared to current tastes. They were timeless, the sort of songs sung by the singers Marvin held in the highest regard: Nat Cole and Frank Sinatra, Billie Holiday and Ella Fitzgerald. In short, this was the material that, ever since initiating his professional career, he had longed to interpret.

"I can't sing these songs at the Motown studio," he told me. "Word will get back to Berry. Berry will have a fit. He'll start demanding that I churn out hits. No, I'm not going to record at Motown. I need a place of my own."

That place turned out to be a customized recording studio contained in a small single-story building on Sunset Boulevard that, together with the house in Hidden Hills, became a central focal point for Marvin and me for the next several years. The location was both logical and alluring. It was logical because it was a piece of prime real estate in the middle of Hollywood. It was alluring because it was situated on that portion of the Strip populated by prostitutes. The illicit sex trade that Marvin found so enticing operated right next door at the Copper Penny, a coffee shop where the working ladies liked to congregate.

Inside, the Marvin Gaye Recording Studio was all Marvin. He chose the colors; he designed the decor. It was cooler than cool: dark wood, soft lighting, plush carpet, an upstairs loft apartment with a waterbed and Jacuzzi. It was a musical cocoon, a heavenly hideaway in the midst of Hollywood's hellhole sex trade. I saw how the studio symbolized every one of Marvin's baffling paradoxes. It was in the world, yet not of the world. Its purpose was to free his art from earthly distractions, even as it positioned him closer to those distractions than ever before.

For days at a time Marvin was locked up in the studio, where he worked with his trusted and skillful engineer Art Stewart, a wonderful man whose calm personality, good humor, and brotherly devotion helped Marvin in every possible way.

Marvin lost himself in the sounds of these standards. When I was invited to hear the music haunting Marvin's mind, I was mes-merized. The orchestrations were lush and enormous: violins, cello, oboes, flutes, harps.

I observed how Marvin sat as he sang, his mouth practically touching the microphone. He sang effortlessly. His eyes were closed. Even singing songs with well-known lyrics, he improvised new lyrics of his own, making the story completely personal.

"I'm singing these songs about you," he told me. "You are the subject of every song."

I was both pleased and confused.

"They weren't written about me," I said. "They were written by other men for other women."

"I'm rewriting them for you."

"But why?"

"Because that's what love demands. Tell Jan the story of how it all began," Marvin urged Art.

"In the late sixties," said Art, "Marv hired an orchestrator, a brilliant musician named Bobby Scott, to write arrangements for a suite of songs like 'The Shadow of Your Smile' and 'Why Did I Choose You.' Every one is a classic. Bobby rose to the occasion. His orchestrations are great. Sinatra would kill for these charts. So Marvin immediately went into the studio and began singing over the arrangements. His vocals were good, but not great. This was before *What's Going On*, before he knew how to overdub his own voice and accompany himself. He sang the songs straight. He sang the songs honestly, but in one voice and one voice only. I believe he sang them with the intention of revising his career as a pop singer—as opposed to a rhythm-and-blues singer."

"I hate those original vocals," said Marvin.

"Why?" I asked.

"Because they're immature and superficial. This material required a knowledge of love—I'm talking about romantic love—and

that's something I had never really known. You can't fake this material. These songs demand everything you've ever felt about love. I
simply hadn't felt enough. And then I met you."

My heart began to race. His words suddenly erased all our
problems.

"These are your songs," he said. "And now I can sing them."

He sang them not for an hour or two or three, but all night
long, and the next night, and the night after. He sang these songs—
building new harmonies, merging his many voices, sweetening the
lyrics, augmenting the melodies—utilizing every essential tool available to him as not only a former doo-wopper but a musician who, like
Miles Davis, understood the improvisatory genius of jazz.

"He's already sung these songs a hundred times," Art told me.
"And never the same way twice."

"I'm trying to understand what they're about," added Marvin.
"I'm searching for the meaning. If you stay here next to me while I
sing, I can feel the meaning come into focus. Will you stay?"

"I will."

"Then roll the tape, Art, and let me sing."

The sessions went on and on. It was as though they happened
outside of time. Marvin adhered to no schedule. He had no plans to
release them.

"Why not?" I asked.

"Motown wants singles," said Marvin. "Motown wants hits. And
I want love."

"Your fans will love these songs."

"Motown will say they are not current. Motown will moan and
groan about how I tried to do this before. Motown will remind
me that it didn't work then and won't work now. I don't need to hear
that from Motown. I don't need to play these songs for Motown. I
just need to birth these songs the way you will soon be birthing our
baby boy."

A month before I gave birth, Marvin told me he was flying to the East Coast.

"What's the trip about?" I asked.

"A secret mission."

Two days later, his purpose was revealed. Newspapers across the country carried a formal photo of Marvin, elegantly attired in custom-tailored suit and tie, sitting next to Shirley Temple Black, former child star and US ambassador to Ghana, and United Nations secretary general Kurt Waldheim.

"Did I look distinguished?" Marvin asked me.

"Very."

"The UN wants me to spearhead a campaign underscoring the plight of the poor in Africa."

"That's wonderful."

"They say that because of the respect I command the world over, I can make a difference. I can bring awareness where awareness is sorely needed."

"I'm proud of you, dear."

"But there's only one problem."

"What is it?"

"They see me as a responsible and decent human being."

"Why is that a problem?"

Marvin's eyes narrowed. He allowed a few seconds of silence to pass before uttering words that chilled me to the bone.

"It's a problem," he said, "because it's a lie."

On November 16, 1975, our son was born. A great blessing for all. His name was Frankie Christian Gaye. His first name was in honor of Marvin's brother and his middle name in honor of my brother Mark's middle name. We called him Bubby.

Circumstances surrounding the birth were dramatic. Marvin

was due to fly out to a gig in Denver. At the hospital, his manager
Stephen Hill kept looking at his watch and urging Marvin to leave.
But he wouldn't budge.

"Let the promoter sue me," he said. "I don't care."

The night of the fourteenth, as we approached midnight, everyone in the room—Marvin and his whole family—was urging me to
have the baby so his birthday would be the same as his namesake
Frankie's. Unfortunately, I couldn't comply. Our son was born the
next day. It was a breech birth during which our precious newborn
broke his arm: it had to be taped to his body.

Like a fool, I was feeling guilty about everything—guilty that
Marvin had to miss his gig (and was eventually sued for a ton of
money); guilty that I couldn't deliver on Marvin's brother's birthday; guilty that the breech birth caused harm to my son. Of course
I knew that none of it was my fault. That was my rational mind. But
my irrational mind, which so often ruled the day, kept burdening me
with the blame.

And yet joy prevailed. Marvin and I had another beautiful baby!
Unfortunately, joy was short-lived. Like so many women, I was hit by
a serious case of the postpartum blues.

So much was happening at once. Marvin's former family with
Anna was falling apart as his new family with me was coming
together—at least for now.

On any given day, documents and demands arrived from Anna's
lawyers. Marvin was required to attend a series of court hearings
concerning spousal and child support. He refused. His lawyers kept
warning about dire consequences, but Marvin was adamant. Anna
responded by refusing him visitation with their son, Marvin III. The
animosity between Anna and Marvin intensified.

"She's going for my money," Marvin told me. "She's using my
child to hurt me. But what she really wants is me. She wants me back.
And that will never happen."

Another battle was the political fury over the case of Rubin

"Hurricane" Carter, the boxer who many thought had been wrongly imprisoned for murder. Bob Dylan had written a song about the injustice. Marvin identified with Hurricane and, like Dylan, was convinced that the fighter was the victim of racism.

In an act of solidarity, Marvin shaved his head.

"When the press wants to know why I've done this," he told me, "I'll tell them that my head is clean shaven to let the world know that the case against Hurricane is dirty."

Bald as a cue ball and dressed in white from head to toe, Marvin appeared at a charity event for Reverend Cecil Williams's Glide Memorial Church in San Francisco, barely making it to the stage on time.

I was back in Hidden Hills, dealing with depression. Because this particular form of blues had hit me before, this time was a little easier. But I was still down. More than ever, I felt unable to help Marvin sort out his problems. And when it came to my problems, I was still fixated on my body. I was still a teenager, worried about whether, after this second birth, Marvin would find me less appealing.

When I thought about my own largely unspoken dreams—to sing or dance, to have some role in show business—I understood that, given Marvin's supreme self-preoccupation, those dreams would be given little consideration. In this relationship there was room for only one career. A large part of me accepted that. Yet a smaller part of me clung to the hope that Marvin would one day help those dreams.

At the same time, watching Marvin's dramatic dismissal of Anna from his life, I worried that the same fate might befall me. In order to avoid that fate, I had to be understanding, put his needs before my own, and make sure I slimmed down so he'd still find me sexy.

If he was happy with me, he'd protect me from his family who had moved from Washington to LA. He'd seen that they were cold to me—his mother was disapproving and his father, who had also decided to relocate to the West Coast, was creepy.

Marvin would provide me with the warmth and security that I so badly needed. He'd make our new family—me, Nona, and Bubby— his first priority. He'd see that this time he had a chance to achieve what he had always wanted: peace in his heart, peace in his mind, peace at home.

He'd realize that either romance grows or withers. And he'd decide to do all he could to make our love grow.

He'd stand up against the negative forces.

He'd protect me; he'd protect our children.

He'd do what was right.

He'd make sure that we all lived happily ever after.

A Deepening Maze

Marvin's brother Frankie was flattered that our son was named after him. But he confided in me that he also expressed bewilderment. He couldn't understand why Marvin was going out of his way to help the other Frankie—Frankie Beverly—and not him.

"I know he wants to help you," I said, recognizing the love and mutual admiration between the two brothers. "But right now he's really busy."

"Not too busy to get Beverly and his band a meeting with Capitol Records. I heard they already have a deal."

"You know your brother," I said. "He adores Stevie Wonder. He knows that Stevie idolizes him. He knows that if it weren't for *What's Going On*, Stevie wouldn't have found the courage to take on Berry and produce his own records. Marvin loves those records. We listen to them night and day. But every time Stevie wins another Grammy, Marvin sinks into a depression. All these years and all these hits, he's never won one—not for 'Grapevine,' not for 'What's Going On,' not for 'Let's Get It On.' He can't help but feel competitive with Stevie. Or, for that matter, with you. That's his nature. You were the one who first told me that your brother was haunted by insecurities."

"He is, but at the cost of others. Seems like the ones closest to him—those of us who love him most—are the ones who wind up getting most hurt."

"He speaks of you lovingly," I said. "I promise you he does."

"And that's how he speaks of you, Jan. But is he letting you sing? Is he doing anything to help you build a career free of him?"

"I don't want to be free of him."

"He knows that and he uses that. He wants you—he wants me, he wants our mother and father and everyone around him—to be dependent on him. That way he controls us."

"You make him out to be so manipulative. You make him out to be almost evil, Frankie."

"He has more love in his heart than anyone I know. But he also has all this fear. And the fear takes the form of control. If he feels like he's in control, the fear subsides."

"So what can we do?" I asked.

"Wait," said Frankie. "Wait and hope that with all his crazy success he'll feel more confident and not have to shut us out."

"I don't feel like he's shutting me out," I said.

"He loves you, Jan. He loves his babies. That's how it should be. It's a beautiful time in his life. You've brought out so much beauty in him. I'm just praying that he can feel worthy of this beauty. Because if he doesn't, if the devil stays in his ear and tells him that he's not worthy, he'll do what he always does."

"What's that?" I asked.

"Find a way to turn heaven into hell."

Meanwhile, Marvin was deeply involved with his wife. Yes, the involvement concerned divorce; and yes, the divorce grew more acrimonious by the day; and yes, Marvin was infuriated by her legal assaults. But from my point of view, the truth was that he was still passionately engaged with Anna, even if the engagement had assumed a malicious tone. As a result of the furious warfare, Anna was receiving far more of Marvin's attention than me.

There were still sunny days and moonlit nights when we were alone together. There was still passionate love. There were drives up the coast with our family of four in the camper. There were stops along the ocean's edge, the kids playing in the sand, Marvin and me filled with joy at the sight of our precious angels.

Marvin was a proud and doting father. I was an affectionate and protective mother. I loved those babies with all my heart; couldn't have loved them more.

There were long nights at his Sunset studio where, again and again, Marvin returned to record the love ballads that excited his soul.

But there was also a negative undercurrent, very subtle, not always apparent. Case in point was Marvin's relationship with Frankie Beverly.

"He's coming to town to meet with Capitol at the end of week," Marvin told me one afternoon. "I think it'd be nice if you picked him up at the airport."

The suggestion took me by surprise.

"Why me?" I asked.

"You guys are buds. You introduced me. You're his girl."

"No, I'm not!"

"You know he wants you," said Marvin.

"He's not my type. He's too hairy."

"Right," he responded with wicked sarcasm.

"Marvin, why are you starting up this mess?"

"Mess?"

"Yes, mess. Just be nice. Be cool."

"I still want you to pick him up at the airport."

"I will," I said, "if you back off."

For the rest of the week Marvin went out of his way to shun me, especially during the midnight hour when I hoped my frilly negligees would lure him to bed. Yet he regarded me indifferently.

"What's wrong?" I wanted to know.

"Nothing's wrong. Just wanna go out and shoot a few hoops."

"At this time of night?"

"I have energy to spare."

"I love your energy," I said, hoping that he'd say, *I love yours.*

Instead he said, "Save your energy for Frankie."

"You won't even look at me," I said, dropping the negligee to my waist. My breasts were still firm and, while not as perfectly sculpted as when we'd met three years ago, surely they were alluring.

Yet Marvin wouldn't look. He was out the door and headed for the basketball court, leaving me to consider all that was wrong with me.

His rejection stung. In his eyes, I did not appear in the least desirable. At the same time, he did not relent in his insistence that I pick up Frankie Beverly at the airport.

Well, if Marvin wasn't turned on by me, Frankie was. And, in anticipation of picking him up, I dressed accordingly. I wore a revealing red sleeveless leotard and tight jeans that showed every last curve. The outfit excited me. I wanted the outfit to excite Marvin, but he had left the house. He had continued to avert his eyes from me.

I wanted Frankie's eyes on me. I wanted the absolute reassurance from another man that, after birthing two children, I was still desirable.

I was only half conscious of the fact that Marvin had understood my emotional vulnerability. He perceived my need to be appreciated. And by not appreciating me—and encouraging me to seek such appreciation from Frankie—he had set me up. He had set up a scenario in which misery would prevail.

Driving to the Burbank airport in my Benz, I was anything but miserable. I was wary yet stimulated by the danger ahead. When I pulled the car up to the curb where Frankie was waiting with his luggage, I waved to him and flashed a big smile.

"Not sure I'm worthy of such personal service," he said.

"Marvin insisted," I said.

"Marvin's the man."

I felt Frankie's eyes all over me. I put down the top and headed out on the highway. My hair was down, my curls bouncing in the breeze.

"You look fantastic," he said.

"You must be happy about your deal," I rejoined in a weak attempt to change the subject. "I don't see how Raw Soul can miss."

"There's no more Raw Soul," he said.

"What happened to the band?"

"The band's the same. The name's changed."

"I always liked Raw Silk better."

"We're going to be Maze."

"Wow. That's different."

"Marvin's idea."

"He didn't mention it to me."

"I'm surprised. I thought he told you everything. Did he tell you that he's invited us to open some shows for him?" asked Frankie.

"No, but I think that's great."

"He's a prince."

"He is," I said, still feeling the heat of Frankie's gaze.

As we rode the rest of the trip in silence, I was certain that the connection between Frankie and me was powerful. His attraction to my body had me feeling powerful. And heady.

The joint he offered added to my headiness. The smoke melted what little tension remained between us. I drove us back to Hidden Hills, where Marvin was waiting. I then made myself scarce.

My mind was reeling. I didn't want to do right. But I also didn't want to do wrong. Something in my head said that Marvin was pushing me to do wrong. He'd delight in my wrong. But wrong was wrong and right was right.

It was only right to avoid Frankie.

Marvin was the man I loved, the father of my children, and the reason my life was worth living. I couldn't conceive of any life other than the one I was living with Marvin. I couldn't risk losing him, even if he was the one provoking me to take that risk.

Motown was provoking Marvin. The label had no choice. His contract demanded that he turn in a new product. When he allowed the label execs to hear the ballads on which he had lavished such loving artistry, I saw that they were unimpressed. They didn't consider it new product. These were old tracks, after all, that he had been reworking for years. Besides, they had no currency in the marketplace of the mid-seventies. In the view of the suits, the collection did not contain even a hint of a hit single. I heard them tell Marvin that he was wasting his time. He needed to get off his cloud, come down to earth, and give his fans another "Let's Get It On."

"Is Miles Davis's label telling him to come up with a hit record?" asked Marvin.

"Miles is a jazz artist," the execs responded. "Jazz is different. Jazz is an experimental art."

"Art is art," Marvin responded. "Miles goes where all true artists go. He goes further out because that's where his muse takes him."

"Miles's market has nothing to do with yours."

"And markets have nothing to with anything," Marvin snapped back. "Miles is looking for the truth, for a way to awaken man's mind to something other than markets."

Miles Davis was, in fact, in touch with Marvin. I heard them speak about a project. The conversation was easy; the two men were in sync. They came to a quick agreement to record together. Nothing would be prearranged—no orchestrations, no advance song selections. Improvisation would be given free rein. They would create in the Eternal Now. Marvin was convinced that this, more than another commercial outing, was exactly the nourishment his artistic soul was seeking.

But Miles, like Marvin, was a proud man with a sturdy ego. He wanted Marvin to come to New York to record. Marvin preferred that Muhammad come to the mountain—that Miles venture to California and work at Marvin's own studio. I witnessed the negotiations breaking down. The meeting of the two masters never happened. If it had, what miraculous music would have been made!

Now without Miles and without Motown's interest in Marvin's extravagant treatment of standards, what would happen next?

"It's another Marvin standoff," brother Frankie told me. "Just like he's relishing this standoff with Anna, he'll push this standoff with Motown as far as he can. He'll push them to the point where they'll threaten to sue if he doesn't turn in some new tracks."

Then, suddenly, fate intervened. In the course of a few hours, I saw the script flipped. Motown gave Marvin a set of tracks created by another Motown artist that caught Marvin's ear, awakened his imagination, and spoke to his wildest erotic fantasies.

Just like that, a new Marvin Gaye suite of songs—by far his most sensuous—was underway.

Wanting

The ego is a funny thing. No matter how we humble or deny ourselves, we all have one. I think back to my own ego in the year 1975 when Marvin began to record the album *I Want You*. From the moment I met him, I felt my ego melting into Marvin's. It was all about him. How could it not be? He was a superstar. I was a less-than. He was a man of the world. I was a teenage girl looking for a world where I could feel safe.

In my mind, all I had going for me was my body. You could say that I was witty and bright; you could say that I had the precociousness to keep up my end of a conversation with people twice my age. You could say that I had a flair for fashion. You might even say that I had hidden musical talent. I had a good ear. I could blend harmonies. I could appreciate the most subtle motifs and messages in Marvin's music. I could appreciate the sincerity of his spiritual attachment to the god of love. I shared that attachment. I shared everything with him—but all to the point of denying myself as I celebrated him.

My positive qualities might have been obvious to others, but I couldn't even begin to recognize them. The simple fact was that I had lost myself in Marvin. And whenever I felt that I was losing him, I didn't know what to do. Of course it hardly helped that after the birth of our babies I returned to a daily routine of getting high on grass. As Marvin's use of cocaine increased, so did mine. It isn't that he forced me to keep up with him. Like most people in his circle, I simply wanted to live life on his cloud. His cloud, colored by the most beautiful music imaginable, appeared to offer the safe love I was seeking.

The fear of being banned from the cloud was always on my mind. And even though the fact that we shared two children seemed to guarantee me a permanent place on that cloud, I had learned that in Marvin's world there were no guarantees. In short, I was obsessed with him.

"He's obsessed with *you*," my daddy Earl Hunter would tell me. Earl and Marvin had become buddies. "You're the only thing he talks about, baby. When he's singing, you're the woman he's singing to. Everyone knows that."

"But everyone doesn't see how he doesn't look at me the way he used to."

"That's because you're more than his girlfriend. You're now the mother of his children. You gotta give him time to get used to that. The important thing is how he's taking care of you. Hell, he's even taking care of Slim."

Earl was right.

At the beginning of the *I Want You* project, I was both gratified and concerned about the reemergence of my crazy-ass biological father.

One afternoon at the Sunset studio, I saw that Slim Gaillard was helping Marvin organize his tape library.

"What's up with that?" I asked Marvin.

"Slim's cool," he said. "I like having him around. I like hearing his bebop stories. I feel like it's my responsibility to help you take care of your family."

"Slim never helped take care of me," I reminded Marvin.

"That's not the point, dear. The point is that now we're in a position to help him. The cat's a little down-and-out, so why not give him something to do in the studio?"

"That's sweet of you, Marvin."

"I'm growing sweeter by the day," said Marvin with a smile.

But on those days when Marvin was not sweet on me—when, for example, he felt that my mom was interfering in our life or dropping by the house too frequently—he punished me by threatening to fire Slim.

"Why are you taking your anger at me out on him?" I asked Marvin.

"Anger has nothing to do with it," Marvin answered. "I can only take so many of Slim's bebop stories."

The new music Motown gave Marvin was simply too good to resist.

I was at the studio when Marvin was studying a track of startling sensuality.

"Who is that singing?" I asked.

"Diana's brother," he said. "T-Boy Ross. Berry put him together with Leon Ware. They've been writing together."

"That happened a while back," I said. "They wrote 'I Wanna Be Where You Are' for Michael Jackson."

"Well, now they've written something else. Listen to it."

I listened and said, "I think it's beautiful, Marvin. I think it's a smash."

"Berry thinks it's tailor-made for me."

"Berry's right."

"But Berry's just looking to lure me back into the studio."

"The motives don't really matter, Marvin. What matters is the music. If you feel that the music suits your soul, why not go for it?"

"I'm tempted."

"What's it called?"

" 'I Want You.' "

"I love it," I said.

The longer he listened, the more passionately he wanted to take the song and turn it into his own. As it turned out, it was more than one song: T-Boy and Leon had written an intricate set of innercon- nected songs.

Marvin and Leon, who was an exceptional vocalist, producer, and writer, were musical soul mates. Leon's lush orchestrations were perfectly suited to Marvin's sensibilities. Adding fuel to the fire was the fact that both men were deep into cocaine. The drug drove the creative work to a feverishly high level.

Soon Marvin was so deep into the album that, for all practical purposes, he had moved out of the Hidden Hills home into his studio on Sunset.

"I want you and the kids to be with me when I'm cutting these tracks and laying down the vocals," Marvin told me. "I want to be able to look at you when I sing these songs."

I was elated. Just as Marvin projected the war story of his brother Frankie returning from Vietnam into *What's Going On*, he was using our love story to inform *I Want You*. The result was that, during the year-long process of making the record, our love was renewed.

"It's like it was when we first met," Marvin said. "That's the feel- ing I'm getting when I'm singing these songs."

"That's the feeling that I want to keep forever," I said.

The feeling in the studio was magical. And it was more than the impossibly seductive music. It was the feeling of the family—Marvin, myself, Nona, and Frankie—living in the loft while the songs were sculpted into a form that was distinctively Marvin. The extraordinary harmonies—the blend of Marvin's many voices—were mirrored in the emotional harmony between us.

In "Come Live with Me Angel," he flashed back to the early days when he asked me to leave my mother's house and come to Cattaraugus so he could explore all my "treasures" and indulge in "freakish pleasures."

In "Feel All My Love Inside," he opened by asking for another joint before painting a picture of sweet sexual passion, stroking me "in and out . . . up and down . . . all around" because he loved to hear me "make those sounds."

In "Soon I'll Be Loving You Again," he fell into a daydream where he documented the first time he performed cunnilingus, describing how, despite past reservations, he had made up his mind to "give some head."

But there was more than the ecstasy of physical pleasure; there was the prospect of pregnancy. Love must lead to family. Family is formed by his desire for me. At the end of the song he calls me by name. "Oh, Janis," he cried. "I love you, I love you, Janis."

In "After the Dance," he fantasized about seeing me on *Soul Train*, my sinuous movements an invitation to a lifetime of love. It didn't matter that I was never a *Soul Train* dancer. He invented the scenario.

In "All the Way Around," he sang about "getting down to the skin," exciting himself at the thought that I might be "promiscuous."

In perhaps the most moving moment of all, Marvin made a brief visit to a song previously sung by Michael Jackson, "I Wanna Be Where You Are." On the actual track, he acknowledged our family, saying, "Good night, little Frankie, Nona . . . good night, little Marvin . . . I love you all . . . I'll always love you, Janis . . . I want to be where you are . . . oh, my children, I'll always be where you are . . ."

My heart had never been happier. In the midst of the most erotic suite of songs he had ever sung, he had once again—as he did with *Let's Get It On*—reaffirmed me as his muse. He had placed me in the center of his bed and his dreams. At the same time, he had placed himself in the center of our family.

"Did you hear what I said in the song?" Marvin whispered to me after he layered his harmonies on "Feel All My Love Inside."

"I heard you sing about making love to me," I whispered back.

"Before that I said, 'I want you for my wife.'"

"Is this a formal proposal?"

"It will be."

"Well, I accept—when you are free."

"The divorce is coming soon," he said.

"The way these endless hearings are dragging out, I'm not sure *soon* is the right word."

"The name of the song was 'Soon I'll Be Loving You.' And the name of this chapter in my life was 'Soon I'll Be Marrying You.'"

The chapter was blissful. During those long months blending lovemaking and music making in the Sunset studio, there were sights and scenes I'll always cherish.

Marvin seated on a couch in the control room—the speakers mute, the room perfectly silent—as he quietly read aloud from the Book of Psalms:

> In peace I will lie down and sleep
> For you alone, Lord, make me dwell in safety

Marvin in the loft, playing hide-and-seek with Nona and Bubby.

Marvin playing the tracks from *I Want You* for a smiling Stevie Wonder, Stevie's head circling to the rhythm.

I was thrilled to be a witness to the making of a masterpiece.

Return to the Maze

There was the beautifully peaceful Marvin, the Marvin who spent endless hours in the studio with his music, honing his harmonies and constructing melodies and countermelodies of astounding grace.

This was the Marvin that I held closest to my heart—the Marvin who voiced the deepest emotions and transformed pain into beauty.

This was the Marvin who, even in realizing an extravagantly erotic work like *I Want You*, was able to ascend beyond the flesh into the realm of the mystical.

There was also the Marvin who was determined to clean up his act and stop smoking Camels and Marlboros. He'd renounce pot and coke and swear never to eat meat again. He'd turn over a new leaf by going on a super-strict health routine for a month and expect everyone to follow. Everyone did. We wanted to please him. We also wanted to get healthy ourselves. Suddenly it was all about organic food, long hikes, bike rides, basketball games, and strenuous jogs.

But then someone would offer him a joint, he'd accept, and we'd all be back at square one.

One of his cleanest periods came after Muhammad Ali invited us to his home in Hancock Park. At the time he was married to Veronica Porsche, with whom I'd gone to high school. Marvin and Ali played basketball and became great friends. It was only a few weeks later that Marvin was asked, along with Sammy Davis and Richard Pryor, to face Ali in the ring as part of a charity event. Of course it was a lark, but Marvin didn't take it that way. He went into training and dreamed of actually knocking down the champ! He bought all the professional gear, hired a trainer, and went to work. At the event itself, he entered the arena with a full entourage and even had it filmed. Sammy and Richard never took it seriously and, once in the ring, ran from the champ. The audience howled. But when Marvin got into the ring, he actually began to box. It didn't take more than a minute for Ali to knock him to the ground. Because Ali loved him, he didn't hurt him. But Marvin was nonetheless humiliated. When it came to sporting feats, Marvin had delusions of grandeur.

The footnote to this story happened at a Motown picnic where Ali and Marvin ran a hundred yard dash. Marvin beat him—and saw that as something of a consolation prize to what had happened in the ring.

Marvin had other friendships that he found satisfying. Ray Charles had us up to his home in Baldwin Hills and was a kind and attentive host. He and Marvin admired each other enormously. Ike Turner has us down to his Bolic Sound Studios in Inglewood where he charmed us with funny stories and carried around his coke supply in a suitcase. Needless to say, we got blasted. Same goes for Redd Foxx, who invited us to his home in Studio City and kept us both high and in stitches. Natalie Cole, then married to Marvin Yancy, adored my Marvin and hosted us on several occasions.

We spent a wonderful evening with Bill Cosby and his wife,

Camille, in Las Vegas where Marvin and I stayed in the Elvis Suite at the Hilton. And in Chicago, Jesse Jackson had us over to his house where he and Marvin enjoyed a highly competitive game of basketball.

Every once in a while Marvin liked to break loose and go out on the town to have some fun.

After his performance at Radio City in New York, he and I were invited by Mick Jagger and Jerry Hall to join them at Studio 54, the hottest disco on the planet. During the show itself, I stood next to Mick in the wings. Mick watched Marvin reverently.

Studio 54 was a trip. Cutting through the long line of eager souls begging for admittance, we were whisked inside and escorted up to the balcony, where everyone was openly snorting coke. When we learned that the star attraction of the night was Sylvester, Marvin led me down to the dressing room so we could say hello. Both Marvin and I adored Sylvester. We saw him as the greatest of all the disco artists. He was a beautiful man. It was fascinating to see how he and Marvin were attracted to each other. Yet I wouldn't call the attraction sexual. Sylvester had a freedom that Marvin admired, and Marvin had a sophistication that Sylvester found alluring. They chatted like old friends. Their common link was Harvey Fuqua, the man who had discovered Marvin and produced Sylvester. The mood was altered when Grace Jones and Dolph Lundgren showed up, two outsize personalities who sucked all the air out of the room. Marvin and I wished Sylvester well and went back upstairs, where we watched his fabulous show. With flashbulbs popping, I was certain our picture would wind up in *Rolling Stone*—and it did.

During that same New York trip, we met Andy Warhol, who spoke as though he worshipped Marvin. He gushed how he just had to paint Marvin's portrait, and Marvin agreed, but never followed up. Typical Marvin.

One time he did follow up. We had hung out with Argentinian jazz saxophonist Gato Barbieri and his Italian wife, Michelle, in their Manhattan apartment. During the evening Gato kept praising Marvin's writing and asked whether he'd compose something for him. Marvin agreed to do it and did. A few weeks later he wrote "Latin Reaction," one of his best instrumental efforts.

Marvin liked the hot spots. Back in LA, we'd sometimes cruise over to Beverly Hills and lunch at the Daisy, a happening bistro. Once, looking across the room, Marvin spotted a woman he described as gorgeous enough to stop traffic.

"I can't think of her name," he said.

"I can. That's Candice Bergen."

When I kept sneaking glances, Marvin accused me of having sexual designs on her. He was wrong. I was simply bowled over by her beauty.

During that same lunch we noticed Ryan O'Neal. In this instance, it was Marvin who seemed obsessed. He couldn't stop staring. I didn't see it as physical attraction, but merely fascination. O'Neal was an incredibly handsome movie star.

I told Marvin, "If I can see that you're not sexualizing Ryan—just admiring him—than I hope you can see that I wasn't sexualizing Candice. Beauty is captivating."

"It's certainly is," said Marvin. "And it seems as though your beauty has captivated Ryan. He's coming over to say hello."

He arrived at our table and shook hands with Marvin, who introduced him to me. I was thrilled. The thrill took a different turn, though, when O'Neal stood behind my chair and pressed himself against my neck, which was covered over by my long, wild hair. He made his move with great subtlety, but there was no mistaking the feel of his penis against my neck. As he spoke with Marvin, he kept pressing ever so slightly. I had a funny smile on my face. I didn't know what to say or do. So I did nothing. When he left, I didn't share the experience with Marvin. I was afraid it would only lead to a fight.

On another evening, Marvin and I were dining at Mr. Chow in Beverly Hills. We were about to leave when Bud Cort, the actor who had played Harold in *Harold and Maude*, ran up to our table and told

Marvin how he adored him. He said he had a friend who he wanted us to meet. The friend, who was waiting outside for his car, was the great Groucho Marx. We all exchanged numbers but, as with nearly every chance meeting with Marvin, there was no follow-through.

As free spirits, we lived in Marvin's studio with Nona and Frankie. Where we went, most of the time our children went with us. When Marvin and I needed alone time, we would call on loving family members to care for the children.

In 1975–76, Marvin was working on his *I Want You* album. The studio was bursting with incredible music and the energy was at times surreal. We also designated 6553 Sunset, the studio, our home, as party central. When there was a birthday, anniversary, listening session or really any occasion to celebrate it usually happened there. Our parties were legendary, for those who worked at the studio and for those who visited and wanted to hang out. They wanted to be near Marvin, to be inspired, to get high, to have fun, and to create music. Real music.

With the living quarters upstairs and with a closet here or a bathroom there, there was always someplace for the kids to hide— and sometimes the adults. It provided us, and those that we knew, a second home. The windows upstairs had two-way glass that allowed us to look down from our bedroom and see who came and went. It always made for interesting conversation. We knew who was hitting on who, who had the drugs, when to hide if there was someone we didn't want to see, and when to go down and greet any new arrivals.

Once people got there, they didn't want to leave, especially if we were having one of our celebrations. We would go all out, having food, drinks, drugs, celebrities, music, music, and more music.

I threw a party for Marvin in 1977. It was one of the best parties ever. Muhammad Ali; Cecil Franklin, Aretha's son; superagent Phil Casey; superproducer Leon Ware and his wife Carol; Don Corne-lius; Richard Pryor; *Jet* photographer Ike Sutton, who became a dear friend; Jayne Kennedy; Smokey Robinson; Thomas "Hollywood" Henderson; Azizi Johari; Denise Nicholas; and many other stars came to enjoy a great party. At this particular party, we let the kids hang out for a little while, even though they were only two and three. Marvin had finished "I Want You," and his massive hit "Got to Give It Up," which we played whenever we wanted to get people moving. Before the party really got going, Nona insisted on showing off her dance moves to anyone who would watch. "Got to Give It Up" was playing and she went to work! She jumped and bumped, hooped and hollered, went into a spin at one point and fell on her bottom. Never missing a beat, she spun around on the floor, jumped up, making the fall a part of her dance. She was pleased with her performance. We laughed, clapped, and cheered for her. Being a big ham, she wanted to do it all over again, but it was time for her to head to bed. My mother arrived to pick Nona up and take her to her house to get some sleep.

Stevie Wonder showed up that night and we gave him a tour by describing this and that. We took him up to our living area. Stevie knew acoustics so well, with his heightened senses, that he stood in the middle of the room and said, "Wow! I'm digging the surround sound." He instinctively knew that the room was round. I was amazed by his perceptibility.

Even Slim ended up working at the studio for a while. He would primarily hang with my brother Mark and Marvin's brother Frankie, who took care of our day to day. It was nice having family around. There was a lot of laughter, pranks, and good times. One of my favorite occasions was Marvin wearing his pyramid hat. He said it made him smarter and made it easier to create music. It looked ridiculous but he swore by it.

"Don't touch Daddy's pyramid," he would tell the kids.

Of course that made them want to not only touch it but throw it about, bend it, and put it on each other's heads.

The studio was next door to a health food store where we were always finding interesting items like the pyramid hat or biofeedback machines. Marvin was way ahead of the times when it came to natural health and metaphysical concepts. He taught me a lot about vitamins, or "mins" as he called them, and herbs for every ailment. He read *Back to Eden* and bought numerous copies to give away as gifts, convinced that he knew how to live forever.

He would also read Edgar Cayce to me. Marvin scared the shit out of me with stories about Cayce, Virginia Beach, and how we should all move there to survive the end of the world—one of his favorite topics. The more I cried out in fear, the more he laid it on. Then he would do his best to make me laugh. It didn't always work, though. He was incredibly hip and smart, open-minded, and forward thinking.

Jane Fonda was another star drawn to Marvin. One day she came bouncing into his Sunset Boulevard studio looking like a little girl in a candy store. I was there when he played her some of his new music. Afterward, she talked of plans to start up an aerobics center. Would he be interested in investing? He was. I was afraid, of course, that his interest had more to do with Jane than with her aerobics. The two had engaged in super-intense eye contact.

A week or so later, Jane invited Marvin to see the space that she had rented on Robertson Boulevard. He decided to take me along. The center was impressive—gleaming wood floors, expansive mirrors, bars along the walls. Marvin thanked the assistant who showed us around and then asked when Jane would be arriving.

"I'm afraid she won't be," the assistant said.

I wondered whether that was because she had been told that I was there. In any event, I was relieved. Marvin didn't invest. I'm not sure he ever saw Jane again.

But he did see Dyan Cannon, famous for rooting on the LA Lakers from her floor seat at the Forum. When friends told me of the rumor that Marvin had been hanging out with Dyan at the Forum Club, I grew alarmed and confronted him.

"We both love the game of basketball," he said. "That's all there is to it."

"But why am I learning about this through friends? Why didn't you tell me you were seeing her?"

"I'm not 'seeing her,' as you put it. I'm just hanging out with her—and only once in a great while. It's an innocent thing."

"And not an affair?"

"A friendship, yes. A love affair, no."

When it came to Marvin and other women, I was always on guard, especially as he escalated his divorce war with Anna. As those wars threatened his emotional and financial well-being, Marvin became more vulnerable. He refused to retreat or listen to reason. He also grew more hostile. When he faced the prospect of losing all his material possessions, he responded with, *"Après moi, le déluge"*—"After me, the flood"—the foreboding words allegedly ascribed to Louis XV. Marvin saw himself as a king about to lose his empire. But rather than alarm him, the prospect of ruin excited him.

He was further excited by the notion that I might be unfaithful. It took me a long time to understand why. Why would a man who had declared his love to me with the most romantic words—and the most romantic music—want to see that love tarnished and broken?

Why design drama that would lead to heartbreak? Why ask for chaos and confusion?

I was deeply confused when Frankie Beverly drove to the ranch in Round Mountain to meet with Marvin about an upcoming tour and, once again, Marvin forced me into a situation calculated to both tantalize and traumatize.

Just as Marvin went out of his way to avoid sex for the weeks preceding Frankie's first trip, he repeated the pattern with the second trip. He did this to play on my insecurities.

When Frankie arrived, I was filled with uncertainty about my attractiveness. I was ashamed of my post-baby body. Marvin used my insecurity to further upset me.

What seemed unreasonable, though, was when Marvin told me that he had reserved two rooms at a nearby motel in Redding—one for Frankie and one for me.

"Why in the world would you do that?" I asked.

"I want you to be comfortable, dear," he said. "I've got work to do."

I argued that it was a weird arrangement. I saw it as a setup.

"I need to be alone," was all Marvin kept saying.

A few hours later, Frankie and I were checking in to the motel when we discovered that Marvin had arranged for us to have adjoining rooms.

Not an hour passed before Frankie knocked on my door.

"Can I come in?"

I hesitated. I was aware of his desire for me. And I couldn't deny that I also desired him. I wanted to be desired. I wanted to feel that, despite Marvin's recent rejections, I was a woman men found sexy. Frankie was a sexy man. Our relationship had been flirtatious from the start. At the same time, I had no intention of sleeping with him.

"Sure," I said matter-of-factly. "Hold on." I unlocked the adjoining door.

Frankie was standing there, all smiles.

"D-d-d-do you want to smoke a joint?" he asked.

"I was just rolling one. Come in."

"Well, this is w-w-w-weird that we're neighbors. But I'm glad you're next door."

"Me too," I said.

We both tried to play off our awkwardness.

There were two beds. He sat on one. I sat on the other.

Before we could do any talking, though, there was loud banging on the door. It was Marvin telling me to open up.

My heart started pounding as Frankie dropped to his hands and knees and crawled back to his room. Marvin's knock got louder.

With Frankie back in his room, I opened the door to let Marvin in. He looked around suspiciously.

"I smell weed," he said.

"Of course you do. I just smoked a joint."

"Where's Frankie?"

"In his room, I guess."

I tried to lighten the mood and act like Marvin was the crazy one. He finally relaxed and stayed for an hour or two. When he left and went back to the ranch, he took Frankie with him. I was relieved to see them both go.

Less than a month later, Marvin invited Frankie and Maze to open for him in Atlantic City. As usual, Marvin dreaded the event. His performance anxiety had reached new heights. To beat back the fears, he got high and was nearly two hours late to the venue.

Finally, we got into the limo. The driver sped along the highway while Marvin insisted that I twist him yet another joint. Something didn't feel right. I sensed imminent danger.

"Hurry, my man," Marvin urged the driver. "Do whatever you have to do—but get us there in ten minutes."

"We're a half hour away, sir," said the driver.

"Not if you throw caution to the wind," said Marvin. "I'll pay the speeding ticket. Just press on. Hit it, man, hit it hard!"

In response, the driver went crazy, as if being chased. He floored the pedal and started speeding at what felt like a hundred miles an hour, swerving from lane to lane and barely avoiding one collision after another. We were scared to death. I was certain that Marvin and I would both be killed. I tried to tell the driver to slow down, but fear blocked my words.

And then it happened.

The limo crashed head-on into a telephone pole.

I was thrown into the front seat. As I was carried out of the car, I moved in and out of consciousness. Marvin, unhurt, was by my side.

"You have to stay alive, baby," Marvin was saying. "You can't go.

You can't leave me. I want to marry you. I want you to be my wife. Do you hear me? Please, Jan, please say yes. Please marry me."

The timing of this, still another proposal from Marvin, was definitely strange. It came when I was suffering a concussion. At the same time, I was happy to hear the words. I was happy to accept his proposal. And then, hearing the siren of the arriving ambulance, I passed out.

When I awoke, I was back at the hotel. Marvin was still by my side.

"You're here, dear," he said. "You're safe. You survived. Our love can survive anything. God was watching over us. You said you loved me. You said you'll marry me. Say it again."

I said it again before falling back into unconsciousness.

When I awoke a few hours later, Marvin was holding my hand. He gazed deep into my eyes and said, "I knew God wouldn't take you from me. I knew he couldn't be that cruel."

Later that night I learned that the driver had been killed on impact. The news broke my heart. I thought about this tragic loss of life and his grieving family.

"It could have easily been you," said Marvin. "Or me. We were spared. God spared us."

The concert was canceled. Frankie Beverly never got to open for Marvin Gaye.

Repeating his proposal to me over and over again, Marvin concentrated on making me happy. It was now Marvin who wanted me for himself, Marvin who insisted that I come with him on his tour of England. He insisted that I be with him every minute of every day; I must vow never to leave him; I must believe him when he said that—despite all the delays and legal complications—he *will* have his divorce from Anna; he *will* create comfort and bliss; he *will* be sweet; he *will* be true; he *will* honor and safeguard me; he *will* love and protect our precious children; he *will* make our life heaven on earth.

He will.

He will.

He swears he will.

Family Love

At the start of the seventies—before Marvin had left Detroit, before his marriage to Anna had fallen apart, before his move to Hollywood, before his meeting me had thrown him into a romantic obsession that deepened by the day—Marvin sang, "Father, father . . . there's no need to escalate."

The escalation, of course, referred to the Vietnam War, but he was also talking about brutal battles fought with his own father.

"Mother, mother," he sang to the mothers who had lost sons overseas, but he was also singing to his own mother, who had struggled to protect him from her husband's cruelty.

"Brother, brother," he sang to his brother Frankie and to all his brothers, black and white, brown and yellow, who opposed the tyranny of a heartless establishment.

"Love your mother," he sang. "Love your father. Your sisters, your brothers."

From the day I met him, I had seen Marvin as a man whose capacity *to* love was matched by his need *to be* loved.

As much as he fought his father, he also sought the man's love; he sought to reconcile the friction in his family by buying homes and cars for his parents, by keeping his sisters and brother close, by trying to re-create the very thing he lacked as a child—a happy home life.

And yet a happy home life is exactly what eluded him.

As it turned out, he had created three homes: one was the sprawling suburban home in Hidden Hills; a second was the secluded studio home in Hollywood; and the third was the enormous old house he bought for his parents on Gramercy Place in Mid-City LA.

As time went on, he went from one home to another, seeking solace in one family even as he ran from the other. When he was suspicious of me, he ran to his mother; when the presence of his father chased him from his mother's house, he ran to the studio that, from time to time, was being supervised by my brother Mark—Slim's son who's seven years my senior—Marvin's brother Frankie, or my father Slim. When he grew angry with Slim, when he felt that his sister Zeola was pressing him too hard to employ her as a dancer or his brother Frankie was pressing him too hard to sponsor his career as a singer, he ran back to Hidden Hills.

On any given day in Hidden Hills, I might see George Clinton and Bernie Worrell shooting hoops. They were the funk geniuses who loved Marvin as much as he loved them. The three of them loved to get high on acid.

On any given day in the Sunset studio, I might see Rick James with his protégée Teena Marie. Like all the young soul stars, they idolized Marvin. More smoke, more coke, more high times all around. The studio had a magic all its own.

On any given day in the house on Gramercy Place, I might see Bishop Simon Peter Rawlings, a fellow minister of Father Gay, who had come all the way from Kentucky to read Scripture to Marvin. Marvin loved the man. I witnessed their prayer sessions, which went on for hours.

On one afternoon in Hidden Hills, my mom showed up with one of her friends, an engaging black man named Ernie Barnes. Ernie was a fabulous painter. In addition to his artistic talent, he had also once been a pro athlete. As a young man he was drafted by the NFL's Baltimore Colts to play on the same team with Johnny Unitas and Big Daddy Lipscomb. With his own dreams of playing professional ball, Marvin was enchanted by Ernie's stories.

He was also enchanted by Ernie's most famous work—an enormous panorama of black couples dancing sensuously at a neighborhood nightclub. The great painting had been used in the background of the television series *Good Times*. Marvin had long loved the work and wanted to know how this particular image came about.

"When I was kid," said Ernie, "I wasn't allowed to go to dances."

"Me either," Marvin chimed in.

"So when I snuck around and peeped through the window of the local juke joint, I got my first look at the sin my folks never wanted me to see. And I loved it. A lifetime later I remembered that scene and painted it. I called it *Sugar Shack*, and over the dancers' heads I drew a banner that says 'WSRC,' the soul station I listened to when my folks weren't home."

"Sounds like we have the same story, brother," said Marvin. "Mind if I play you something I just finished cutting?"

"Are you kidding? Lemme hear it, man."

Marvin put on *I Want You*.

Ernie was all smiles, his head bouncing to the groove.

"You thinking what I'm thinking, Ernie?"

"I'm thinking that the dancers in *Sugar Shack* look like they're getting down to *I Want You*."

"That's it, brother! That's exactly it! As a musical artist, I don't like anyone coming along to change what I've done. So I'm a little hesitant about asking you this. But, with all due respect, is it even remotely possible for you to add a little banner that says something about Marvin Gaye?"

"You're thinking of using it as the album cover?"

"It's beyond perfect. It's so right I can't begin to consider anything else. I really want it."

"A Marvin Gaye album without Marvin Gaye's picture on the cover?"

"There are enough pictures of me on my album covers. Your picture does what no other picture can do. It makes the music come alive. Will you give me permission to use it?"

"Permission granted. And with much respect and love."

Marvin bought it along with several other Ernie Barnes works with football and basketball scenes. One especially sensuous painting called *Circle of Love*, depicting a couple lying on tousled sheets in tones of brown and purple, was absolute genius. It hung over our bed.

A month later, when the first copy of the *I Want You* album with the Ernie Barnes cover was brought over to the house, I asked Marvin, "My mom has some pretty cool friends, doesn't she? Don't you love Ernie?"

"I do. And I gotta give your mom some credit this time for doing something good. In addition to giving birth to my sweet Jan, yes, the woman does know some hip brothers."

On any given good day—and there were many—Marvin demonstrated deep family love. He tried over and over again to reconcile the pain of his past with the good fortune of his present and the beautiful prospect of his future.

I saw how he wanted to spread the love that he saw at the heart of the teachings of the God he called Jesus. Yet for all his noble efforts and valiant attempts to live the life of a man of goodwill, he trapped himself in a battle between good and evil. He didn't want to be a hypocrite. He didn't like people who were duplicitous and lied, even though he sometimes displayed these actions. He was complex, but he strove to live by higher moral principles when it came to his treatment of others.

"There is the devil," he told me. "And the devil is real."

"But isn't God greater?" I asked. "Isn't God stronger? Didn't God defeat the devil?"

"The devil can't be defeated," said Marvin on one of his many dark days. "The devil simply changes form."

"You don't actually believe in a demonic figure who's running around with horns and a red cape, do you, dear?"

"I believe in a devil that is already inside us. We each have a devil of our own making. That devil is designed to destroy all the joy in our life."

"But can't the devil be confronted? If you know the potential for destruction is there, can't you do something to avoid it—like pray?"

"The devil is tricky," Marvin insisted. "The devil is sly. The devil knows to offer us temptations we can't resist. The devil knows our weakness. The devil *is* our weakness."

"I'm not sure," I said skeptically. "I think that if we really believe the devil is all that powerful, we're contributing to his power. We're building him up. In truth, the devil may not even exist."

"You don't believe in negative energy?" asked Marvin. "You don't see evidence of evil in the world?"

"I do, but that's different from subscribing to some superstition that has you fearing a demon who's out to get you. Maybe I'm wrong, Marvin, but I have a feeling that superstition comes from way back in your childhood. Didn't your father's church give you all these ideas about the devil?"

"Do you believe my father's the devil?"

"Now you're asking a different question."

"I've heard you call him the Beast."

"I've heard you call him worse."

"I've heard him preach," said Marvin, his demeanor changing as he conjured up memories. "That was when I was a boy. He preached beautifully. Have I told you that, dear?"

"You have."

"He sang beautifully. He understood God's Word beautifully. He understood that there was a devil in him that had to be defeated."

"And did he?" I asked.

"No. The devil prevails—in him, in you, in me. The devil prevails the world over. And just when we think we have his number, he comes at you in another clever form with another sweet temptation and, just like that, you're back in his arms."

The words frightened me. I wouldn't accept the premise. "That won't happen," I insisted.

"You say that now," said Marvin, "but you will fall. We all will."

"I hate it when you talk like this. It's depressing. Please stop."

Marvin sensed my fear and put his arm around me. "I'll do all I can to protect our little family," he said.

The public adored *I Want You*. It quickly sold over a million copies. Marvin was gratified. But then someone brought over a copy of *Rolling Stone* with a review that said, "With Barry White on the wane, Marvin Gaye seems determined to take over as soul's master philosopher in the bedroom, a proposition that requires little but an affectation of constant, rather jaded horniness."

The write-up in *DownBeat* was even worse: "Slush for disco dancers in the bogus overblown manner of Barry White."

Marvin was furious and hurt. He loved what he had created with Leon Ware and T-Boy Ross.

"The critics are tin-eared idiots," he said. "They want to insult me by comparing me to Barry White, whom they detest, except that Barry is a genius, a brilliant orchestrator, writer, and singer with a vision all his own. I love Barry. Is it a crime to make music that celebrates the joy of sex? Didn't all the great composers want to seduce us with sensuous sounds? Didn't Mozart? Didn't Beethoven? Of course they did. But the critics don't want me to seduce. They want me to save the world. They think because of *What's Going On* I have to keep writing socially conscious songs. Well, how about sexually conscious songs? Besides, sex is social."

"The fans love *I Want You*," I said. "The DJs love it. Motown loves it. Who cares what a couple of writers say?"

"I care."

I knew that there was no consoling him. The bad reviews kept him down for days.

During that same summer of 1976, he went even further down. He failed to pay alimony and child support to Anna and was about to be served a contempt-of-court subpoena. That would mean ten days in LA County jail. Rather than run the risk of serving time, Marvin disappeared for two weeks. Not even I knew where he was. In the meantime, his lawyers did what Marvin had consistently refused to do: they tried to negotiate an intermediate settlement with Anna. Nothing doing. The divorce war raged on, draining Marvin's dwindling supply of money.

To make money, Marvin accepted some questionable gigs. He called me from Buffalo, where he was supposed to give a concert that never came off.

"The promoter promised I'd get my money up front," he said, "but when I got here I learned that he'd run off with the advance ticket sales."

"So what did you do?"

"Nothing."

"You didn't sing?"

"I never left the hotel. But it turns out they're having an NAACP convention right here, so I'm going to sing for them tomorrow—for free."

The next day the papers ran an article about thousands of ticket holders who had waited in the rain for three hours in front of Buffalo's Memorial Auditorium, only to learn that Marvin was refusing to appear.

"Happy ending, though," Marvin told me.

"What happened?"

"They caught the promoter before he could escape with all the money."

"This is the same guy you trusted?"

"When it comes to judging promoters, I've never had the most discerning judgment, have I?" he asked with a laugh.

His judgment about other business deals also proved disastrous.

I watched as Marvin ignored warnings from his advisors against investing in speculative oil deals and sketchy sports franchises like the World Football League that, shortly after he had kicked in $96,000, went belly-up. It was as though he did his best to lose all the money he was making.

Watching this made me feel increasingly insecure. I had no earning power of my own. I was counting on Marvin for everything.

"I can always tour," he reassured me. "I have fans in Latin America, in Europe. I have fans in Asia."

But because of his fear of flying, Marvin refused dozens of overseas tours. Again and again, he passed up chances to cultivate foreign markets.

"I'm not interested in marketing," he told his money men. "I'm an artist."

"An artist who's about to lose everything."

"I can't lose my art. It's a gift from God. And God's not taking it back."

I saw that, when faced with the impending reality of losing the Hidden Hills house or the Sunset studio, Marvin eventually changed his mind. He agreed to a tour of Japan. But then a week later, he canceled. Same routine with Brazil. Finally, though, he saw that, given the cash-flow crisis, he had to stop the foolishness. Come hell or high water, he was going to London to play the Palladium, followed by an extensive tour of England. The payday was too big to pass up.

I was thrilled to learn that he was taking me along. My mom would care for the kids. His brother Frankie and sister Zeola made the trip along with my sister Cass, who designed and made his stage outfits.

Marvin loved London. It felt like his natural habitat. The Brits treated him like royalty. He was charmed by their lordly accents; they were charmed by his soft-spoken candor. He told me that he could live there forever.

The day before the big show at the Palladium, we spent time shopping the avant-garde boutiques on Carnaby Street and the more conservative shops on Bond Street. Marvin bought me a wardrobe of edgy fashions—short skirts and high boots—while, for himself, he preferred the look of an English gentleman in elegant pinstriped suits and sport coats of Harris tweed. He also acquired an instant British accent.

That night there was news that Flo Lyles, one of Marvin's singers, was suffering with laryngitis. It was Flo who sang with Marvin on the hit duets that he'd originally sung with Mary Wells, Kim Weston, and Tammi Terrell. Even before attending dozens of Marvin's shows, I knew these numbers by heart—"You're All I Need to Get By," "Your Precious Love," "It Takes Two," "Ain't Nothing Like the Real Thing," "Ain't No Mountain High Enough."

"I can sing them," I told Marvin.

"Oh, dear," he said, "that's just too much."

"I can do it."

"You really think you can handle it?"

"I know I can. You've heard me sing those parts in your ear. You know I know them."

"Maybe."

"Not maybe, dear. *Pleeeease . . .*"

"That would really make you happy, wouldn't it?"

"Yes, yes, yes!"

"All right, dear, tomorrow night will be your grand debut."

I could hardly contain my excitement. The night before the show I got little sleep. I saw this as the start of a new phase of my relationship with Marvin. Once he heard how well I sang these songs, he'd make me a permanent part of the performance.

True to form, Marvin missed the rehearsal and sound check, but I was there, gratified that all went well. Frankie stood in for Marvin. We sang the duets flawlessly.

An hour before show time, I started to dress. The outfit—a low-cut full-length cap-sleeve jersey dress—was the sexiest I could find. It fit perfectly.

When Marvin finally showed up he asked, "Are you sure you know the lyrics to the songs?"

"Positive."

"And are you sure that appearing before a live audience won't freak you out?"

"I'll be fine."

"And you really, truly have it under control?"

"Really and truly, I do."

"And you'll stay on key?"

"I will."

"And when you sing, you'll be able to look me in the eye and mean it?"

"Of course. These are love songs. And I love you. I've always wanted to sing to you."

"All right. I'll see you during the show."

My heart beat wildly. I couldn't wait for my moment in the spotlight. Standing next to Marvin and singing those songs would be a dream come true.

Ten minutes before showtime, the dream shattered.

"Sorry, dear," said Marvin as he entered the dressing room, "but I have some news that won't make you happy."

"What news?"

"Flo tells me she's up to perform. No need for you to bother yourself about performing."

"Need! Bother!" I exclaimed. "It's something I've been dreaming of."

"I understand, dear, but, after all, Flo is a professional. I can't stand in the way of her work."

"Flo gets to sing every night. Why not give her a night off? She can rest her throat."

"She's well rested. She's ready to sing."

I was ready to tear my hair out. But what could I do? I had no choice but to comply. Adding to my frustration, Marvin asked whether Flo could wear my dress. I couldn't say no. But I wasn't happy saying yes.

"You'll have other opportunities to perform," said Marvin.

But no such opportunities ever came about.

I was inconsolable.

"Have faith," said Marvin. "You must have faith."

Faith

Faith was the topic.

Back in the US, Marvin decided to take our kids and me to Kentucky to visit Bishop Simon Peter Rawlings. It was time, he said, to reestablish his ties to his spiritual roots.

I saw how Bishop Rawlings, a patient and compassionate man, acted as a surrogate father to Marvin, who never stopped seeking the paternal approval denied by his own dad.

It was there in Lexington, where Marvin's father had grown up, that I learned the original name of the Pentecostal church that shaped Marvin's childhood: The House of God, the Holy Church of the Living God, the Pillar and Ground of the Truth, the House of Prayer for All People.

"It is a combination of Scripture from the Old and New Testaments," the bishop explained, "a mixture of Isaiah and First Timothy."

The bishop broke down the history of the small sect—of how in the late forties a disagreement over theological doctrine divided the congregants. Both Rawlings and Father Gay became leaders of the breakaway church. But when Rawlings was named chief apostle, jealousy set in. Father Gay withdrew into dark seclusion. This happened over the course of Marvin's early life.

The bishop explained a great deal.

"Your father was a gifted rhetorician," I heard him tell Marvin. "As you yourself saw, he could preach the angels down from heaven. He could also sing like an angel. But he was also deeply in love with the world and its many pleasures. Like so many of us, he found himself locked in a battle between the spirit and the flesh."

"I understand," said Marvin. "I'm engaged in that battle myself."

"We all are, son," said the bishop.

"Some worse than others."

"Yet the family you have brought with you—your beautiful woman and two beautiful children—shows me that you're winning that battle."

"My father was convinced that on the day I refused to become a preacher myself, I had lost the battle forever."

"A battle that he himself is convinced he has lost. You see, he did the very thing he warned you not to do. He left the church. But God's love is not restricted to a physical church. God's love is something we can never lose."

"I lost it a long time ago."

"How can you ever lose God's love?"

"I'm talking about my father's love."

"If you reach out, it's there."

"I tried," said Marvin. "I wanted him to come to London with me, Jan, and the kids."

This was news to me. I was startled when Marvin said, "I wanted him to see me perform in a great European concert hall. I thought it would give him pleasure and pride. I wanted to see him in the first row, standing and applauding me. Is that an unreasonable request from a son to a father?"

"Not at all," the bishop assured Marvin. "What did he say?"

"He said no. He said he had no interest in attending one of my concerts."

"I'm sorry to hear that. Sorry that he doesn't understand that, after all is said and done, you have become a preacher, Marvin. You preached a mighty sermon with *What's Going On*."

"But after that I returned to songs of sin, songs that celebrate and even encourage lust."

"It sounds to me that you judge your work harshly."

"No more harshly than my father," said Marvin.

"Which is harsh indeed," the bishop stated. "All this judgment coming down . . ."

"Isn't that the religion you and Father teach?"

"Your dad gave up teaching a long time ago, but I teach that Jesus said, 'Judge not, lest ye be judged.'"

"Will you call Father and tell him that?" asked Marvin.

"He doesn't recognize my authority."

"Whose authority does he recognize?"

"Only he can answer that question."

As Bishop Rawlings entertained Marvin's questions for hours on end, I could feel the strength of Marvin's sincerity in his search for spiritual answers. He was deeply conflicted. He embraced the all-encompassing love and forgiving heart of Jesus.

"I was born a Christian," he told me time and time again. "I will always be a Christian. I will always call Jesus my Lord and savior."

Yet he couldn't free himself of the pre-Jesus Old Testament judgment.

"I'm caught up in sin," he confessed when we were walking to a nearby park, the kids in tow. "You know that as well as I do. You see it. You must hate me for my weakness. My weakness must disgust you."

"We all have our weaknesses," I said, "but we also have our strengths. Together, Marvin, we're strong. Look at Nona. Look at Bubby. Look at the amazing lives that have resulted from our love."

Marvin took us all in his arms and held us tight. He wouldn't let go. I felt his beating heart. I saw tears streaming down his cheeks.

"Why is Daddy crying?" asked Nona.

"Because Daddy is happy," said Marvin. "Because Daddy knows that he's the luckiest man alive."

At the park, young children and their parents recognized Marvin. They followed him and our family until there were dozens of admirers encircling him.

"Sing for us!" said one of the kids.

"Yes! Yes!" shouted another.

Standing in front of this group of admirers, he closed his eyes, stood in the sunshine, and sang the words that Jesus spoke when he ascended the mount:

> Our Father, who art in heaven
> Hallowed be thy name
> Thy kingdom come
> Thy will be done
> In earth as it is in heaven
> Give us this day our daily bread
> And forgive us our debts as we forgive our debtors
> And lead us not into temptation
> But deliver us from evil
> For thine is the kingdom
> And the power
> And the glory
> Forever

After the song was sung, a little boy of five or six years old, whom Marvin had never seen before, came running up with open arms and embraced him.

"I love you," said the child.

"I love you, too," said Marvin. "I love everyone here. Let today mark a new life of love for everyone!"

The loving new life did not last long.

The divorce proceedings continued to separate Marvin from his money. It was clear to me that Anna's lawyers were sharper than his. Beyond that, Marvin's self-sabotage never stopped. The more he needed to conserve his earnings, the more recklessly he spent, and the more he needed to do what he disliked most: tour.

Performing in Dallas, Marvin and I accepted the gracious invitation to stay at the palatial home of soul singer Johnnie Taylor, whose "Disco Lady" was the hottest single in the country. Taylor was on the road but had left behind an ample supply of top-grade weed and cocaine for his guests. It was there where, after the show, Marvin and I met friends of Johnnie's, a handsome couple eager to get high.

After all four of us consumed copious amounts of stimulants, Marvin took me aside and said, "I think they're swingers."

Floating on a cloud miles above the earth, I wasn't sure.

"I am sure," said Marvin. "I think they want to take this party to the next phase. I also think they're quite attractive. Wouldn't you agree?"

"I haven't been looking at them in that way."

"Well, they've certainly been looking at you. He definitely wants you. And I suspect she'd love to participate."

"I don't know, Marvin."

"I do. A small intimate orgy is just what the doctor ordered. Just the four of us. Let's just have a little more of the goodies that brother Johnnie has provided and go with the flow."

A lot more smoke and coke, and it was apparent that Marvin was right. The couple was ready to rock.

Marvin was the ringleader. I remained hesitant. Marvin insisted.

He told me that this would make him exceedingly happy. It would be a new thrill, a beautiful moment of physical freedom filled with boundless pleasures.

The problem was, Marvin didn't participate. He watched. He egged me on. He closely observed the three of us engaging in a long sexual dance. Yet he himself stood to the side. I don't know whether it was the coke or the jealousy, but Marvin claimed that he couldn't perform.

Hours later when the couple left, he told me, "You loved it, didn't you?"

"Not especially."

"Oh, dear, please don't deny it. You were an animal in heat. You couldn't get enough. This was your dream come true."

"Not my dream, Marvin. Yours."

"After this," he said, "I'll never be able to satisfy you again. From now on you'll require this sort of extravagant stimulation. One man will never be enough for you."

"If the one man is you, yes, he will be enough."

"That's what you say now. But I saw you. And now I'll never be able to trust you."

The next night the couple returned looking for more. This time the woman was hoping that Marvin would participate. But Marvin refused to even see them.

"Send them away," he said. "They bore me. You go off with them if you want to. I can't stop you. I won't try."

"I have no interest in them."

"You did last night."

"Why are you using them to torture yourself? What's the point of this whole fiasco?"

"To watch purity turn to perversity is a fascinating thing," he said. "You were once my angel. But now you have fallen. And yes, I do admit, it is exciting to watch the fall."

Other than certain artists like Sylvester, Marvin watched the rise of disco with growing alarm.

"It is too far from the roots of rhythm and blues," he told me. "Too mechanical. Too calculated. Too much the product of a producer rather than an artist."

"Isn't it just dance music with a new name?" I asked.

"Maybe, but when I create music, my purpose is not to get people to dance."

"What is the purpose?"

"To get people to see below the surface of reality. Disco is surface music."

"You like Harold Melvin and the Blue Notes' 'Don't Leave Me This Way,' don't you?" I asked.

"*You* like Harold's singer Teddy Pendergrass. I saw you watching him on *Soul Train*. You think he's hot, don't you?"

"I like the song."

"Motown had Thelma Houston cover it. They souped it up with even more disco than the original. They say it's going to be number-one pop. Now they want a disco song outta me."

"And of course you told them no."

"I told them what I always tell them—I'm not interested in marketing trends. I'm interested in music that gets down to the soul of the matter."

"And dance music can never do that?"

"If dancing were my thing, perhaps. But whatever movements I'm able to pull off onstage, I do with a certain self-consciousness."

We laughed over the fact that neither of us was exactly a world-class dancer.

A couple of days after Marvin's antidisco rant, I was with him at the Sunset studio. Nona and Bubby were upstairs napping on the waterbed. Marvin was stretched out on a couch in the control room. He loved singing while reclining on an easy chair or sofa.

At one point he wasn't singing at all. He was listening to a throw-away rhythm track that his engineer, Art Stewart, had decided not to throw away.

"There's something here, Marv," said Art. "Listen to it."

The track had a quirky, funky feel to it, a snare offset by a cow-bell, a low-tech quality that added to the seductive groove abetted by Bugsy Wilcox, Marvin's drummer. The groove was sparse and loose. In its imperfection it sounded absolutely perfect for a spontaneous Marvin Gaye vocal.

I watched as Marvin started singing over the track. He did so in his falsetto. This was his gentlest voice, the one that expressed the most longing. As I had noted before, I saw that Marvin's writing process did not entail a pencil and pad. Nothing was written down. Like a jazz musician, he wordlessly scatted over the track. He kept scatting until the scats took the shape of actual words. Eventually, he strung enough words together to make a story.

I heard this story as a reaction to our recent antidisco discussion. He sang about a man who has been afraid of dancing his entire life, a wallflower who lacks the courage to strut his stuff. But the force of this infectious groove is too much to resist. The wallflower has to get out there. He has to get down. He's got to give it up.

"Got to Give It Up" became the name of the jam, an under-the-radar, denial-of-disco song perfectly suited for the overblown disco era.

"Is this your story?" I asked Marvin after he improvised the lyrics.

"Well, kind of, sort of," he admitted.

The song was all about Marvin's insecurity. I was moved by how freely he exposed his vulnerability. He wasn't afraid to say, "I'm shy, I'm fragile, I'm afraid of making a fool of myself, I need to sing this song to get over my fear."

"Can I sing on this? *Pleeeease* . . ." I begged.

His honesty gave me the courage to honestly express my own need.

"I was about to do the backgrounds myself," said Marvin.

"Can't I sing just one part?" I urged just as Marvin's brother Frankie happened to show up.

"Can I get in on it too?" asked Frankie.

"Everyone wants to get in on the act," Marvin said with a smile.

"You know that's true!" Frankie and I shouted in unison.

"It's just two lines," I said, "'Keep on dancing' and 'Got to give it up.'"

"Okay, dear," Marvin finally relented.

I covered him with kisses.

Frankie and I sang the backgrounds.

"Not bad," said Marvin. "Y'all can sing."

"We've been telling you that," I said, laughing.

"We're gonna have to do this more often," Marvin added.

"Can't wait till the next time," said Frankie.

For all the enthusiasm, for all the genuine camaraderie, for all the sweet harmony in that moment, the next time never happened.

Neither Frankie nor I ever sang on a Marvin Gaye song again.

Before the final mix, "Got to Give It Up" kept evolving. Whoever happened to walk into the studio heard the jam and spontaneously added to it. Frankie Beverly, for instance, put on a percussive feel with a bottle and a spoon. Don Cornelius strolled through and ended up on the track. My sister Cass spoke the line, "I heard *that*." I asked Marvin if Johnny McGhee, guitarist for LTD, could add a guitar part—and Marvin agreed. It all worked. It all contributed to the song's bubbling funk. Even before its release, we put it on an endless loop and played it everywhere we went.

The single took off like a rocket. Everyone loved dancing to a story about the painfully timid man who allows positive vibrations to overwhelm his fears and force him to the dance floor. In 1977, a dizzy disco year when Leo Sayer's "You Make Me Feel Like Dancing" dominated the clubs, "Got to Give It Up" hit No. 1 and became an anthem of its own.

I had to laugh when I heard a Motown executive tell Marvin, "You have a disco hit."

"The hell I do," said Marvin. "This is just a lonely little song about a lonely little guy trying to overcome his loneliness."

"Call it whatever you want," said the suit. "All I know is that it's going number-one pop."

Despite his protests about the crassness of the disco era, Marvin was happy to be back on top.

"Got to Give It Up" became the final track—the only studio cut—on the double album culled from his show in England. As a result, *Live at the London Palladium* sold two million copies.

I wasn't surprised when Motown urged Marvin to do an all-disco album.

"Never," he said.

"At least consider making music suitable for dancing," said the suit.

"The music I'm considering making," said Marvin, "could not be more *unsuitable* for dancing."

"Then what's its appeal?" the executive wanted to know.

"It appeals to my sense of irony, my sense of poetry, my sense of justice, and, perhaps most importantly, my sense of humor."

"When will you start recording? When can we hear something?"

"It may be a month, it may be a year, it may be a decade. There's no way of knowing when the spirit will move me."

"You need to move quickly," said Marvin's accountant, "if you don't want to lose everything you own. The IRS is coming down hard on you. And so is Anna. You're on the brink of bankruptcy."

"A true artist transforms discord into beauty," Marvin responded. "In the hands of an artist, adversity is a gift. Adversity provides the conflicts that birth creativity."

Finally Free

I watched Marvin make his new record. Since meeting me four years earlier, this was the first music he was making where I wasn't his muse. This time—except for one song—it was all about Anna.

Marvin was lost in the memories of a marriage that had fallen apart, even as he reassured me that he was completely devoted to me, Nona, and Bubby.

I was now twenty-one; Marvin was thirty-eight. We adored our two young children. We adored each other. In spite of the psychological challenges we both faced—including a growing dependence on drugs to beat back depression—we were more deeply in love than ever.

Our dream was to live out our life free of drama and enjoy simple happiness in our Hidden Hills home.

"The dream can be realized," Marvin told me, "once this divorce is behind me and we can get married."

His divorce from Anna had been a ferocious battle, in and out of the courtroom, dragging on for months. Finally, though, there was hope for resolution.

A judge had issued a final decree, ordering Marvin to pay an exorbitant amount of money for child and spousal support. Marvin's accountants had proven, though, that he was broke.

The judge was not convinced. He stated that as an enormously popular recording artist, Marvin was still capable of substantial earnings. With that in mind, it was decided that, to satisfy the terms of the settlement, Marvin would give Anna all the profits from his next record.

Marvin embraced the notion.

"When I refused to go to the studio to record," Marvin told me, "Anna was the only one strong enough to get me in there. So it makes perfect sense that, even at the end of our marriage, she still has the power to make me work. The irony is that the music I intend to make will have no commercial value. I will not contribute to the Gordy wealth in any way. If I have to make an inferior album to satisfy the divorce decree, so be it."

But as I watched Marvin begin to work in the Sunset studio, I saw proof of what I had long known to be true—Marvin Gaye was incapable of making inferior music. Once he started to write and sing, all prior agendas flew out the window. All he could do was follow the dictates of his heart.

"Not every song is a hit," he said, "but every song does tell a story."

He ignored Motown's demands that he make a commercially viable follow-up record to "Got to Give It Up." In fact, as he worked on this divorce settlement record, he banned the Motown suits from his studio. Aside from myself, his engineer Art Stewart, and a few select backup musicians, no one was allowed inside.

The record became an obsession. Within days of observing Marvin putting together the pieces of this new music, I saw that it was evolving into nothing less than a saga. Marvin was not writing

three-minute songs; he was composing a grand suite in the style of
What's Going On in which one melodic motif seamlessly merged into
another. The motifs were chapters in a novel. The subject was his
long and tumultuous marriage to Anna.

When he showed me some of his original song titles, like "You
Never Really Cared," "Fourteen Years of Nothing," "A Messed
Up Mind and a Pocketbook to Match," and one referring to me—
"Younger, Prettier and Twice the Woman"—I told him that he had
gone too far. He had to tone down his attitude and become more
subtle—which is just what he did.

In the final version, he started out the story with a musical creation of his marriage to Anna. Marvin restated his vows and sang
of the beautiful optimism that surrounded the couple. But that
optimism was short-lived. There was infidelity. There was jealousy.
There were breakups and breakdowns. There was tremendous anger.

But as I watched Marvin sing of his anger at Anna, I saw the
anger dissipate. I heard him sing how anger could only make him
sick; how he must purge himself of rage by expressing his rage in
song. And yet that expression was far from furious. It was poetry.
Miraculously, Marvin transformed anger into beauty.

In telling the tale of not only his marriage but of the divorce
proceedings themselves, he asked Anna, "Is that enough?" I sensed
that the question referred not only to the amount of money she was
extracting from him, but the emotional damage they had done to
each other. He detailed those times when she called the cops, the
nasty legal skirmishes, the vicious fights in court. She may have won
the battle, but Marvin warned her that "Daddy will win the war."
He was convinced that she wanted to "break a man." But he wouldn't
permit it. He wouldn't let her win.

Remembering that Anna herself once used this phrase, he named
one song "You Can Leave, but It's Gonna Cost You."

While much of the record was about money, it was more about
the mystery surrounding the loss of love, the sentiment expressed

A "portrait" done by a friend. I thought I could model.

Me as a school girl, hard at work for those A's and B's.

Me at sixteen. I would meet Marvin months later.

Marvin loved anything
on wheels.

Marvin on one of his toys at
Round Mountain.

Mountain man Marvin in
Topanga Canyon, 1973.

My mother with baby Nona, circa 1974. (*Carol Vitz*)

From the left: big brother Mark; our father, Slim; me; and my youngest brother, Michael, at my home.

Ed Townsend, the matchmaker, always working, even after Marvin's death.

Marvin and his beloved mother in her kitchen in DC, 1974. She had just made her famous chicken. That kitchen was one of his favorite spots.

Mother Gay and her sister, Tolie May, in Hawaii, 1979.

Mother Gay, Bubby, and Marvin in our home in Hidden Hills, 1976. Marvin designed the kitchen.

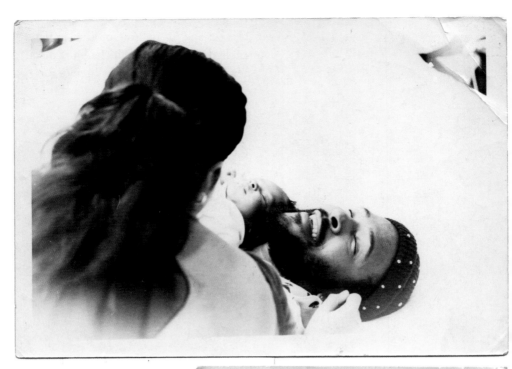

Nona at three weeks, on tour with her dad in New York. Sammy Davis put us up at the Essex House!

New mommy with Nona, September 1974. I'm wearing the dress that Marvin's singer would later wear in New York.

A *Jet* cover that never made it, circa 1975.

On our way to the Brown home for our wedding. Note, Marvin is holding a baby bottle!

Me with my dear friend Laura Brown, before the wedding, at her home in New Orleans.

Marvin, moments before the wedding, watching football!

Signing the marriage certificate, October 10, 1977.

The wine.

The race for the first bite.

Nona and Bubby at our wedding.
Laura Brown in the foreground and
Mama Fontenette in the background.

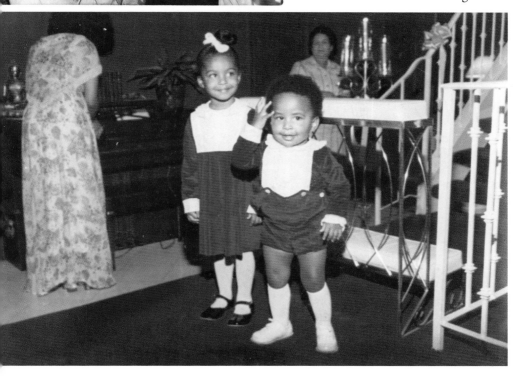

Me with Marvin before a show, circa 1974.

Marvin signing autographs after a show and me feeling out of place but with a smile.

Marvin and me at Pips, the hot backgammon hangout on La Cienega. We were guests of Don Cornelius. We didn't play, but we were introduced to Pimm's Cups.

Marvin Gaye not only has a new recording coming out soon, but a new light in his life, fiance Janis Hunter.

Me with Marvin on a flight to Paris. We both had a fear of flying. Alcohol helped even though we were not really drinkers, instead preferring weed. As much as possible, whenever possible.

Marvin insisted we wear surgical masks whenever we were in the Excalibur. "The fumes will kill us," he would say, never mind the freeway. We're parked here outside Gil Friesen's office at A&M. Marvin seriously considered leaving Motown for them.

Frankie Gaye with his wife, Judy, in our RV for a road trip to Round Mountain, 1974.

Marvin with my right foot in Jamaica, 1974. He love my feet . . . without polish

Cheesy 1983 tour photo.

Having a meal at Mother Gay's apartment in LA, circa 1976.

Me "dancing" with Marvin at a Long Island party, circa 1976.

Me holding a slippery baby Bubby, my sister Cass, and Nona clinging to Frankie Beverly, 1976.

Bubby, Daddy, and "Pie," Marvin's nickname for Nona, in Montego Bay on our "honeymoon," 1977.

Father and son in Ostende. I love
the way Bubby is looking at his dad.

Me with Bubby in Ostende,
Belgium, circa 1981.

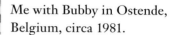

Nona; her dad, with "that look" he could
put on you; and Bubby in Brussels.

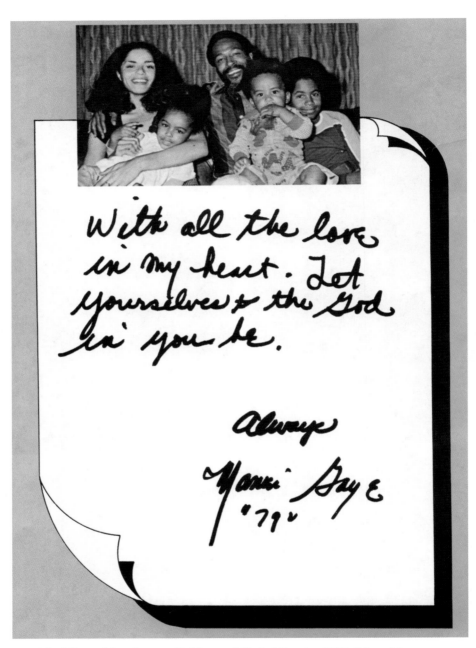

With all the love in my heart. Let yourselves + the God in you be.

Always

Marvin Gaye

"79"

Me, Nona, Marvin, our Bubby, and little Marvin, 1979. I love his words of wisdom.

in the motif of "When Did You Stop Loving Me, When Did I Stop Loving You?"

Yet I was convinced that the answer to that question was *never.* Marvin never stopped loving Anna. I was sure of that because of the song that sat at the center of the suite—"Anna's Song." This was the high point. The passion with which Marvin shouted her name— "Anna! Anna!"—revealed the passion of a man forever bound to this woman, no matter how bitter their separation.

"With this record," Marvin told me, "I'll be done with her."

I knew better, but didn't argue. I saw that Marvin wanted to feel that he was free, but the record itself said otherwise. The enormous creative output proved that Marvin was—and would always be—tied to Anna. In fact, it was the only time in his career that he had written enough material on a single topic to fill two LPs. The record that delineated his relationship to Anna was twice as long as *What's Going On.*

Even when she was at odds with Marvin, Anna still motivated him to work. According to Marvin, Anna browbeat him. In some sense, this new album was a response to that browbeating. I took another approach entirely. When Marvin was reluctant to go into the studio, I'd say, "How can you deny the world these brilliant songs? How can you keep these beautiful melodies to yourself? You need to share. You to need to express all these amazing ideas that live inside you."

In the case of the divorce album, he did just that. He wrote with fearless honesty and complete sincerity. He didn't sing a note that he didn't mean. He didn't write a lyric that didn't expose his raw feelings.

For all the lamentations about how Anna had wronged him, he boldly confessed his own wrongs. In a funky song he called "Time to Get It Together," he addressed his weaknesses, singing about how he had wasted time by blowing coke up his nose and chasing down midnight hoes. He declared the end of that chapter in his life and swore to do better.

It was only love, he realized, that would make him better. In the midst of his divorce dispute, he sang "Everybody Needs Love," a quiet prayer for the love of Jesus, the love required by everyone from "a beggar or even a superstar."

In the symbol of a sparrow, Marvin saw the source of his creative energy. "Sparrow" became a song in which he elongated his prayer, asking the bird to reveal life's deepest secrets—"sing before you fly away . . . sing to me, Marvin Gaye."

I watched as Marvin flew away on the poetic wings of the sparrow into outer space, where he created "A Funky Space Reincarnation," a funked-up fantasy about escaping into a world of musical make-believe.

In the end, though, I was gratified to be included in this long-form composition. When Marvin fell back to earth, he was finally able to look away from his obsession with Anna and turn to me. I was there in the studio, sitting next to him, when he wrote the final song in this remarkable suite, "Falling in Love Again."

"You are my muse," he told me. "You are my happiness. I've lost out on love once, but I won't lose twice. When someone real comes in, when someone you *feel* comes in, love is renewed. I am renewed. Once I turn in this record, I will be a new man. Our love will be born again."

"What are you going to call it?" I asked.

"Dick Gregory gave me the title. He said, 'Call it *Here, My Dear.*' I will hand the album to Anna and say, 'This is the record that the judge ordained. This is the record that our marriage made possible, the one that our divorce demanded. *Here, my dear.* This record belongs to you, but I belong to Jan.'"

I wanted to believe him but was moved to say, "I wonder whether you'll ever belong to one woman and one woman alone?"

"You are that woman—I swear. How better to prove that than to ask for your hand in marriage?"

"You've asked before, Marvin."

"And I'm asking again. The divorce is final. I'm free. We can do this. Marry me."

I was thinking:

His words are pretty, but don't let them deceive you. Don't fool yourself into thinking he can defeat his demons. His faith is great, but his fears are greater. The strength of his spirit is under constant attack by his gnawing insecurities. He may seek happiness, but in fact he thrives in chaos. How will that ever change?

At the same time, I was praying:

He is sincere; he is in love with the God of love; he loves me; he loves our children; he has sworn off the crazy drama; he has dedicated himself to peace and harmony.

My thinking, no matter how delusional, was reinforced when Marvin, in fact, married me. It happened in October 10, 1977, in New Orleans while Marvin was on tour. The ceremony took place in the home of our friends Andrew and Laura Brown. Neither Marvin's parents nor mine attended. A judge officiated. I wore a beige peasant blouse and a flowing skirt in dark maroon. Nona and Frankie wore matching outfits. Marvin and I wore expressions of fear, excitement, and love. I fell ill about an hour before the ceremony but made it through. In spite of being blasted on the best smoke and coke available in the state of Louisiana, Marvin and I functioned pretty well.

Being blasted was the norm. It had been the norm for Marvin since his Motown days back in the sixties. It had been the norm for me since moving in with my mom in the seventies. This was our culture. No one was chiding us or warning us or even mildly advising us about being blasted.

This was the white-out cocaine blizzard of the times.

We hung out with Richard Pryor at the Circle Star Theater in Northern California, and the blizzard was in full force. Richard was one of Marvin's biggest fans. And Marvin loved him back.

"I wanna be Marvin when I grow up," Richard told me.

And this, I thought to myself, *is the great Richard Pryor talking!*

So how could anything be wrong with Marvin when a genius like Richard Pryor looked at him as a god?

When Richard invited Marvin and me for an evening to watch bikini-clad dancers having sex with each other, I was introduced to the term "freaky deaky." We became obsessed with the phrase and even named one of our puppies Freaky. The evening was uncomfortable for me, but I went along with the program. Who was I to object when Richard Pryor and Marvin Gaye were having so much fun?

When at a dinner party at Richard's house he referred to me as "Peach Juice Johnson," I accepted it as a term of endearment. When at that same party he got so coked up that he hit his wife over the head with a wine bottle and called everyone at the table "a fuckin' whore" except me, Marvin laughed and said I should be flattered. That night we were the last to leave the party.

Coke may have been making Richard crazy, but I remained convinced that Marvin and I could handle our drugs.

After all, Marvin was getting health advice from Dick Gregory, another close friend. Dick spoke of Marvin in the same breath as Duke Ellington, Charlie Parker, and Miles Davis. Dick was not only funny, but a brilliant thinker and author. Seeing Marvin through Dick's eyes, I fell in love with my husband all over again.

"His music has changed our world," Dick told me. "And as long as he's healthy, his music will become even more profound."

Marvin accepted the regimen of vitamins and supplements from Dick and vowed to double his exercise and stop drugging.

The good times were not rare. Lem Barney and Mel Farr, his friends from the Detroit Lions, would come visit with their wonderful wives. They were the sweetest, most welcoming people in the world. Whenever they stayed with us in California, our mood turned happy and our burdens seemed to lift.

There were always good times when Marvin played the Circle Star Theater in San Carlos, California. It was run by Don Jo Medlevine, who had once owned the Chez Paree in Chicago, where he had booked Frank Sinatra, Dean Martin, Sammy Davis, and Wayne Newton. An old-fashioned tough guy, Don Jo adored Marvin. Marvin saw him as a second father—a kind and understanding father. Don Jo's go-to gal and second-in-command was Barbara Stroum, who became my best friend. When things got rough in my life, I could always turn to Barbara for support. She was the surest and steadiest ally I've ever known. She also worked tirelessly for Marvin to make sure that his tours went smoothly, a thankless task. Her contribution to his success was great.

Don Jo loved to indulge Marvin. He once took us to Frank Sinatra's retreat in Palm Springs. Frank wasn't there, but we got a private tour. Don Jo also got Jilly Rizzo to work with Marvin on several dates. Marvin and I had met Jilly at Matteo's, an Italian restaurant in Westwood. Given how Marvin revered Sinatra, he was thrilled to be associated with Jilly. He loved the link to the Rat Pack.

"Just like Jilly's got Frank's back," said Don Jo, "he'll have your back. You're as good as gold, Marvin. Only the best for you."

Maybe the best time of all was our belated but beautiful honeymoon in Jamaica. It would have been that much better had we not traveled with an entourage of a dozen or so hangers-on. No matter: it turned out to be a lovely respite from the road, a few days in paradise where just watching Nona and Bubby run along the beach in the golden glow of a spectacular sunset was enough to bring tears to our eyes. We were dedicated to making this marriage work. This blessed family would thrive.

Marvin rededicated himself to health. I did the same. Once off the road, Marvin was all about basketball games on the court of our

Hidden Hills home. I was all about jogging, tennis, and swimming. We were both all about purging the toxins from our bodies with long fasts. After the fasts, we were all about consuming great quantities of raw vegetables and fruits.

Marvin was also all about cuddling with Nona and little Frankie and reassuring me that this time the change was permanent. The good times were here to stay.

In January 1978, the good times led us back to New Orleans and Super Bowl XII in the Superdome, where the party was just too great to resist. How could he not get stoned at the Super Bowl? I followed his lead, and soon we were flying high as Dallas crushed the Broncos. By then we had become friends with Cowboys Thomas "Hollywood" Henderson, Tony Dorsett, and Ed "Too Tall" Jones. Marvin loved hanging out with star athletes. Their company made him feel good.

"Good times are getting better," said Marvin.

"Not so good," said Marvin's lawyer, who had gotten a telegram saying that federal marshals had seized his Sunset studio because of unpaid back taxes.

"Just pay the taxes," said Marvin.

"With what?" asked the attorney. "You're seven million dollars in debt. You're about to lose everything—the house in Hidden Hills, the cars, the boats, the property."

"You've said that before."

"Before, I said that the wolf was at the door. But now the wolf is inside. He's at your throat, Marvin."

" 'The wolf shall dwell with the lamb,' " said Marvin. "Do you know who I'm quoting?"

"No," said the lawyer.

"Isaiah eleven, six through nine. 'The leopard shall lie down with the young goat, and the calf and the lion and the fattened calf together; and a little child shall lead them.' "

"I applaud your optimism, Marvin, but I think this is something more like a financial apocalypse."

All this talk of an apocalypse frightened me.

"If the apocalypse comes," said Marvin, "if, in fact, these are the last days, then the prophecy will be fulfilled. 'I was in the Spirit on the Lord's day, and I heard behind me a loud voice like the sound of a trumpet.' The last book of the Bible is Revelation. The last great battle is Armageddon. Two lords wage the final war. The Lord of Love and the Lord of Evil. Who will win?"

"I suspect," said the attorney, "the IRS."

Hawaii Is Heaven/
Hawaii Is Hell

A big gig in Hawaii came at a fortunate time. Hawaii was where Marvin and I escaped the realities of a mainland where his financial empire had crumbled. It was only through the offices of Berry Gordy that Marvin was able to hold on to his studio and home. Gordy paid the IRS bill for Marvin while, at the same time, binding him to a new long-term contract.

"It's humiliating to still be in Berry's debt," Marvin told me as we walked along the private beach in front of the Kahala Hilton on the island of Oahu.

"What other choice did you have?" I asked. "Who else would bail you out?"

"No one. That's why the irony is so thick. I declared my independence from Berry long ago. That was the point of *What's Going On*. Free myself of the Motown machine. Go my own way. Now look . . ."

"What I see, dear," I said, "is that you're still doing what you want to do, still making the music you want to make."

"That will never change."

"Then everything is all right."

"Until Berry and Anna listen to *Here, My Dear.* How is he going to feel about putting out a record on his label that slams his own beloved older sister?"

"I told you," I reminded Marvin, "that there are lyrics that went too far."

Marvin chuckled. "Either way, Berry won't be happy. He adores his sister. She has been as much a mother to him as she has been a mother to me. Now that I am casting aspersions on her, how can he not be pissed off?"

"But you have creative control. You can put out any record you want."

"That, my dear, is exactly right. And I will."

"And you'll take care of all those money matters that your accountants say you can't afford to ignore."

"We can't afford to ignore this splendid Pacific Ocean that calls to us like the Siren's song. The spirit of the islands is on us. It's calm and healing and soothing to our souls. This is where we need to be, Jan—far away from everyone."

"It'll be fun. The Jacksons are opening. You love them."

"The Jacksons only make it worse. After Michael's through dancing, the crowd will be ecstatic, and in no mood to hear me."

"That's not true. You and Michael are totally different," I said.

"We are, but at the same time I do not underestimate Michael Jackson."

"Michael idolizes you," I said.

"But not enough to keep him from putting on a show that will put mine to shame."

"Stop it!" I shouted. "You are Marvin Gaye!"

That night the kids had fallen asleep and Marvin and I were chilling in our suite. The windows were wide open. The tropical breeze
was blowing strong.

A knock on the door.

"Who is it?" I asked. I looked through the peephole.

The high-pitched voice was tentative. "It's Michael. If I'm disturbing you two, I'll go away."

I opened the door. "No, no . . . come on in, Michael. Hey, dear,
look who's here."

"Hey, Mike," said Marvin. "Pull up a chair. Have a toke."

"Oh, no thanks," said Michael, refusing the joint. "I don't ever . . ."

"So I've heard. Well, that's great. More power to you, brother.
What's happening?"

Twenty years old at the time, Michael fought his shyness to say,
"I just wanted to come by and say hello to my favorite singer."

"Love you too, Michael," said Marvin.

"I wanted to know if I could come by the studio when we get
home. You could give me some tips."

"Man, I should be getting tips from you, Mike. You should be
teaching me some of your moves."

"They're nothing."

"They're dynamite. I know Berry's kicking himself for letting
you guys off Motown. He should have met CBS's price and then
some. Are you happy over there at CBS?"

"Very. They finally gave us what you got from Mr. Gordy a
long time ago—creative freedom. I tried to follow your lead, Marvin. My hope was that if you could write and produce your own
material, I should be able to do the same. But Mr. Gordy didn't see
it that way."

"Now radio won't stop playing that dance hit of yours. What's it
called?"

"'Shake Your Body Down to the Ground.'"

"Sing a few bars," said Marvin. "Show me your moves. Let me see if I can follow."

"Sure you can," Michael reassured Marvin.

When Michael started singing, Marvin did his best to follow a few of Michael's signature moves. He was not successful.

"Making a fool of myself," said Marvin.

"You're doing just fine," Michael reassured him.

Michael kept singing as Marvin tried negotiating a few spins. Mocking his own attempts to keep up, Marvin broke out laughing.

"I'm hopeless," he conceded.

"You're great," Michael exclaimed with a little giggle.

"I'll never be Michael Jackson," said Marvin.

"And I'll never be Marvin Gaye," said Michael.

As they hugged, I thought, *This is a very cool moment to witness.*

Michael's visit did Marvin a world of good.

The concert came off beautifully. Marvin's dance moves remained modest but effective. His singing was sweeter than ever. Even though the Jacksons were enjoying a huge pop hit at a time when Marvin was not on the charts, they treated him with great respect. After the show, Michael wanted to come back to the suite for another long hang with Marvin.

"Tell him another time," Marvin instructed me. "I love Michael, but I want to be alone."

When we returned to America, Marvin's money problems continued to mount. Motown's payment to the IRS satisfied only one creditor. There were many others. The only thing that could save Marvin was a blockbuster album. Yet the only music Marvin returned to after completing *Here, My Dear*—clearly not a blockbuster—was the collection of ballads that would eventually be titled *Vulnerable.*

"Vulnerability is the necessary condition for producing great art," Marvin insisted. "The more vulnerable, the more human, the more honest the feelings."

I saw how he felt especially vulnerable when it came to be time for Anna to listen to *Here, My Dear*, a month before it was released. That's why he made sure not to be around when she came to the Sunset studio. Engineer Art Stewart was at the controls. For the entire time it took the two-disc album to play, Anna sat without expression as she listened to the story of her life with Marvin. When the last track—"Falling in Love Again"—was over, she got up, politely thanked Art for his time, and quickly left.

"What did she say?" I heard Marvin ask Art the next day.

"Nothing."

"Was she okay?" he asked.

"I couldn't tell," said Art.

Weeks later there were rumors that Anna would sue for slander, but she never did.

In LA, Marvin's world was increasingly pressure-packed. His money managers showed him that the only way he could hold on to the studio and the Hidden Hills home was to generate income immediately. That meant touring. When a promoter offered still another tour of Japan, Marvin refused. Still uncomfortable on planes, he hated the idea of a twelve-hour flight. When I suggested that we cut the trip in half by stopping over in Hawaii, Marvin's eyes lit up.

"Not just a stopover, but stay a while," he said. "Only this time let's take the kids and go to Maui. Maui has a spiritual vibe that's sure to chill us out."

Marvin and I required a great deal of chilling out.

Although marrying my man was the fulfillment of a dream, the dream was dissipating before my very eyes. I wondered whether our vows had changed the chemistry. Was Marvin happier when he viewed me as his girlfriend rather than his wife? Did the formal institution of marriage feel restrictive to Marvin? Did it bring out the rebel in him? Did he see the commitment as another prison, just as he felt imprisoned by his long-term marriage to Anna?

Even worse, I worried that Marvin was simply tiring of me.

That's why I hoped this trip to Hawaii might restore the romance that had been eroding.

In the beginning, there was a restoration of sorts. Maui did have a magical quality that put Marvin in a mellow mood. Seated on the balcony of our beachfront condo, we held hands as we looked at the landscape before us: the orange sun sinking into the green-blue sea, the gulls sweeping across the majestic sky, the distant mountains shrouded in mist.

Marvin put his arm around me and said, "We are blessed to be in paradise, aren't we, dear?"

"Yes," I said, my heart filled with the hope that this trip would ease the tension and bring us closer.

"I love you, dear," he said.

"I love you, too."

"I know you do, but things are changing."

"What does that mean?"

"It means that while I love you, I'm no longer certain that I am *in* love with you."

I had heard him say this before—and then recant. It was his way of hurting me. I wanted to believe that he would recant again. But even if he would, to hear him doubt his love for me caused incredible pain. My heart sank. I thought my life was over. In my mind, I even saw him going back to Anna.

"I don't understand," I said, my heart pounding. "You always said our love is forever."

"People change. Feelings change. Love changes."

"Love should grow stronger. I know our love has."

"Has it?" asked Marvin.

"Of course it has. You know it has."

"All I know is that I see you differently, dear. There are changes in your character, changes in your body."

"So that's it—my body?"

"There's a big difference between pleasure and excitement. As a man, I can't help but seek excitement."

"I've never stopped you. When you asked me if you could 'ride out,' you think I didn't know where you were going? I knew you were going off to be with someone else."

"This discussion isn't going anywhere."

The talk ended, but the pain lasted. The pain worsened.

With a dark cloud over our heads, the next day Marvin suggested we go out in the sunlight and visit a nude beach. Nona and Bubby were delighted to run around naked. Marvin was also not in the least self-conscious about shedding his clothes. But I was hesitant.

"Why?" Marvin asked me.

"You know why."

"Your stretch marks?"

"I hate them," I said.

"No one will notice," Marvin tried to reassure me.

"I don't care. I'm not taking off my bathing suit."

"Then you'll be out of place," he said with an edge of disdain.

The hours spent on the nude beach proved difficult. Marvin made no secret of his appreciation of several women who, like me, were in their early twenties but, unlike me, displayed flawless bodies. I felt hurt and ashamed. Except for my legs, I kept my body covered. I tried to play it off like it wasn't ripping me to pieces, but it was. I was dying inside, telling myself that I would never regain the figure that I'd once had. I was barely twenty-two, yet convinced that I had lost my youth forever.

Marvin didn't help by saying my breasts were sagging. He remarked how the sun made my freckles that much more prominent. And when he pointed to another woman's perfectly proportioned nose, I took that as a criticism of my own nose. If there was cruelty, the cruelty was camouflaged in Marvin's peculiar mixture of slyness and charm.

The cutting comments increased during family outings to quaint towns like Lahaina and the beaches at Kaanapali and Kapalua. In a deserted section of the island, Marvin and I watched Nona and Bubby run through a beautiful open field, only to realize that the field was filled with psychedelic mushrooms. Afraid that our kids might be breathing in the spores, we gathered them up and hurried down the windswept coast, but not before we took our shrooms to go. A local taught me to mix the shrooms with honey to put in the tea that we drank twice a day.

The Maui trip became more entangled with the arrival of Marvin's brother Frankie, sister Zeola, and mother, Alberta. Joining the entourage was the ever-affable Wally Amos. Marvin was one of the original investors in Wally's Famous Amos chocolate-chip cookies. Jazz guitarist and pop singer George Benson, a longtime resident of Hawaii, also knocked on our door. Marvin and I were big Benson fans. He and Marvin shared a passion for the Bible and spent long hours discussing Scripture. George was a wonderful guide, graciously taking us to his favorite spots on the island.

All these people vied for Marvin's time and attention. He welcomed the distractions.

"I thought we came here to be alone," I said one night while Marvin and I were driving back to our condo in the midst of a punishing thunderstorm. The kids were in the backseat. We'd been to dinner with a large crowd of family and friends, each of whom had sought and secured Marvin's ear for one request or another. Those requests almost always came with a price tag.

"What's the point of being alone?" asked Marvin. "When we're alone, all you do is harp at me."

"And you ignore me."

"I can't stand your bitching!" Marvin screamed.

"I can't stand your insults and your nasty attitude!" I screamed back.

"And I'm tired of you looking at other men!"

The fighting quickly escalated. At one point Marvin lost all control and began to wildly swerve the car.

"I'll drive this thing off the road!" he screamed. "I swear I will!"

"Daddy, don't!" Nona shouted. "Don't kill us!"

I knew he wouldn't—and he knew he wouldn't—but the kids didn't know that.

Marvin brought the car to a screeching halt.

"What the hell is wrong with you?" I asked. "What in God's name were you thinking?"

He didn't respond. Instead he just sat there behind the wheel, his face in his hands, reciting the Lord's prayer.

"Our Father, who art in heaven . . ."

Mind Games

If Marvin had common sense, he would not have pushed me into the arms of another man.

If I had common sense, I would have resisted all such moves on Marvin's part.

Common sense told us that we were in desperate need of righteous counsel. We were in desperate need of psychotherapy—both as individuals and as a couple. We had to immediately get off marijuana and cocaine. If there was any chance of renewing our relationship and salvaging our marriage, we had to seek help. We were smart people with progressive ideas. Surely we understood that if we could openly and candidly address the issues tearing us apart, we'd have a fighting chance. We'd be able to see that we were surrounded by people who wanted to ruin our relationship—those who were envious, those hell-bent on stirring up the chaos in our lives. We'd be able to extricate ourselves from those negative forces.

And yet we did nothing.

We did not reflect inwardly. We did not employ outside counsel. In our multidimensional disease of dysfunction, we got worse.

We were still on the island of Maui.

Marvin lit a joint, inhaled deeply, and passed it to me. I took a hit, reached for his hand, and told him that I loved him.

When he didn't respond, I said, "Let's just go to the market. Our neighbor will take care of the kids. Let's just spend the afternoon alone."

"The market sounds good," said Marvin.

The market was crowded with locals and tourists buying baskets and beads, surfboards and painted seashells. Shapely women were parading around in bikinis. Several recognized Marvin and made a fuss. He graciously signed autographs and posed for pictures. Strolling along, he noticed a tall young black man who was strikingly handsome.

"Your type, dear?" he asked me.

"Please don't start, Marvin."

"Don't tell me you don't get off on those rippling muscles. He must be an athlete. And he's about your age. A perfect fit, I'd say. Let's introduce ourselves."

The guy's name was Steven, and of course he was thrilled to meet Marvin Gaye. He was, in fact, a college football player.

"My wife couldn't wait to meet you," said Marvin, embarrassing me. "Will you join us for a glass of wine?"

Steven turned out to be a charmer. Like Marvin, he had an easy banter and a kicked-back style. He answered Marvin's questions about his feats on the football field, and Marvin answered his questions about the life of a superstar. All the while, Steven was throwing furtive glances in my direction. Marvin caught one of those glances.

"We're going out tonight," said Marvin. "Why don't you join us? Meet us at our place and we'll have dinner first."

Later, when we were alone, I asked Marvin, "Why did you invite him? What's the point?"

"He's a cool brother. I like him. You like him. Don't lie and say you don't."

I didn't say anything. To do so would have only added fuel to the fire.

That evening Steven showed up and had dinner with Marvin, me, and the kids. The conversation was easy. Everyone was pleasant. Once again, there were quick glances from Steven in my direction.

"Tonight's my night for taking care of the kids," said Marvin. "So why don't you two go dancing at the beach club? Have a good time while I play Mr. Mom."

"No, no, man," said Steven.

"It's cool," Marvin reassured him. "Jan's been dying to go dancing."

"Well, if you insist."

I protested, but neither man would be moved. I knew I was being set up. Part of me wanted to defy Marvin by refusing to play this game. But another part of me was gratified and even excited. For weeks Marvin had been distancing himself from me in bed. Then along came a man—a drop-dead gorgeous man—who desired me.

When we arrived at the club, Steven's desire was apparent. He couldn't stop praising my beauty. I wanted to resist his advances—and I did—but I also knew that he knew that my husband had not only arranged this meeting but relished it.

We had a drink.

The DJ spun Marvin's "Got to Give It Up."

Steven smiled.

"Don't we need to do what the song says?"

"I'm singing on the song," I couldn't help but say.

"All the more reason to give it up. At least on the dance floor."

We moved to the dance floor. Our dancing was restrained. If there were sexual suggestions in our moves, those suggestions were subtle.

After Marvin's song was played, we returned to our table and ordered another drink.

"Your husband is really great," said Steven.

"Here's your chance to tell him that in person," I said. "He's walking through the door right now."

Steven abruptly turned around. Marvin was walking directly to our table.

"I thought you were taking care of the kids," I said.

"I found a babysitter and thought I'd check in on you guys," said Marvin, who seemed disappointed that he hadn't caught me and Steven in some passionate embrace.

"They just played your song," said Steven.

"Which one?" asked Marvin.

"The one where you say you're too shy to dance," said Steven.

"Was my wife too shy to dance?" asked Marvin.

"It would have been impolite not to ask her."

"And she accepted, right?"

"She did, and she's a good dancer," Steven lied.

"Good in all ways. But now I'm afraid that I must take her home. It's way past her bedtime."

"I hope we all get to see each other again," said Steven.

"We will," said Marvin.

Riding back to the condo, I lashed out at Marvin. "You humiliated me!"

"Why?"

"You acted like a father spying on his daughter's first date."

"So that's how you see me?"

"I see you torturing yourself."

"And aren't I justified? Weren't you dreaming of falling on your knees and giving him head? Weren't you dreaming of having that hunk on top of you?"

"Your dream," I said. "Not mine."

"I know my baby. I know what she craves. I know she's insatiable. Admit it."

"I admit nothing except that I'm tired of these goddamn games, Marvin. Stop it!"

"You like the games. You love the games. You love fantasizing."

"You sound like you're writing lyrics to a song. That's not real life. Real life has to do with me and you and the kids."

"That's just the point, Jan. You don't understand me as an artist. You're killing my spirit."

"And what are you doing to *my* spirit?"

"I'm afraid of your sexual spirit. It's so powerful it will consume us both. It's clear that I can no longer satisfy you. You need a Steven. He can fuck you right. I can't. At least that's the message you give me."

"And what message do you give me?" I asked. "That my body is repulsive. That I'm past my prime."

"Well . . ." Marvin started to say.

"Well *what*?" I shot back.

"Aren't you?"

When it came to verbal jousting, I had learned to give as good as I got. But in becoming a more aggressive combatant, I had also learned that there were consequences.

As a result of our nasty spat in which I'd accused Marvin of supreme manipulation, he decided to punish me. He left me and the kids behind in Maui as he and his sister, brother, and mom traveled on for his performances in Japan.

I relished the time alone with Nona and Frankie but felt a growing resentment that the man I loved so deeply had so much power over me. The more strained our romantic relationship, the more twisted our sexual liaisons.

Given the presence of inhibition-loosening drugs, there was physical pleasure in such encounters. The aftermath, though, brought me deep humiliation. Why hadn't I found the wherewithal to resist Marvin's maneuvers?

Because I loved him and wanted to please him.

Because I was afraid he would leave me.

Because I was intimidated by his power.

But as I continued to give in, anger built inside me. I lacked the self-confidence to challenge him, yet I had enough self-knowledge to realize that I was disrespecting myself. I felt trapped, frustrated, and confused.

The confusion compounded when Marvin returned from Japan bearing gifts. He'd bought me a gorgeous kimono. He spoke to me lovingly.

"I missed you, dear," he said. "I was wrong not to take you and the kids along. I was terribly lonely. Can you forgive me?"

"I can, I do."

"And will you confess that you got together with Steven? Will you be honest and tell me that it was the hottest night of your life?"

"Don't start, Marvin, please. I didn't see him."

"I don't believe that he didn't call you."

"He called but I never called back."

"And I'm supposed to believe you?"

"Yes. I was with the kids every minute of every day. And I loved it."

Marvin felt my sincerity and stopped the questions.

"Well, let's gather up our babies and go to the beach," he said. "Let's just be a family."

Marvin's mood was back on the mellow tip. It was a perfect day for a long walk along the shore. The sky was cloudless and the ocean calm. The world was blazing blue. The kids scurried into and out of the water. The animosity between Marvin and me had disappeared. He took my hand.

"Let's just let love lead us on," he said. "The scripture says a perfect love casts out all fear. Today I'm not feeling afraid—not one bit."

I put my lips to his cheek and whispered in his ear, "I want this moment to last forever."

A few minutes later, walking calmly along the beach, we saw a man approaching us. From a distance it seemed like I knew him. Yes, I was almost certain I did. But it couldn't be. It shouldn't be. The coincidence was almost too much. He was probably just a look-alike. It was just my imagination. Or was it?

"Frankie!" Marvin exclaimed. "Frankie Beverly! Hey man, fancy meeting you here!"

The two men stopped and chatted for a minute. When Marvin learned that Frankie was going to be in Hawaii for another week, he said, "That's great, man, 'cause tomorrow night I'm going to have to jump to another island to do a show. While I'm gone, please keep an eye on Jan for me. I know she'll like that."

"No problem," said Frankie.

Betrayal

The first night that Marvin flew off and left me alone, the phone started ringing.

"What are you doing?" asked Frankie.

"I'm bored," I said.

"Well, let's just get together and hang out."

"If we get together," I said, "we could wind up doing more than talking."

"That's my hope."

"Stop it," I said.

I couldn't help but laugh. I couldn't help but feel the pressure, couldn't help but fantasize about the pleasure, couldn't help but enjoy the attention.

I closed my eyes. My imagination was on fire.

"I hear you thinking," said Frankie. "You're thinking what I'm thinking. See you tonight."

Our kids were with island friends. It didn't take long to pick out a provocative outfit—a white maxi dress. When Frankie showed up, he was wearing a black leather vest, no shirt, drawstring pants, and flip-flops.

We went to a quiet bar where we sat at a dark, secluded corner table and sipped wine.

A little later we were in his car, where we shared a joint. At his place we snorted more than a few lines. He approached me. I did not resist.

We both thought back to when Marvin had broken up our near connection the first time we'd been alone in a room together. Frankie worried that history might repeat itself.

"It won't," I said. "I drove him to the airport. I watched him get on the plane."

"There are return flights."

"He has a show."

"He's been known to cancel shows."

"Not this time."

Another joint and Frankie's fears went up in smoke. He changed the tone of the conversation and admitted, "I've been dreaming of this."

"Me too," I confessed.

The lovemaking was intense.

For the first time in months, a man was whispering how deeply and completely I satisfied him.

But satisfaction was soon overwhelmed by guilt. And despite the thrill that came with the forbidden, I carried the great weight of betrayal.

The next day, I thought about both the thrill and the betrayal.

Part of the thrill came from my recognition that I had battled back in the war waged by Marvin. He had assaulted me with insults and called me undesirable. Now I could assault Marvin with the fact that another man had found me desirable.

Yet when Marvin returned, I was unable to attack him with the truth.

"Did he fuck you?" Marvin asked.

"No," I lied.

Marvin detected the lie and pressed the case.

"Why can't you say it?" he asked. "Why can't you admit what you did? Why don't you just say how much you loved it?"

Days passed before I could say the words. By then we were back in Los Angeles. Marvin and I were alone in the home in Hidden Hills, which was on the verge of foreclosure because of his refusal to face his financial reality. He had also refused to accept my story that Frankie and I hadn't slept together.

"No, we didn't do it!" I kept crying and denying.

"But you wanted to do it," Marvin insisted.

"No. Nothing happened."

"I don't believe you."

"Ask Frankie."

Marvin did just that, and Frankie denied it as well.

But the fighting went on. The battle zone was toxic. It was not only awash with literal toxins like highly potent pot and coke, it was where Marvin felt most powerful. It was where he operated. In the battle zone, he was a master manipulator.

Once drawn into the battle zone, I was forced to rely on my greatest weapon, one I had used to snare Marvin initially: my sexuality. And the more Marvin undermined my belief in my desirability, the greater my need to reestablish that belief.

"Maybe Frankie Beverly wants you," Marvin told me, "but no one else does. Not really. Not the way you're looking these days."

The uglier his remarks, the more my determination to disprove them. That meant seeking the approval of other men.

I felt Marvin slipping away. I felt myself slipping away.

When Marvin called Frankie Beverly, he insisted that I listen in. In the brief conversation, Marvin assumed a calm tone. He never raised his voice.

"I don't blame you," said Marvin. "I know she's been after you for years. You're a man and men do what they do. I'm not interested in hurting you, Frankie, but you are no longer my friend. I never want to hear your name or see your face again."

Frankie denied anything had happened, but Marvin didn't believe him and hung up.

"Now are you satisfied?" Marvin asked me. "You've ruined a perfectly good friendship."

"Nothing happened," I said, keeping up the lie.

I argued the same argument I had been expounding for months—that it was Marvin, not me, who was obsessed with ruination.

Marvin was also obsessed with Teddy Pendergrass, who was being called the next Marvin Gaye. When Teddy left Harold Melvin and the Blue Notes in 1977, his solo career took off like a rocket. Reporters couldn't resist comparing him to Marvin. While Teddy's star was rising, Marvin's was fading. After "Got to Give It Up," Marvin fell off the charts.

In 1978, while Teddy was red-hot with super-sexy hits like "Only You" and "Close the Door," Marvin released *Here, My Dear*, the divorce narrative that flopped both commercially and critically. Reviewers called it "self-indulgent" and "irrelevant." The highly personal nature of the material was too obscure for all but the most devoted Marvin Gaye fans. Marvin also complained that Berry Gordy would never promote a record that demeaned his sister, even if she did stand to make money from it.

"*Here, My Dear* has no singles," Marvin told me. "I did that on purpose. I didn't want people to read a short story, but rather a whole novel. Most people don't have the patience. So they're switching allegiance. They're all over Teddy. They're calling him the new sex symbol and calling me last year's news."

"Your fans are loyal," I tried to reassure him.

"No more loyal than you. It won't be long before you fuck up. Teddy thinks that I'm weak, and that means he'll be coming after you."

Marvin's obsession with Teddy manifested in a song he called "Ego Tripping Out."

The result was a proto-rap record with Marvin reciting, rather than singing, a story about a man who had the baddest cool, the biggest house, the flashiest car, the most sexual prowess. The boasting continued until, halfway through the song, Marvin broke off a melody set to unexpectedly meditative lyrics. He sang about how egomania led to pain, how self-centeredness was rooted in fear, and how "the toot and the smoke"—cocaine and marijuana—wouldn't "fulfill the need." The goal was to transform the fear into energy and find a way back to God.

I realized that, although the song had been written to ridicule Teddy, it had become self-reflective. The song was really about Marvin and his struggle with his own ego.

When it was released as a single, there was little airplay, thus doing further damage to Marvin's sense of self-worth. I saw how "Ego Tripping Out" only served to deflate Marvin's already wounded ego.

But Marvin didn't stop there. He was motivated to do an entire album that would compete with Teddy and reestablish himself as the sultan of sex. Marvin tried to write a suite of love songs with the intention of outselling *Let's Get It On*. The tunes had titles like "I Offer You Nothing but Love" and "A Lover's Plea." He planned to call the album *Love Man*.

"The lyrics might be superficial," Marvin told me, "but no more superficial than Teddy's. Besides, the grooves are more seductive than his. The album's going to bring me back and knock Teddy off his throne."

Marvin's efforts were in vain. I saw how he could work only periodically. Blocked by self-doubt, he fell into a deep depression. His antidepressants were the drugs, pot and cocaine, which only compounded his emotional instability. Meanwhile, his life remained in ruins.

He was lost.

I was lost.

For a few hours he might be loving. For a few hours romance might be renewed. For a few hours he might attend to the children. For a few hours I might hold on to the hope that our family could be preserved. We'd fly back to Hawaii for a week, leaving the children with my mother.

"The peaceful spirit of the islands will renew our spirits," Marvin would say.

But peace didn't last. Even in that serene setting, Marvin sank back into despair. On a day when he had been drinking mushroom tea and eating mushrooms from the ground and topping it all off with cocaine, he went on a bad trip. He brought up my betrayal and became enraged. His fury turned to madness. This time the madness reached a new and dangerous level. His eyes turned red with hatred. I was filled with fear.

At one point he took a kitchen knife and put it to my throat. I was petrified, paralyzed. I thought it was all over.

"I've loved you too much," he said. "This love is killing me. I beg you to provoke me. Provoke me right now so I can take us both out of our misery."

I was too terrified to say a word, too frightened to move.

Fortunately, his rage subsided and he put the knife away.

But by then I knew what I had to do.

I had to protect myself and my babies.

As soon as we arrived back in Los Angeles, I took the children and fled.

The Dance

If a man threatens you, you call the police. You seek protection. You leave him. You have nothing to do with him ever again. You preserve your safety by putting great distance between him and you. Your course of action is clear. Only insanity will allow you to continue the relationship.

Reflecting back to 1979, when I was twenty-three years old, I have no doubt that I was, in fact, insane. So was Marvin. One definition of insanity—doing the same thing over and over again and expecting different results—applied to virtually all my actions.

The dance looked like this:

Marvin lost his cool. He cursed me. He threatened violence.

I left.

Marvin called to apologize. He sent flowers. He promised to change. He said that he'd been on his knees all night asking for forgiveness.

He wrote songs in which he pleaded to me—"If God in heaven can forgive me, why can't you?"

I forgave. Reconciliation was forged. Romance was renewed. Sex happened. Sex was satisfying. The dance recommenced. The cycle started anew.

This crazy cycle drained me of all self-confidence. I couldn't trust Marvin's sanity any more than I could trust my own commitment to avoid him at all costs. When he was stark raving mad, it was easy to stay away. But when he reemerged as his charming self, filled with love for me and the children, I'd watch my resistance melt like butter in the sun.

At the same time, I had life-threatening problems of my own. My own drug addiction was dragging me down. At one point, out on tour with Marvin while the kids were back in LA, I broke down completely. All that cocaine flipped me out. I locked myself in the hotel room and swallowed a fistful of antidepressants. I ODed. One of Marvin's security men had to knock down the door and rush me to the hospital. Were it not for my dear friend Barbara Stroum, who came running to my aid, I would have never made it. It was Barbara, not Marvin, who got me on my feet again.

I needed my mother, and thank God my mother was there for me. The kids and I moved into her place in Hermosa Beach at the same time Marvin lost possession of both the studio on Sunset and the sprawling estate in Hidden Hills. His world was falling apart.

I struggled to keep my world intact. It was summertime. I took the children to the beach practically every day. My mother was a conscientious and loving grandmother. I desperately needed her help. She was also my drug buddy.

Mom lived on Fourteenth Street in a funky green beach house right on the strand. There were two bedrooms and a sunroom and barely enough room for everyone. But it was home, my only safe haven.

Mom's collection of odd male friends came and went. Some were sweet; some were strong; some provided the household with dope.

Mom did her best to shelter us. She warned me to keep Marvin at bay.

"How can I?" I asked. "He's their father."

From time to time Marvin drove to Hermosa to visit the children. They adored him and he adored them. For an hour or two or three, the world was at peace. The world was wonderful. But then the attention would to turn to me.

During one trip, he said he never wanted to see me again.

During another, he said he couldn't live without me.

I believed him one day and disbelieved him the next. I wanted to reconcile; I didn't want to reconcile. I loved him; I hated him; I hated myself for loving him; I hated myself for hating him. My sense of self was completely shattered by the viciousness of his assaults—and my nasty self-assaults.

One day, in the midst of my emotional devastation, I came back from an afternoon with the kids at the beach.

"You got a call," said my mother.

"Who from?" I asked.

"Teddy Pendergrass."

"What did he want?"

"I presume," said Mom, "he wants you."

Mom was right.

Teddy wanted to see me. I asked my mother to set up the date.

I had met Teddy earlier, through my best friend Barbara Stroum, who also introduced me to Shep Gordon, Teddy's manager. Barbara and I spent an afternoon with Teddy at the Beverly Wilshire Hotel. He was a fascinating man. He was rough around the edges, but he had a charm all his own. His self-confidence was a large part of his sexiness. He also had enormous amounts of blow, another reason Barbara and I were pleased to spend time in his company.

I was excited that he wanted to see me alone. All the pain inflicted by Marvin was gone—at least for the moment. I was wanted. I was worthy. Teddy had his choice of any woman in the world, and he had chosen me. How could I not feel good about myself?

Surely Marvin would find out. And when he did, he'd have to face the truth that other men—famous and powerful men—desired me. The truth would hurt him.

But wasn't that what he wanted? Didn't he want to suffer deeper pain? Wasn't he the one who predicted that Teddy, the man seen as his successor, would replace Frankie Beverly as my next lover? Didn't he speak of the scenario as something he hoped would happen? Didn't he relish the prospect?

Well, I relished the fact that Teddy had called. Teddy was interested. Teddy was asking that I meet him back at his suite at the Beverly Wilshire Hotel.

I dressed in brown suede palazzo pants and a matching midi coat. I was feeling good. I was feeling confident. I was feeling sexy, but not sexy enough to give it up in this first meeting.

I got off the elevator on Teddy's floor. Walking down the hall, I passed by a woman who had obviously just come from Teddy's room. We purposely ignored each other.

I knocked on Teddy's door.

"Well, hello," said Teddy, dressed casually in a sport shirt and jeans. He was tall and devilishly handsome. His beard was trimmed close to his face. His eyes were smiling.

I saw that he was high on coke. I decided to take a chance and speak my mind. "Wasn't that La Toya Jackson who I passed in the hallway?"

"It was. We're old friends."

He was unapologetic about La Toya's visit. He was unapologetic about everything.

"So glad you could make it," he told me. "I've been thinking about you ever since we met."

It was a line, but I liked it. I liked the praise. I needed the praise.

Teddy and I fell into easy conversation. He was delighted to learn that I could talk intelligently about the music business. He saw that I had superb taste in artists and songs. He liked that I was funny, articulate, and candid. Within no time, I had Teddy completely charmed.

He couldn't keep his eyes off me. He listened carefully to my every word. Yet he made no move. I was both impressed and disappointed. I was certain that he'd expect sex—and was prepared to deny him that pleasure. Instead he exhibited the behavior of a perfect gentleman. After an hour, he thanked me for dropping by but unfortunately had to prepare for a business meeting. He excused himself.

I got up to leave.

"Before you go, though," he said, "why don't we share a little treat?"

He brought out a vial and laid out several lines on a small mirror.

"Ladies first," he said.

I snorted up as much of the cocaine as I could. It was mighty strong. I wondered whether he would now make his move. He did not. Instead we chatted a few more minutes before saying good-bye. He gave me a hug, not a kiss.

I drove back to Hermosa Beach in a state of happy confusion. I wondered:

Is that it for me and Teddy?

He waited a day before calling me again.

"How 'bout if I drove down there and took you to dinner?" he asked.

"Would love it," I said.

He showed up in a big black Mercedes. Came to the door. Met Mom and Nona and Frankie. Again, the perfect gentleman.

We shared a joint as we drove up to Beverly Hills, where he had reserved a table by the window at the Mandarin restaurant on Rodeo Drive. The place was super sophisticated, fabulous floral arrangements, soft lighting, exotic cuisine. We ordered cocktails.

"I'm excited to see you again," said Teddy. "You look beautiful tonight."

I was moved by the flattery, coming from the man a million love-starved women called the Teddy Bear. In the crazed soul-disco era of the late seventies, Teddy stood tall as black America's new romantic dreamboat. He was also one of the only men self-confident enough to ask me out. Others were intimidated by Marvin, but not Teddy. I was excited to be out in public with him.

"I'm glad you called," I said.

"I had no choice," said Teddy. "I couldn't get you off my mind."

"Sounds like a Teddy Pendergrass song."

"It's the truth."

I smiled before Teddy, looking surprised, said, "Hey Jan, Marvin just cruised by this restaurant."

"It couldn't have been."

"Jan, I know what Marvin Gaye looks like."

"How could he know that we'd be here?"

"He's obviously been following you."

I shook my head and sighed. *Marvin*, I said to myself, *what is wrong with you? Why do you do this to yourself?*

"Don't worry, Jan," said Teddy. "I'm not afraid of Marvin. Let him shadow us all he wants. As long as you're comfortable with me, I'm comfortable with you."

Comfort was one of the many emotions I was feeling. Teddy did make me comfortable. I was impressed that he was not bothered by the fact that Marvin was stalking us. I also couldn't deny feeling some satisfaction that Marvin now undoubtedly knew that Teddy was pursuing me.

Let Marvin see that other men saw me differently than he did. Let him see that other men, unlike him, were eager to praise me to the sky and lure me to bed. Let him see that I could lead my life without him. Let him see that I was finally free of his control.

Let him drive by the restaurant two or three more times before the meal was over. Let him do whatever the hell he wants to do. I'm going to stand my ground.

But when Marvin returned and parked his car right in front of the restaurant, I couldn't take it anymore.

"Would you mind if we left?" I asked Teddy.

"Not at all."

We went out the back door and Teddy drove me back to my mom's house in Hermosa. He saw me inside and had a nice chat with Mom. Unlike Marvin, he treated her like a queen. He gave me a sweet kiss good night, and that was it.

My next date with Teddy was more intimate. This time he had a luxurious suite at the L'Ermitage hotel. I was ready. Snorting copious amounts of cocaine, I was happy to fly high over my doubts and confusions. I was willing to let the big man have his way with me. Not just for a few hours, but all night and all morning. Time out for food, time out for blow, but then back to bed—talking, sleeping, loving, snorting, drinking, and loving some more.

Two days and two nights in Teddy's suite.

When it was over, he said, "We've got a good thing. Too good to stop."

"Hmm," was all I could say. I wanted to believe him.

"I leave tomorrow for New York. But I'll be calling you. I'm doing a gig at Chino for the lady prisoners. It's a captive audience."

"Terrible joke," I said.

"Sorry, but come to the show with me."

"I have two kids to look after."

"You'll bring the kids with you. I love kids. I want you and the kids to come to all my shows."

Teddy was true to his word. He sent me and the kids first-class tickets to come to his concerts in faraway cities. Once he had me meet him at the Brown Palace in Denver. While Teddy was at rehearsal, the phone rang. It was Frankie Beverly.

"I know you're with Teddy," he said. "I know Teddy from back in Philly. You need to get out of there. You're in the wrong place with the wrong guy."

I ignored Frankie and stayed put. It turned out to be a wonderful weekend.

Back in LA, we'd pile in to Teddy's Rolls and he'd take me and the kids to Universal Studios. He loved visiting us in Hermosa Beach. There were times when I saw Marvin's car parked down the street from my mom's house, but I paid Marvin no mind. I had moved on. If Marvin wanted to torture himself, that was his business.

When Teddy played the Greek Theatre in LA, I couldn't make the show. Later he told me that Marvin had sent him a dozen red roses—all dead. Teddy laughed it off.

"He's obsessed with you," I told Teddy.

"No, he's obsessed with *you*," Teddy told me. "He'll always be obsessed with you. He'll always want you back. You just have to find the strength to resist. You have to keep him away."

But how was it possible when he was the father of our children?

A mother in possession of her full sanity would see that keeping her children away from a father like Marvin would be an act of protection, not punishment.

I was not that mother.

I was acting out my anger at Marvin by juggling affairs with both Frankie Beverly and Teddy Pendergrass, knowing that both men had other women. And when Rick James, whose *Fire It Up* was the hottest album in the country, came to call, I found myself forging a friendship with still another superstar whom Marvin viewed as a competitor.

The attention and praise lavished upon me by these men kept me from sinking into a deep depression. They boosted my sense of self-worth. They kept me high.

And yet underneath I was miserable.

My marriage had fallen apart. My husband was falling apart. I was falling apart. My family was falling apart.

I entertained the hope that my marriage, husband, and family could all be saved. That hope was sparked when Marvin called.

He was not manic; he was mellow. Mellow Marvin was beautiful Marvin, loving Marvin, sweet Marvin, soft-spoken well-mannered Marvin, the Marvin I had met six years earlier who was all charm and graciousness, a man in tune with his heart, a man whose soul radiated warmth.

"Dear," he said, "we need to talk. I need to come down there to Hermosa. We need to discuss our relationship. We need to get it together."

"I don't know," I said.

"I do. I clearly see what I need to do. I have a lot of making up to do."

"Marvin . . ."

"Don't argue, Jan. Just listen to reason. It is reasonable to allow your husband to visit you with a plan for reconciliation. It is reasonable to let your children enjoy the company of their father. It is reasonable to assume that love—pure love, deep love, everlasting love—is strong enough to heal even the deepest wounds. It is reasonable to believe in God and the undeniable truth that God wants us all together, happy, strong, and united. How can you argue with that?"

I couldn't.

War

void war at all cost.

Do anything to protect my children and myself from the fallout of a romance turned rancid.

Stay away from any encounter with a man seething with anger.

When Marvin called me, though, I didn't hear his anger. I felt his hunger for reconciliation. To resist reconciliation was to risk a chance to finally make things right.

"I need to go back to him," I told my mother.

"Don't," said Mom. "He's playing you. Let go."

I couldn't. I had to hold on to hope. I had to see Marvin again and allow visitations with our children.

Once we agreed to visitations, Marvin showed up in Hermosa at a time when I wasn't home. He greeted Mom, who was caring for the children, with great contempt. He played with the kids for a short time and then took little Frankie with him.

"What are you doing?" asked Mom.

"I'm taking my son."

Before Mom could object, Marvin and Frankie were gone. Mom was alarmed, but there was nothing she could do. Nona was devastated. Her dad had taken her brother and left her behind. A half hour later he returned for Nona and whisked her away, too. When I returned home, my children were gone.

Now the game had suddenly changed. Now the children were in play.

Marvin was using the children to wound me, just as my affairs had wounded Marvin.

More than feeling wounded, I was feeling frightened—even terrified. I didn't fear that Marvin would harm his children, but I worried that he'd never return them to me.

Marvin took Nona and Frankie to the home he had bought his parents on Gramercy Place in an old neighborhood in Mid-City LA. The house was huge. The kids had their own bedrooms and a large yard to play in. Marvin's mom was a doting grandmother. Nona and Frankie were made to feel safe there.

After a couple of days, Marvin called me to say, "I have an out-of-town gig. Please come and get your children."

His voice was calm. When I arrived, the kids were happy to see me but disappointed that they wouldn't be going on the road with their dad, where his entourage spoiled them to no end.

"Thank you for letting me care for our babies," Marvin told me with seeming sincerity. "They missed you something terribly. They need their mom."

I was comforted by Marvin's words. I was convinced that, when he was right—and today he seemed very right—I had been right not to throw a fit when he took the kids. I was right to keep cool.

"When I get back to LA," Marvin said with his customary cool, "I'll come down to Hermosa and we'll have that talk I've been wanting to have. Is that okay with you, dear?"

"I'd like that," I said. "There's no reason not to be civilized—especially when the children are involved."

"Civilization is based on mutual respect," Marvin added. "And the great civilizations are built on love. I'm always going to follow the path of love."

A week later Marvin followed the path to Hermosa Beach. I was careful to make sure Mom left before he arrived. The animosity between my mother and husband would have only harmed the chances of a harmonious meeting.

In the first minute of the meeting, though, I realized harmony wasn't happening. Marvin was coked up. I was too.

"I can't talk to you in this house," he said. "It's filled with your mother's evil spirit. If we're going to talk, it's going to have to be outside."

I suggested that we take a walk to the beach. We had no choice but to bring Nona and Bubby with us.

Eager to get to the beach, the kids ran ahead.

"It's over, Jan," Marvin blurted out. "It's been over for months. I'm no longer fooling myself about who you are and what you want to do to me. I have no choice but to save my own soul. I'm out. I want a divorce. And I want it quickly. We can go to Vegas."

Feeling Marvin's manic mood, I didn't want to provoke him.

"Can't we talk about cooperating—"

"There is no cooperating with you."

"I don't want to argue with you, Marvin."

"Then don't."

"I'll agree to a divorce, but not before we work out the financial details—"

"What details!" Marvin screamed. "There are no details! You deserve nothing! You'll get nothing!"

I started to cry. "And how will the children live?" I asked.

"They'll live with me. The courts will see to that. You're an unfit mother. The courts will see you as the slut that you are, and that mother of yours—"

"Shut up! The kids can hear you!"

"I'm going to have my children, no matter what!" Marvin insisted.

The kids were further down the beach, oblivious to what was happening.

Marvin's fury had unleashed my own rage.

"Just leave us alone!" I screamed. "Just get the hell out of our lives—and stay out!"

Marvin snapped. He pushed me, and I fell onto the sand. Marvin was all over me, straddling my chest, talking about how we could both die right here on this beach.

Hearing the commotion, the kids ran to us. They were hysterical. Marvin grabbed Bubby's right hand, I grabbed his left, and we started pulling the poor boy in opposite directions. A neighbor called the police. A squad car was in close proximity. Within a minute or two, four cops were forcing Marvin off of me. He resisted but was quickly restrained. He cursed them wildly. One of the policemen punched Marvin in the eye.

"All I want is my son!" Marvin screamed. "This woman won't let me have my son!"

Nona heard this. Nona couldn't stop crying.

Marvin was hauled off, thrown in the squad car, taken to jail.

I remained dazed, devastated.

Within hours Marvin was bailed out. The next day I learned that he and his mother were driven to Las Vegas, where a fighter in whom Marvin had invested heavily, Andy "the Hawk" Price, was facing Sugar Ray Leonard. Before the bout, Marvin and Mother Gay attended Diana Ross's big show at Caesar's Palace, where they ran into Berry Gordy. Marvin had a huge shiner.

Word had it that if Price could beat Leonard, Marvin's financial problems would be dramatically lessened.

But his problems—emotional as well as financial—were dramatically increased when Sugar Ray knocked out Andy Price in the first three minutes of the first round.

Marvin was down and out.

A week later, Marvin was frantically calling me again.

"You sent your daddy Earl out to kill me," he said.

"Earl's not trying to kill you," I said.

"But he's looking for me, isn't he?"

"He doesn't have to look. He knows where you are. But I'd never let him hurt the father of my children."

"I don't believe that," said Marvin.

"Believe what you want. But stay away. There's a restraining order. If you come back to Hermosa, you'll be arrested."

"If Earl isn't looking for me, someone else is. You've got gangbanger friends. You've got gangbanger lovers. You've got gangbangers hunting me down."

"You're paranoid. You're paranoid out of your goddamn mind. You gotta get help!"

It was clear that Marvin was sinking into spells of insanity. And yet how could I call it insanity when Marvin sent me songs that he was recording, beautiful new songs filled with remorse and pleas for reconciliation?

"I hate that *Love Man* album," he told me. "I'm keeping some of the tracks but none of the lyrics. They meant nothing. Instead I'm writing about the state of the world, the state of my soul, and the state of our relationship. My point is to repair the relationship. Listen to the music and you will hear my heart."

I was unable to listen to Marvin's music without falling in love all over again. One song called "Praise" was just that—an open invitation to praise the God of love every day in every way. It was among Marvin's most uplifting anthems. "Heavy Love Affair" was a synopsis of everything that had been right and wrong about his relationship with me. He sang about "loving the pleasure sweetly" but also "loving the pain as deeply." He sang about how he thought of me "every day" and in "all kinds of ways"—hating me, loving me, obsessing over me.

But the obsession was more than personal or romantic. The obsession concerned the apocalypse. It was clear that his early religious upbringing, first learned at the feet of his father, had come back to haunt him. He told me that these were the end days. The world was on the brink of destruction. "In Our Lifetime?" was the key song in this suite, a question that referred to the annihilation of the planet— *Will it happen in our lifetime?* If it was going to happen—as Marvin increasingly believed—then all we could do was "live and play and laugh and be happy." All we could do was make love every day. Since the end of the world was just around the corner—"Revelation's prophecy nearly fulfilled," he sang in a song called "Love Party"—all we could do is celebrate the here and now.

As much as he tried, Marvin could not reconcile the two sides of his nature or, for that matter, mankind's nature. The spirit and the flesh were at war. God and the devil were at war. War raged within Marvin's heart and soul. In a song he would eventually call "Life Is for Learning," he saw himself in the role of the suffering artist. "The artist pays the price," he sang, "so you don't have to pay." We just have to listen to what the artist has to say.

What did Marvin have to say?

Return to love. Return to God. Bring out the best in your character. Praise the power that can heal all wounds. Believe in that power.

When I heard those songs even in half-completed form, I realized what Marvin's violent behavior had made me forget: that he was a genius. I felt his genius being expressed in not simply a single voice of indescribable sweetness, but in many voices—all of which were woven in a tapestry of enchanting harmony. Marvin's musical expression broke me down—broke down my animosity for all the ways he had hurt me, broke down my vow to protect our children from his presence, broke down my pledge to Mom and Earl that I would never again respond to his overtures for reconciliation.

In short, to hear Marvin sing was to forgive him. Any man who sang so soulfully must possess a loving soul. Any man who sang so lovingly must be incapable of living without love. Marvin required love. Every song he sang said so. Marvin required my love, Nona's love, Frankie's love.

"I'm going back to Hawaii," Marvin told me during one of our midnight phone calls.

"When?"

"Tomorrow."

"Why?"

"It's all over for me here. The house, the studio, all my money. My family is gone. My spirit is depleted. Hawaii is the only place where I've ever been able to find peace. Hawaii will be salvation. When I get settled, I'll send for you and the children. By then I know you will have forgiven me for all the suffering I caused. By then all will be well. God will be served. We will be together. I will see you in Hawaii, Jan. Until then, just remember—I love you, and I always will."

I spoke the words that I had sworn never to say again:

"I love you, too, Marvin. Always."

Escalation

I n the album eventually titled *In Our Lifetime?* Marvin wrote a song he called "Love Me Now or Love Me Later." I heard it as Marvin's version of the creation myth. For the album cover, Marvin commissioned an artist to draw a twin version of himself—Good Marvin with angelic wings and a halo sits across from Evil Marvin, with horns on his head and a black cape around his body. They are engaged in a life-and-death chess game in the clouds. Beneath them the planet is being destroyed in a nuclear holocaust.

At the end of the seventies, as I watched him escape once again to Hawaii, this was Marvin's vision of himself and the world in which he felt trapped. He was filled with love; he was filled with hate. He was filled with hope; he was filled with despair. He was filled with creative energy; he was filled with destructive energy. There was nothing he wanted more than reconciliation with me; there was nothing he wanted more than ongoing warfare with me. I wanted him to forgive me, but I kept up the ridiculous and destructive behavior. I kept making the same mistakes.

When Marvin called me to come to Hawaii with the kids, it was the loving Marvin that I heard, the Marvin who expressed his great need for us. But when I arrived, it was the angry Marvin who greeted me. He wanted details of my current affairs. There were no details to report. My relationships with Frankie Beverly and Teddy Pendergrass were mere diversions. They involved lust, not love, and had run their course.

"What about Rick James?"

"He's my friend, not my lover," I said truthfully.

"And you expect me to believe you?"

"The only thing I expect of you, Marvin, is to make good on your promise to try and bring us all back together."

My words had an impact on him. He wanted peace. He and I walked on the beach, swam with the kids, watched the glorious sunsets. There were a few days of calm, a few nights when intimacy was restored. My sweet Marvin was back.

We rented a condo in Kihei and went for long drives around the island. We hung out at Longhi's in Lahaina with John McVie of Fleetwood Mac and visited friends in the hills. We moved from Kihei to Kaanapali and went house hunting with George Benson, who already owned three properties on the island. He urged Marvin to move to Maui.

"I'd love to," Marvin said. "I feel like it's definitely in my future."

Optimism returned. Our hearts filled with hope. But then, like the purple sun sinking into the ocean, hope vanished.

We couldn't escape the darkness.

Was it the drugs?

Probably, because he and I kept getting high.

Was it Marvin's ongoing battle with chronic depression? Was it my similar battle with acute depression?

Certainly. There were prolonged periods of darkness that separated us from everyone and everything.

Whatever it was, Marvin moved from mellow to manic, then

from manic to violent. His arguments with me got physical again. I feared for my life. I prepared to flee with my children.

"You're not taking them anywhere," he insisted. "They're staying here with me."

I was terrified, confused. I didn't know what to do. I couldn't leave without my children, but Marvin was adamant. Then he offered a compromise.

"Take Nona back with you," said Marvin. "But Frankie stays with me."

At first I rejected the offer. I also saw the pain that the compromise was inflicting on Nona: Marvin wanted his son but was willing to lose his daughter. I wanted both my children. But Marvin wouldn't let me have them.

Lacking the resources to hire a lawyer, I reluctantly accepted the proposal. Openly weeping, I embraced my son. I could barely speak the words:

"Be a good boy, Bubby. Listen to your father."

"Say good-bye to your mother," said Marvin. "You won't be seeing her for a long time."

"Not too long," I told Marvin.

"We can't foresee the future," said Marvin.

Back in LA, living with my mom and Nona, I grew more fearful that my son was not safe. Word came down that Marvin was growing more despondent. His money had run out completely. He was down to begging old friends like Smokey Robinson for loans.

A week later, another report came back from Maui: unable to pay the rent, Marvin was evicted from his condo. He and Frankie were living in an abandoned Helms Bakery truck.

"I've got to go back over there," I told my dad Earl. "I've got to go get Bubby."

"I know Marvin," said Earl. "He won't give up his son voluntarily. Your only chance is to go over there with a court order—and that's going to take time."

I started those proceedings, but they were slow going. For every step forward, there were two steps back. Because I was high a good deal of the time, I just couldn't pull it together.

Another report from Maui: Jeffrey Kruger, a big-time promoter out of London, had traveled to Hawaii to convince Marvin to tour Europe. It was Kruger who called me with the news.

"Your son is safe," said the Englishman, "and he is eating well. He looks fine. His father, however, looks terrible. Marvin is close to a complete breakdown. I suggested that we immediately fly you over here to care for Bubby. But Marvin has flat-out refused. So I've convinced him to allow me to send for his mother."

I was both relieved and crushed—relieved that Frankie was all right, crushed that I could not come to claim him. I continued to work through my lawyer as Kruger prepared Marvin for his European tour.

When Mother Gay arrived from the mainland, she, Marvin, and Frankie moved into a condo in the town of Lahaina. Kruger also brought over Marvin's band, led by Gordon Banks, a fine guitarist who had married Marvin's sister Zeola.

Frantic phone calls from me, concerned about my son's welfare, went unanswered. Marvin had instructed his mom not to speak to me. Only Kruger kept me in the loop.

The winter of 1980 had come and gone. Kruger returned to London. Realizing that Marvin required more time to build up his strength, he postponed the tour. In the spring Marvin went into a recording studio in Honolulu to work on what was once *Love Man* and was now *In Our Lifetime?* His philosophical-theological writings continued.

Money for production came from Motown, which was clamoring for the release of the record. It had been three years since the commercially unsuccessful *Here, My Dear.* Berry Gordy had done nothing but pour money into Marvin. Marvin had squandered and mismanaged that money. He was on the verge of being indicted by the IRS.

I was on the verge of losing it. I had to see my son. I had to get him back. I had to find a way.

After months, good news. My lawyers persuaded the Superior Court of California to issue a writ of habeas corpus. In June, when Marvin was due to fly into Los Angeles to change planes for London, he would be served and forced to give up Bubby. I'd have my son back.

But someone tipped off Marvin's mother about my plan—and Mother Gay tipped off Marvin. To avoid the writ, he avoided LA and instead flew into San Francisco. I was enraged, but there was nothing to do. Even though Marvin had lost his passport, Kruger managed to convince the authorities to allow him and Bubby to leave the country and make the transatlantic journey.

In June of 1980, Marvin and Bubby arrived in London along with an entourage that included Mother Gay.

Having failed to reclaim my son, I fell into despair, the deepest and scariest of my life.

The Pipe

Ed Townsend introduced me to the pipe.

Oh, the pipe . . . freebase cocaine . . .

The pipe was addictive beyond imagination.

The pipe warped one's imagination.

The pipe destroyed one's life.

The pipe led to utter madness.

Crack cocaine is like no other drug. It has a life of its own and a dark, dark spirit. It obliterates your senses. You become married to it and it leaves you with no moral compass. It's true, once you try it, you forever chase that high.

I had an apartment of my own in Reseda, a suburb in the San Fernando Valley outside LA. This was not only the first place I had lived without Marvin since meeting him seven years earlier, this was the first place I had lived on my own—*ever.* It was just me and Nona.

Nona was at daycare. Ed had come to visit. As a housewarming gift, he brought the pipe. This was not an unusual act. In the drug culture, sharing the newest high was customary.

Cooking up this high required a kit with baking soda, a torch, a giant plate, a bottle of rum, and the cocaine itself.

"This is taking forever," I said impatiently. "I don't need to be bothered."

"Oh, yes you do," said Ed as he prepared the pipe. "This high ain't like no high you've even known. You're gonna love it."

Ed was wrong. I didn't love it. I worshipped it.

The pipe took over my life, seducing me with a euphoria I had never known before. Every three or four days, Ed returned to my apartment with a fresh supply. He overcharged me like crazy. I didn't care. Just keep the shit coming.

In a monumentally ironic and tragic way, the pipe reconnected me to Marvin, who, while in England, was also freebasing cocaine. During his first high in London, he called me.

"I'm seeing something I've never seen before," he said. "I see myself floating above myself. I look down and see all my selfishness. I see how spoiled I am. How destructive. How I hurt everyone around me. I see how much I need you, Jan."

"I need you too," I said. "But I have to be sure that Bubby is okay. Are you taking care of him?"

"My mother is right here," Marvin assured me. "She guards him with her life. He's never been safer, never happier—except for how much he misses you. Why don't you fly over with Pie?"

Floating on the same high as Marvin, I was ecstatic.

This time he means it; this time he is really reconnected to his heart; this time his soul and mine are in perfect alignment; this time nothing can keep us apart. This love is real! This love is right! This love is forever!

A day later, though, when I called him to make plans, he was too fucked up to talk. Two days later, when he called, I was too fucked up to talk. Another week passed while our love for the pipe deepened.

When we finally did talk, he was enraged because I was asking for money. I had no choice. I was dead broke.

"Get it from Teddy P," he said. "Get it from Frankie B. Get it from all those friends of mine who you've been fucking. But don't expect a dime from me."

I had no choice but to look cold reality in the face. I needed to work.

I got a job answering phones. I got a job as a housekeeper and nanny for a professional single mom. At one point I couldn't pay my rent and had to turn to my dad Earl. He had a big house in Mid-City LA but instead sent me and Nona to live with his hooker friend I'll call Miss Thing. Nona and I slept on pallets on the floor of Miss Thing's living room. After a few weeks, Miss Thing threw us out and kept my clothes.

Ultimately, all roads led back to Mom's house in Hermosa Beach. I would have liked to declare independence from my mom, but I couldn't. Mom remained the most dependable character in my undependable life.

Mom got me drugs. Mom helped care for Nona when I was too high to manage. When Marvin called and learned that I was back with Mom, he was infuriated. He loathed Mom. During these moments, I loathed Marvin. I got satisfaction from letting him know that Nona and I were living with a lady that he despised.

The animosity deepened.

The addiction deepened.

Rick James, himself an addict, appeared as something of a savior. He called to invite me back to Maui, where he was staying at a posh resort. I flew over, hoping that this, unlike the liaisons with Teddy and Frankie, would prove lasting.

The setting was opulent. The seaside suite was palatial. Rick was expansive. He talked a mile a minute. He had nothing but praise and admiration for me. I saw that, like Marvin, Rick was brilliant. While

Marvin's default mode was mellow, Rick's was manic. But that was okay. It was a sweet manic, a poetic manic. He was interested in politics, religion, art, history. He was a reader, a thinker. He was also a sensualist, but when night fell and we returned to the bedroom, the cocaine he had consumed rendered him impotent. He was embarrassed, but I reassured him. He needed a friend; I did too. At this moment in our journeys, friendship was more important than sex. God knows that each of us had had enough sex to last a lifetime. We fell asleep in each other's arms. We remained close friends and nothing more.

Back in Los Angeles, Rick gave me a job in his office. The idea was that I could write press releases and publicity for his new records. But in the end, he basically used me as an errand girl to bring him drugs. I didn't mind because he didn't mind if I skimmed off the top.

So it went: a scattered life, living here and there, scuffling for enough money to eat and live, to buy drugs, to stay high on the pipe.

My growing friendship with Rick was a blessing. I saw the best in him, just as he saw the best in me. We often talked of quitting drugs but—at least for now—neither of us had the will.

Meanwhile, there were reports from London.

Marvin's mom had returned to Los Angeles but had little to say to me—only that Bubby was fine. I missed my son terribly.

Kruger had Marvin on tour, but the tour proved disastrous. Like Marvin's former manager Stephen Hill, Kruger thought he could control Marvin. But the truth was that Marvin was uncontrollable. No one could manage him. He couldn't manage himself. Marvin manipulated Kruger unmercifully. He got him to give him money, get him gigs, and then wound up humiliating him. When Kruger held a press conference, Marvin avoided the reporters by sneaking out through a bathroom window. When Kruger booked a command performance for Princess Margaret, Marvin refused to appear. In a panic, Kruger called me in LA to ask me to persuade my husband to take the stage. For the time being, I was back in Marvin's good

graces. We'd been having long and loving transatlantic phone con-
versations. I was the only one he'd talk to. Kruger told me that if I
could persuade Marvin to perform, he'd send me a first-class ticket to
England so I could finally see my son.

"What is going on?" I asked Marvin when I got him on the
phone. "Kruger says the princess is a huge fan of yours. Why won't
you sing for her?"

"Because Kruger had me take a six A.M. flight from Switzerland
to London this morning," he said, "claiming that was the only non-
stop. Later I learned there was a noon flight that he didn't tell me
about. He was afraid I'd sleep through it. So he kept me up all night
and drove me to the airport at five A.M. You know how I hate getting
up in the middle of the night. You know how I hate flying. I will not
be played like that. I will not be disrespected. Let *him* sing for the
princess."

"He's willing to pay you an extra twenty thousand dollars," I
said. "He's saying his reputation is on the line."

"Fuck his reputation. Fuck him."

"What about the princess?"

"Fuck her."

"I'm sure she'd like to fuck you," I said, finally eliciting a laugh
out of Marvin.

"There are many women over here," he said, "but they don't
understand me like you do, Jan. They can't make me laugh. They
can't love me. If you were here, dear, you could make me sing. I'd
sing for you, not some silly princess."

"Look, dear," I said, "just be a good boy. Go out there and sing
for the royals. Make your manager happy. He's sending me a ticket
so we can be together. I'll see you soon."

"Yes! And put all this foolishness behind us! That's beautiful,
dear. I'm getting dressed as we speak. I will sing tonight. Thanks for
talking me through this."

But by the time Marvin arrived at the concert hall, he was two hours late and the princess, tired of waiting, had already left. Kruger had no reason to send me a ticket to London. In fact, this marked the end of Marvin's relationship with his English manager.

Motown released *In Our Lifetime?* in January 1981, before Marvin had tweaked his final vocals and approved the final mix; that marked the end of his two-decade relationship with the label. He was enraged and vowed never to record for Berry Gordy again—and never did.

He turned his fury inward and fell deeper into his addiction. And in his fury, he renewed his anger at me. His head was filled with fantasies of me with other men. Our transatlantic calls became bitter and ugly. I responded with a fury of my own. In our verbal battles, I became as nasty as Marvin. I was tired of his broken promises, tired of his bullshit, tired of a ruinous relationship that brought only pain. I was also tired of myself. I was filled with self-hatred.

Only the pipe brought relief.

There were men who would bring me drugs. There were men who would praise my beauty and provide me with comfort. They may not have been Marvin Gaye, but they would do. They would have to. And if my drug buddies didn't come through, I turned to Bacardi 151 rum to drown my disgust.

Marvin was in London with no plans to return. He had a young Dutch girlfriend named Eugenie who, if the rumors were true, was a groupie he'd met after a show. She was willing to do whatever freakish things he wanted to do. She was entirely submissive.

When he tired of Eugenie, there was a sixty-three-year-old English lady, an aristocrat with a great country estate where he spent weekends.

"I have found my true home here," he told me during one of the calls when we were being civil with each other. "I'm certain that in a former life I was English. I adore their speech, I adore their style, I adore the way they appear cold and controlled but underneath they're the freakiest. I could live and die in London."

"But what about Bubby? Who's taking care of him?"

"He is his father's son. He's pampered by Patsy, his nanny. Round the clock women are watching him with loving care. You have nothing to worry about."

"Put him on the phone. Let me talk to him."

"Let me get him."

"Mum," said Frankie with a decidedly English accent, "is that you?"

"I miss you, Bubby. I love you so much. I can't wait till you come home."

"I miss you, too, Mum."

"Are you okay, son?"

"Yes, Mum, I'm okay. I'm reading my Mr. Men books. Mr. Topsy-Turvy is my favorite."

"You see," said Marvin, back on the phone. "Everyone is doing fine."

But no one was doing fine.

Marvin was sick and getting sicker.

I was sick and getting sicker.

Marvin had no money, no record deal, no willpower.

My willpower was less than zero.

In the middle of the night, the phone rang.

Marvin was calling from somewhere in London.

"I can't stop thinking about you," he said. "Have you been thinking about me?"

I couldn't lie.

"Yes," I admitted. "All the time."

"Then it is love," he said. "It's always been love, hasn't it?"

"Yes," I repeated.

"And love will see us through all this garbage," he insisted, "won't it?"

"Yes."

"Are we going to try again?"

"Yes, yes, yes."

Reunited

The summer of 1981.

I was excited, ecstatic even, because Nona and I were packing our bags. We were flying to France to meet Marvin and Bubby, whom we hadn't seen for over a year.

That year had been hell. Marvin had fallen to new lows, and so had I. Several times he nearly overdosed on drugs. Friends visiting him in London were shocked at his appearance. He was thin. He went off on rants. When he called home he was sometimes loving, sometimes crazed, sometimes weeping, sometimes laughing, sometimes remorseful, sometimes resentful, sometimes incoherent, sometimes clear as a bell.

I mirrored him at every turn. I was just as uneven, just as stoned, just as angry and afraid, just as desperate to stay away, just as desperate to reunite. I had sex only to remind myself that I was still desirable.

Marvin had my son. Marvin had my heart. I was still in love with him. He was still in love with me. We spent a fortune on phone calls. Weeks would go by when he would torture me by not allowing

Bubby to speak to me. Other times he would speak of how he could no longer live without me.

Moving about Great Britain, he was very covert. He feared, I believe, that I would hire someone to bring my child back to me. But I would never traumatize my son like that. Marvin kept reassuring me that the nanny was taking good care of Bubs.

The reassurance fell on deaf ears. For most of the time, I was beside myself. I should have sought the help of doctors. I should have sought the help of lawyers—besides the ones who claimed the situation was hopeless. I should have, should have, should have . . . The should-haves were maddening.

My head was high, my heart was heavy, my thinking cloudy. For all the insanity that preceded my trip to France, for all the evidence that argued that reconciliation with Marvin Gaye was not even a remote possibility, I sought reconciliation. Marvin sought reconciliation. We were honestly convinced that this time, for the sake of our souls and for the souls of our children, we would make it work. We chased that idea round the world.

It didn't matter that he had bottomed out in England. It didn't matter that he had spent the last month flirting with self-destruction. What mattered was that, according to everyone close to Marvin—and according to Marvin himself—he was on an upswing. A small-time promoter from Belgium had visited him in London and convinced him to leave England. That man, Freddy Cousaert, had brought Marvin to Ostend, a subdued Belgian city of eighty thousand, and set him up in an apartment overlooking the North Sea. Like Stephen Hill and Jeffrey Kruger before him, Cousaert had convinced himself that he could manage Marvin. Marvin had convinced Cousaert to give him what he needed most—money and an off-the-beaten-track place to regain his health. Cousaert was certain he had Marvin in his back pocket. He held up Marvin like a trophy.

In the face of utter confusion, who didn't want to cling to certainty?

I was certain that my love for Marvin—and his love for me—was the only thing that would save us from annihilation. I was certain that once the family was reunited, minds and hearts would be healed.

I had heard a change in Marvin's voice. Ever since he'd moved to Ostend, he had grown close to Cousaert, his wife, and their two daughters. He had been reminded of the joy of a warm and loving family.

"Being here in this peaceful community with these peaceful people," he told me, "has reminded me how much I need peace. I need the peace of seeing my children play together, the peace that comes with being with the one woman I cherish above all others. That's you, dear. That's always been you."

"I want to believe you," I said.

"I am believing that God has intervened to send me to a place of healing, Jan. It's a blessing to be away from London and all its pollution. You'll love it here. You'll love the quiet. You'll love the people. You'll love how I've cut out the pipe. You'll see how I've cut down on the other stuff. I'm breathing in fresh air. I'm running on the beach. I'm eating good food. I'm meditating in the morning and praying all the day through. I go to sleep early. I'm in a sound and sane place. Maybe that's because I've left Motown and all the madness."

After Motown released *In Our Lifetime?* prematurely—and without his permission—Marvin kept his vow and quit the label. Eventually he was signed to CBS Records through the efforts of Larkin Arnold. He was now cutting a new record in Belgium.

"It's taking me a while to figure out what I want to say," he confessed, "but I'm determined to do something meaningful. I also want to score big. I want to prove to the world—and myself—that I'm still capable of making hit records."

I understood. It had been nearly five years since his last hit, "Got to Give It Up." His records since then—*Here, My Dear* and *In Our Lifetime?*—had been brilliant but strange. While the critics damned them, the public ignored them. For all of Marvin's philosophical leanings, he remained a competitive artist. He didn't like being off the charts for long.

"It will come back together," Marvin told me. "My music, my peace of mind, my family. You'll see all this, dear. You'll feel all this when you come to Europe. You'll come as soon as this summer tour is over."

Marvin's band, led by his brother-in-law Gordon Banks, had been living in Belgium, working on the new record, and rehearsing for a series of gigs around Europe. I later learned that the tour was more dysfunctional than Marvin had led me to believe. Although he had dramatically decreased his drug intake, there were still times when he reverted to his old ways.

Cousaert forcefully spun the story to the press that, under his management, Marvin had foresworn all stimulants and become engaged in a rigorous program of rehabilitation. In interviews Marvin took this same tack. He convinced himself, just as he convinced me, that he had turned a new page.

I needed to turn a new page. I needed to get off drugs. I needed to see my son. I needed to believe that this long separation would soon end. Even though I had heard these words before, and even though those words had proven misleading, I needed to believe Marvin when he said, "Replace your fears with faith. Have faith that we have weathered the worst of the storm. Be assured that nothing is more important to me than making sure that my son sees his mother and I see my daughter and my wife."

Nona and I boarded the long flight to Paris. We were too excited to sleep. We couldn't stop thinking of finally reuniting with Marvin and Frankie.

It was Marvin's idea to meet us at Charles de Gaulle Airport and then drive back to Ostend. After clearing customs, we started looking for Marvin and Frankie. They were nowhere to be seen. I started to panic.

Has Marvin changed his mind?

Is this a trick?

Is this whole venture another terrible mistake?

Have I fooled myself into believing that things could be different?

For ten minutes, Nona and I wandered around the airport.

"Why isn't Daddy here?" asked Nona, crying.

"He will be, honey," I said. "He's just a little late."

"He's a *lot* late," Nona insisted.

The search continued. I put on a good face, but my panic deepened.

Is this another one of Marvin's devious manipulations? Is this another one of his cruel tricks?

"It's Daddy!" screamed Nona loud enough for people to stare.

Yes, there he was: he was standing at the top of an escalator. Frankie was next to him. Marvin was wearing a white suit and colorful knitted skullcap. His eyes were covered with dark aviator sunglasses. He looked beautiful. With his hands in his pockets, he looked detached. Frankie was jumping up and down. Nona raced up the escalator into her father's arms. I followed and gathered up my son who, in his adorable English accent, was screaming, "Mum! Mum!" I was crying, Nona was crying. Marvin's distant demeanor broke down. Now he was crying. Now the four of us were joined together in a huge hug. No one would let go.

The warmth was offset by the presence of Freddy Cousaert, who was waiting outside the terminal behind the wheel of a blue Mercedes-Benz. I immediately felt his disapproval. It was only at Marvin's insistence that Nona and I had come to Europe. Cousaert feared that we would distract Marvin from work on his new record. Cousaert feared that we would lure Marvin back to America. The new manager's agenda was to keep Marvin in Ostend and have him operate out of Europe.

Cousaert drove us into Paris and dropped us at the George V hotel. We were thrilled to be together at long last. In our suite, we ordered room service. The kids jumped on the bed and we all played hide-and-seek. That night Marvin and I made beautiful love.

The next day, on the drive from Paris to Ostend, Cousaert said, "Marvin has found peace here in Europe. To maintain his sanity, he must stay in Ostend."

When it came to Marvin, I felt that Cousaert was selfish, much like Stephen Hill had been. He wanted Marvin all for himself.

"We're like brothers," said Cousaert. "We have adopted him into our family. At this point in his life, he is closer to me than anyone. He knows that my only concern is his welfare."

I doubted that.

"Freddy likes to trip about masterminding my career," Marvin whispered to me. "I let him. Meanwhile, he has provided me with food and shelter in this small city far from London or Los Angeles. It's cool. You'll like it."

I did like Ostend. The place possessed a certain elegance. Marvin's apartment on the strand afforded an expansive view of the North Sea. It was calming to watch the ships sail by. The children were thrilled to be together, and Bubby was thrilled to be with me, Nona thrilled to be with her daddy.

The four of us spent that evening together. The feeling was warm and loving. It was a feeling that each of us had been seeking ever since our family was torn apart.

"This is the dream I told you about," Marvin said to me. "This is the dream that I swore would come true."

That night Marvin and I made love again. The passion was renewed. So was the sweetness. Body and soul, we were one. The lovemaking was powerful enough to erase the pain from the past.

"I forgive you," said Marvin, holding me in his arms. "Can you ever forgive me?"

"I can," I said, kissing Marvin's eyes. "But can you *really* forgive me?"

"Yes," he said.

I heard his words. But in my heart, I did not feel that I deserved his forgiveness.

The fantasy of a happy family was further fulfilled the next morning over breakfast. That afternoon we strolled on the promenade. We went to the beach, to the park, to the Chinese restaurant. Nona and Frankie were holding hands, Marvin and I were arm in arm. The city moved along at a satisfyingly slow pace. The air was fresh and clean. The citizenry was fashionably attired: attractive couples with their pedigree dogs, bikers in professional gear, joggers in flashy outfits.

To me, the world felt new. Marvin spoke about biofeedback and the amazing ways that, drug-free, he'd been able to use his mind to heal his body.

I was delighted to hear Marvin talk this way. He'd been reading books on metaphysics. He'd also gone back to Scripture. We had endless discussions about Psalm 91 and how God is our ultimate protection:

> "Because he loves me," says the Lord, "I will rescue him;
> I will protect him, for he acknowledges my name.
> He will call on me, and I will answer him;
> I will be with him in trouble,
> I will deliver him and honor him.
> With long life I will satisfy him
> and show him my salvation."

Something was happening in Ostend, and in the first week that something felt powerful and positive.

Then came our second week together. The kids had gone to sleep. Marvin and I, still in chilled-out mode, were looking through a large book of the art of James Ensor, a radical expressionistic painter from Ostend who built a reputation in the first half of the twentieth century. Marvin had visited a local museum that featured his work when he was struck by a self-portrait, reproduced in this book, of Ensor wearing a floral and feathered woman's hat.

"Who does this make you think of?" Marvin asked.

"Your father," I said, trying not to laugh.

Marvin scowled. "I knew you'd say that."

"Then why'd you ask me?"

"To test you. To see if you'd jab me."

"Marvin, let's not start up."

"I asked you a question and you answered. I have your answer."

"I don't want to fight, Marvin."

"Then why did you mention my father?" he asked.

"Because that's who came to mind. It was an honest reaction."

"And you honestly wanted to manipulate my mood."

"I wouldn't use the word *manipulate*," I said.

"And why not?"

"Stop! I'm not having this fight over a hat in a painting."

"You wouldn't know anything about hypocrisy, would you, Jan? In the history of our relationship, you've never been hypocritical, have you?"

"Yes, I have. But I don't want to fight. I don't want to be attacked."

"Now I'm the one who's attacking! That's a joke. This whole thing started with your attack on me and my father."

I didn't bother to reply. There was no winning. I stayed silent, hoping Marvin's combative mood would pass.

"Kiss me," I finally said.

He did just that, but as he did there was a knock on the door. He went to answer.

"Cool Black," he said to the man standing there. "Brother, you are right on time. Jan, come meet my man Cool Black."

For all of Cousaert's talk about Marvin being drug-free in Ostend, Cool Black was Marvin's drug dealer from London. I watched Cool Black sell Marvin a supply of temple ball—opium and hashish. The men mixed it with cocaine, put it in a pipe, and lit up. Marvin took the first hit.

"Jan," he said as he offered the pipe, "you wanted to change the subject. This is the very instrument to affect that change. This will change us in a hurry. Have a puff."

I said yes. I accepted the pipe and joined in on the high. The pattern was set: from time to time in the weeks that followed, Marvin and I indulged. It happened at night when the kids were off to sleep. It happened because we both wanted it to happen. It happened because bonding through stimulants had always been essential to our relationship. It happened because the highs allowed us to cover up our conflicts and avoid the bitter fights. It happened until the highs led to even more bitter fights.

The bitterest fight of all occurred when, a month or so after arriving in Belgium, Marvin and I took the kids to Paris for a weekend. It was October and the weather had turned crisp. We were walking over a bridge that spans the Seine River on our way to the D'Orsay Museum. Marvin was explaining how this fabulous nineteenth-century train station had been converted into an elegant repository for some of the world's great art. He led us to another strange painting by James Ensor called *In the Conservatory*. In the picture Ensor showed how musicians and critics were ridiculing Richard Wagner, the German composer, whose work they considered too far-out.

"The cat was ahead of his time," said Marvin. "Ensor knew Wagner was a genius, but the people around him in this painting think he's full of shit. They're too straight to understand Wagner's genius. What you're looking at is a man misunderstood in his own time, a man misjudged by his colleagues and scorned by his critics. So what does Ensor have Wagner do in this painting? He has Wagner put his fingers in his ears. Wagner is blocking out everything the detractors have to say. He's ignoring the wrongheaded critics and jealous musicians. Wagner knows he's a genius, so the hell with the rest of the world. If Ensor were still around, he'd put me in that painting. He'd draw me putting my fingers in my ears rather than listen to the people who called *Here, My Dear* self-indulgent and *In Our Lifetime?* incomprehensible."

"People are going to love your new album, Daddy, aren't they?" asked Nona.

"Of course they are, Pie. It's going to be the biggest record ever because I'm bringing back the love. You guys brought the love to me from Los Angeles and I'm putting it right into the record. It's gonna be nothing but love, love, love."

"What are you going to call it, Daddy?"

"Maybe *Nothing but Love, Love, Love*. Maybe *Love from Nona and Frankie and Jan*. Maybe just *The Family of Love*."

While the record was being slowly put together, a theme hadn't yet emerged. Marvin continued to search for a title, an overall theme to tie the songs together.

"Does the record have a story, Daddy?" asked Nona.

"Of course, Pie. All records have stories."

"So what is your story about?"

"It's all about Daddy getting better."

In spite of the introduction of opium into the mix, Marvin's days were calmer and his nights less frantic. He was devoting time to our children and had even enrolled them in a local school where they wore uniforms and began learning French. He and I were fighting, but in between the verbal battles were frequent long-lasting lovemaking sessions. During those moments, past regrets receded, future fears faded, and we were able to embrace the present.

"Nothing matters but this holy now," Marvin whispered into my ear. "In this precious now, we are in perfect harmony. If we stay in the now, we need never be afraid again. In the now, our love is eternal."

It was in the now, during a stroll down the Champs-Élysées, when all was peaceful for our handsome family of four, delighted by the sights and sounds of the fall afternoon in the most beautiful city in the world. We walked by the old bookstalls by the Seine. We bought croissants. The kids ate ice cream. Marvin and I sipped strong French-press coffee from demitasse cups. We stopped in an old-school record store that carried an impressive inventory of vintage

American jazz. Marvin spotted a long-play vinyl album by Slim Gaillard called *Opera in Vout*, featuring cover art by David Stone Martin, the great American illustrator. He showed it to me with pride.

"Look, kids," he told Nona and Bubby, "this is your famous grandfather, Slim."

Marvin got the shop owner to put on Slim's records. The scat singing got the kids to dancing and laughing.

Back out on the streets, the sun was sinking behind the Cathedral of Notre Dame, which sat alongside the Seine. Marvin stopped to praise the beauty of the amazing architecture.

As day turned to night, Marvin was filled with praise. He was in his God space, where there was room for everyone. He spoke of his gratitude for everyone in his life. "Everyone has a purpose," he said. "Everyone carries a gift. Everyone can have a positive influence, as long as we are thinking positively."

His positive thinking was infectious. The kids had never been happier. I was able to relax again, relieved that Marvin was in good spirits. The mind games had been put to rest—at least for the moment.

We reentered the elegant George V hotel and were waiting for the elevator to our suite when suddenly a woman came up behind Marvin.

She was young—a few years younger than me—and, from my perspective, not attractive.

"You told me you'd call me yesterday," she told Marvin, obviously upset.

"No," he retorted. "I said I'd call you tomorrow."

"Who is this?" I asked Marvin, who didn't answer. Turning to her and looking her dead in the eye, I asked, "Who are you?"

She didn't reply.

"Is this your Dutch girlfriend?" I asked, fuming.

"This is Eugenie," Marvin finally said. "Jan, this isn't the time . . ."

"You kids take the elevator upstairs," I said.

The kids got on the elevator and Marvin followed.

I turned to the woman.

"Step back, bitch," I said between my teeth, "or I will fuck you up."

Eugenie stepped back.

"Why are you here? Don't you see this is a family?"

"Marvin asked me to come here," said Eugenie. "He also told me to come to Ostend next week."

"I don't care what Marvin said. Just stay away. Just stay the fuck away from us."

When I got back to the suite, I told Marvin that he must be desperate, that his taste was slipping.

He said none of this would have happened had we stayed together.

"I can't go into all that," I said. "Not now. I don't want to fight in front of the kids. Just make sure I never see her pasty face again."

The Commotion

The commotion had to do with Eugenie. She was out of sight, but always around.

The commotion had to do with Marvin's procrastination over completing his new album.

The commotion had to do with Marvin's fear that his new album would, like the two albums before it, bomb.

The commotion had to do with Marvin's anxiety that, having been out of the country for so long, his American fans had forgotten him.

The commotion had to do with Marvin's realization that he was not willing to give up either the dream of his reunited family or his relationship with Eugenie.

The commotion was about Marvin's insistence that the kids continue at their school in Belgium while I insisted that they go back home.

The commotion had to do with my recognition that it was over.

I could no longer rationalize or overlook the truth. The truth was brutal. The truth was staring me in the face.

A compromise was struck. We would spend Christmas in Ostend and then talk about what would happen next.

It was a happy holiday for Frankie and Nona. Frankie's English accent was fading. Nona never left her father's side. That Christmas we shopped for toys, cooked a great meal, and watched the snow fall. The beach turned white. We all ran out and built a snowman. The kids named him Luke. A lifetime later, Nona would record a tribute to her dad, a memory of that Christmas, in a song called "Snowman." She co-wrote it with Prince, who produced the track.

For my part, I made it through the holidays, but barely. In my heart and head, the commotion built. The renewed hostility became unbearable. Marvin would not let me forget my past betrayals. Nor would he let go of Eugenie. I would not let go of my fury. Neither one of us would let go of the drugs. The love had not ended—it never would—but toxins, both chemical and mental, overwhelmed it.

In 1981, Marvin and I attempted another of our many reconciliations. We were traveling back and forth between Ostend and London. Marvin had friends there and I loved London. Nona and Frankie didn't care where we went as long as we were together. The ferry ride from Ostend to Great Britain was always fun, docking in Dover, with the exception of this one trip. Around that time, we were smoking something called "temple balls." About the size of a mandarin orange and wrapped in tissue, the temple ball was a mixture of hashish, opium marbling, and cocaine. If I did not know better I could have mistaken it for an orb of granite. We would chip off a bit, add it to tobacco, roll it up and smoke it. At first it was a great high. We had no worries other than making sure our children were okay.

One particular evening, we had left Ostend and were out on the deck of the ferry. It was cold, damp, and dark. It never occurred to me that this time of year that I would need warmer clothing than the red pashmina I had brought along. I was eager to have a smoke. About halfway through the ferry ride and after several deep drags of the smoke, I felt a stabbing sensation in my back. I tried to shake it off.

On the dimly lit deck, Marvin took one look at me and knew something wasn't right. "Are you okay?" he asked.

"I'm in pain," I said barely audible. I tried to inhale the sea air and couldn't catch a decent breath. My breathing was shallow. My lungs felt heavy. Then, I couldn't breathe. I couldn't breathe at all.

Marvin was alarmed. The kids were crying. Marvin tried to lay me on my back. I fought him to sit back up. Marvin left me with the kids to search for a doctor on board. He became frantic when he returned and found my lips blue and me pale as a ghost. The pressure on my chest was unbearable. I just knew I was having a heart attack. All I could think was that this is what my children and Marvin would remember of me—dying on a boat. I realized that I was not invincible, not immortal and that having used drugs for most of my life they were going to kill me.

Marvin began slapping me on the back. He held me. He screamed at me to breathe.

The English Channel was treacherous. The air was frigid. I felt like I was in a block of ice. I was finally carried into a warm, enclosed area. Marvin and the crewman pounded on my back. It worked, with great effort, I could get air into my lungs.

Marvin, Nona, and Frankie started massaging my back, legs, and arms to get my circulation going. It was the longest boat ride of our lives. Their love and fear of losing me kept me alive that night. Did I learn my lesson? Not really. I gave up temple balls but like most addicts, I thought I could just do other drugs and I'd be fine. I continued using cocaine and smoking European cigarettes. Did I see a doctor? No. I was still in denial. I felt grateful to be alive but not grateful enough to stop knowingly using poison. We were relieved to get off the ferry in Dover. We drove to London and Marvin immediately put me to bed. We all slept in the same bed that night.

When I made arrangements to return home with the kids, Marvin did not protest. Cousaert and CBS were pressuring him to complete his album, long overdue. He realized that his family had become a distraction.

"This marriage," he told me, "is the biggest distraction of all."

"So we'll end it," I said. "I'll file the minute I get home."

"You'll have no money."

"You'll have no peace until you find money to feed your children."

"Get money from Rick James. Or, better yet, ask your mother to let you turn some of her tricks. Share in the wealth."

"Is that what you really want to say?"

"Yes, because that's who you and your mother really are."

The flight home was long and sad. The children were more confused than ever.

"Why aren't we gonna be living with Daddy in Europe?" asked Nona. "I thought we were all gonna live together."

"You'll be back to visit him," I assured her. "Daddy loves you. He hates being far away from you, but he has to work."

Back home, I realized that I had to do what I had long avoided: I had to initiate the arduous legal process of divorcing the man who, despite everything, haunted me day and night.

Despite the haunting, despite the fog of confusion caused by a combination of too many highs and too many lows—drugs followed by depression leading to more drugs to relieve the depression—I did what I had to do.

Divorce was inevitable. I couldn't help but think of *Here, My Dear*, the epic album dramatizing the collapse of his marriage to Anna. That album was barely in the stores for a year when my marriage to Marvin was crumbling. As early as 1979, I had decided to serve Marvin divorce papers when he was in bankruptcy court. But his financial woes had so devastated him that I couldn't add on to his misery. He thanked me for backing off. "Now I know how much you really love me," he had said.

Then we reconciled for a short while but soon were back at it. My mother kept insisting that I move forward with the legalities. She was right when she said that I wasn't being fair to my children or myself.

"You're killing yourself, Jan," she said. "You need to make a clean break."

In January 1982, I finally filed the papers. Marvin failed to show at the custody hearings. He didn't even bother to send a lawyer, but that didn't stop the judge from granting Marvin custody. When he said that, I thought I was having a heart attack. My lawyer quickly responded, telling the judge that, given Marvin's crazed lifestyle, he was incapable of caring for these children. The mother was present and ready to assume responsibility. After some legal wrangling, the judge rescinded and granted me full custody.

When Marvin found out, he accused me of doing what Anna had done—denying him access to his children and looking to destroy his life.

By the spring of 1982, Marvin and I were finally divorced. I viewed the decree with deep sadness. How could I view our relationship as anything other than an abysmal failure?

At this point, living in Ostend and preoccupied with completing his album, Marvin didn't bother to contest. He also didn't bother—or was unable—to pay the court-ordered child-support payments. Between the millions he owed the IRS and the complications of his old obligations to Motown and his new obligations to CBS, he was still insolvent. The kids and I received nothing.

Even Marvin's parents, who had never been supportive of me, expressed sympathy by sending me a few hundred dollars. From time to time my daddy Earl helped out. My father Slim was nowhere to be found. My mother Barbara provided shelter and help with the children. The house on the strand at Hermosa Beach remained headquarters.

The fact that Marvin and I were divorced was neither surprising nor shocking. It had been long in coming and, for at least a short while, provided some relief. The struggle to stop struggling was finally over. The trip to Europe proved that, no matter how much Marvin might have longed for reconciliation, reconciliation was never going to happen. Our shared history was too dark, the pain of the past too much. And yet in spite of the court's final decree, the relationship between Marvin and me was far from final. Beyond the bond of sharing children, we shared a unique and permanent knowledge of each other. Marvin knew my heart. I knew Marvin's soul. No legal document could or ever would alter that understanding.

"Marvin is having a hard time over there," I told Rick James.

We were having dinner in Beverly Hills. Seeing Rick, a loyal friend, always lifted my spirits. Free of romantic entanglements, our relationship comforted us both.

"How do you know he's having a hard time?" asked Rick.

"He called last night."

"What! After everything that went down, after all the messes that y'all made, he's still calling you?"

"Yes."

"I don't get it."

"After the divorce, I knew he'd keep calling the kids," I said, "but I didn't think he'd want to talk to me. And I didn't think that I'd want to hear his voice. But that didn't last for long. He knows that I know what he's going through and how he's suffering."

"Suffering about what?" asked Rick. "CBS is letting him make whatever record he wants to make."

"That's the problem. He isn't sure what kind of record to make. He's still crying for the planet. He takes his role as an artist seriously, Rick. You've heard him say that."

"What he needs to see right now," said Rick, "is money. Money for you and the kids."

"He's always cared more about art than money."

"Please, Jan, you're defending a man who's treating you like shit."

"Believe me, I've treated him like shit—more times that I can count. Look, I'm not defending Marvin. I'm just saying that when it comes to making music, he suffers. He really wants his music to have the right effect."

"Like all of us, he wants a hit."

"I know," I said, "but he wants a hit that means something and says something."

"Look, baby, Marvin is a flat-out genius. He'll find the fuckin' hit, and I have no doubt that it'll say something. Meanwhile, though, you gotta take care of yourself. We both gotta cut back on all this fuckin' blow and shit and get ourselves straight."

"I want to," I said.

"We need to," said Rick.

Yet the need was overwhelmed by the compulsion. Like with Marvin in Belgium, we'd attempt to get clean only to see it last little more than a few hours or a few days.

The word from Belgium was that, after over a year of experimenting with different melodic and lyrical motifs, Marvin had finally hit upon a song he liked. Despite the divorce filing, we were still speaking. And when Marvin called to play me an early version over the phone, I was struck by the title, "Sexual Healing." The music brought me joy and its message brought me hope.

"You like it?" he asked.

"Yes," I said, flattered that he was asking my opinion. "I love it. I think it's a hit, it's a smash!" I was genuinely happy for him.

"You think my fans will dig it?"

"They'll love it."

"But will they understand it?"

"*I* understand it," I said. "Yes, they'll understand it. I love the title. I love it when you sing, 'Sexual healing is something that's good for me.'"

"You know that I'm singing to you, dear. The song's about *our* healing. I know that we can . . ."

"Don't get started. We can't go down that road again. We've lied to ourselves too much in the past. It's not good for us. And it only hurts the kids."

"It hurts me, Jan, if you don't hear what I'm trying to say in these songs. CBS wanted a party record. They didn't want any of my personal shit. So I gave them a party record. But if you listen closely, baby, you know I'm talking to you. I call this one tune 'Rockin' after Midnight.' It seems like it's about sex, and it is, but I say what I mean. I say, 'I'm gonna be in love with you for the rest of my days.' In another one, 'Turn on Some Music,' I sing about how I still dream of you every night, how I've missed you with all my heart, and how I have to have you back. 'Third World Girl' is Jamaica. I'm thinking about Bob Marley, but I'm also thinking of our times there. You were pregnant. If you listen to 'Joy,' Jan, you'll hear me say that there's joy in a sweet word, there's joy in a dream come true, and there's joy in every thought I have of you."

The more Marvin insisted that I was still serving as his muse, the more compelling the music he played, the more my resistance started to melt again.

"I'm calling the record *Midnight Love*," he said, "because midnight is when I'm feeling that love. In 'Sexual Healing,' midnight is when I'm on the phone, like I am now, calling you in Los Angeles, so far away.

"It's taken me a long time to record the last song," he continued, "but I found the right one. 'My Love Is Waiting' is about us getting together again. It looks back at what I've been doing since I got to Belgium and began this whole recording process. And what have I been doing, Jan? I've been praying. I've been staying in faith. The song says how I've been making plans to get back to you. I'm saying how I missed you. Listen to what I'm singing . . ."

Marvin put on the rough mix of the music. He was singing about how it'd been so long since we'd been together, but now he was going to make up for it. Now he was going to make our love fresh and new.

Over the transatlantic line, the message came through loud and clear. I was moved, my resistance shattered. Marvin's music always had my heart believing what my mind would not accept: that his heart was pure. I was in tears.

"It sounds beautiful, Marvin. It always sounds beautiful. But what about the bitch?" I asked, referring to Eugenie.

"She was nothing but a toy," he claimed.

"I know how it feels to be used and abused."

"We abused each other," Marvin admitted.

"You and I, or you and your girlfriend over there?"

"She is not the other mother of my children. She is not the love of my life. She does not, as an English poet once wrote, 'haunt my days and chill my dreaming nights.' You are the one, Jan, doing the haunting and chilling."

"Who is the poet?" I asked.

"John Keats. I learned about him when I was living in England. Some critics think he wrote it to a woman who had rejected him, as you have rejected me. Our divorce is killing me."

"The divorce was something we mutually agreed upon," I said.

"I never wanted it, Jan. You know that. All I want is you. All Keats wanted was this woman. But he was dying. He only had a year or two left to live."

"You're not dying, Marvin," I said. "Your new songs don't give me the impression of a dying man. It's a man who's looking for healing."

"A man," added Marvin, "who's looking for his family—and for the woman who makes sense of everything . . ."

"The woman who makes him crazy, and makes herself crazy in the process."

"Love is always crazy," said Marvin. "Love never makes sense. But this new record does make sense, Jan. You can hear it in the songs, and the songs are all about us. *We* make sense. You and Nona and Bubs and I together all make sense. I want you to come back and bring the children. We can live in Europe—away from all the distractions. They can go to school here. We can be happy here. It's what I want. It's what you want. In working on this record, I realize it's what I've been working for. You have led me to the music, and the music must lead you back to me. Listen to the music and you'll understand. Listen to the music, Jan, and you'll know what to do. The music never lies. Our healing is in the music."

"Isn't It Funny
How Things Turn Around?"

It was the late summer of 1982. I was living at the Brussels
Hilton with the kids. During the day the children were attending
school. Marvin was spending much of his time making the final
tweaks on the album. Its first single, "Sexual Healing," was about to
be released worldwide.

Things were rapidly changing. For all my equivocation, I had
returned to Europe. Marvin prevailed, just as Marvin always prevailed. The sincerity in his music, the sincerity in his promises, the
sweetness in his demeanor—there were so many positive forces conspiring to convince me that this time it was different. This time there
was a new album with songs about joy, a record that came as a result
of Marvin's recovery, his absolute determination to put the dark time
in London behind him. He spoke about repentance and redemption.
He spoke about living in Europe permanently and, despite the final-
ity of the divorce, he wanted us to be part of his life.

Back in America, family and friends warned me, just as they

had warned me before: Marvin had made and broken these promises time and time again. Yet even they couldn't deny that something
had changed. For the first time in years, reporters visiting Marvin
in Europe were returning with stories of his remarkable restoration.
They were writing about his robust health, forward-looking attitude,
and powerful new music.

"On one level, it's a party record," Marvin told a reporter. "It's
a record you can dance to and even freak to. But if you listen closely
and go beneath your surface, you'll hear my heart speaking. You'll
hear my heart saying, 'It's time to put the madness behind and let
love lead the way.' You'll hear me testify that I still believe in Jesus,
I still believe in God's miraculous grace, I still believe that the Lord
forgives even when—and especially when—we cannot forgive ourselves."

I was trusting that Marvin's sentiments were genuine. From
both his public and private statements, I was feeling his resolve. The
children wanted to see their dad. The children wanted to see their
mother and father together. For all that had happened before, I was
predisposed to accept Marvin's attitude. He was contrite. As the
author of a new suite of songs, he once again cited me as his primary
muse. No wonder I was drawn back to the center of his world.

Once I arrived in Europe, I saw that world was changing. In
terms of Marvin's management, there had been a profound power
shift. During the course of making *Midnight Love*, Marvin had
grown insecure and called for Harvey Fuqua, one of his original
mentors. Marvin had come out of Fuqua's Moonglows in the fifties.
It was Harvey who had brought Marvin to Motown in the early sixties. Marvin had long looked at Fuqua as a benevolent father figure,
an experienced writer-producer who understood the nuances of the
studio.

Marvin's close bond to Harvey threatened Freddy Cousaert.
Fuqua quickly replaced Cousaert as Marvin's main man. Making
matters worse for Freddy, Harvey had arrived with his girlfriend,

Marilyn Freeman, who began to function as Marvin's manager. Freddy saw the handwriting on the wall. He feared that his days were numbered.

That's why Freddy worked so diligently to keep Marvin in Europe. In Belgium, Germany, and the Netherlands, where Marvin had worked on *Midnight Love*, Cousaert was on home turf. He knew the languages. Here he operated from a position of strength. I heard him argue loud and long for Marvin's permanent residence in Ostend. At one point, Cousaert convinced Marvin to make a down payment on a comfortable country home just outside the city limits.

"To go back to America," Cousaert contended, "is to lose everything you've gained here. The pressures there are too much to bear."

"The money is in America," Fuqua counterargued. "Your fans are in America. We've cut a hit album, and the only way to really cash in is to work it at home. That means media interviews, touring—the whole bit."

Marvin's siblings took Harvey's side. They wanted their brother back in America. They wanted him to put his show back together and take it on the road. They wanted to be in his show. They needed money. Marvin living on another continent had not bettered their lives.

The CBS executives also wanted Marvin back in the USA. Publicity-wise, it would be far more effective to launch the record from America. The pressure on Marvin was intense.

"I want to stay in Europe," he told me one night at the Brussels Hilton after we had slept together.

"The kids and I want to stay with you," I said.

"I want you to," said Marvin, all smiles. "I need you to. Isn't it funny how things turn around? We needed to get this divorce out of the way so we could find each other again."

These were the words I wanted to hear, confirmation of his commitment to finally doing the right thing.

Midnight Love was the name of the new album, and the midnight talks between us revealed the extent of his equivocation. He wanted to stay in Europe. He wanted to maintain a distance between his present and his past. But he wanted a comeback hit. He suffered with indecision about whether to follow his instincts and live a quiet life in Belgium or put all his efforts behind the release of the new record.

"I've decided to definitely stay," he finally declared one afternoon. Marvin and I, along with the kids and the management team, were traveling through the Netherlands, where Cousaert had arranged interviews for Marvin to introduce the album to the northern European market. Afterward, we planned to travel to Paris, Rome, and London before returning to Ostend. Marvin's plan to remain abroad, enthusiastically supported by Cousaert, gave him a measure of peace.

Riding around Rotterdam, everyone was happy—even thrilled—when "Sexual Healing" came on the radio while we were passing through, of all places, the red light district.

"It's going all over the world," Marvin predicted. "It's touching people's hearts—and touching people in other places."

We laughed. It was a moment of healing and happiness.

Yet the ending of his final European foray was neither healing nor happy. I learned that Eugenie was also in Rotterdam, claiming it was Marvin who had called for her. Marvin denied this. But he did not deny her access to his suite.

This was just another version of the same scenario I had seen a dozen times before. Marvin not only created a dangerous form of domestic drama, he thrived on it. He liked hearing me and the other woman call each other names, just as he liked the vicious competition that he had fostered between Fuqua and Cousaert.

In a haze of highs, Marvin and I were back at it, bickering, blaming, and bemoaning the fact that we had even tried to revise a relationship mired in such deep vitriol.

Then came dire news from Los Angeles: Marvin's mother had

been diagnosed with bone cancer and required a risky surgery. It would happen in a matter of days.

"Marvin is petrified," I told my mother when I called her to say that we would all be flying back to LA from Rotterdam the very next day. "I've never seen Marvin so frightened. He's afraid he'll never see Alberta alive again. He's traumatized. It breaks my heart to see him like this."

Just like that, all European plans were scrubbed. Harvey Fuqua was emboldened. Cousaert saw that he was defeated. Knowing Marvin as he did, Freddy realized that once Marvin landed in a place—as he had landed in Hawaii and London and Ostend—he remained there for a very long time. The chances of Marvin returning to Belgium were remote.

At Rotterdam the Hague Airport, Marvin, the kids, Harvey Fuqua, Marilyn Freeman, and I boarded the plane, leaving Cousaert behind. Marvin's great European adventure came to a tumultuous conclusion. To calm his fear of flying, Marvin drank heavily as the plane winged its way across the Atlantic. I watched him fall into an uneasy sleep. I also glanced at Marilyn, another manager who thought she could control Marvin. I thought, *Lady, you need to go away; you don't stand a chance.*

Frankie and Nona were also sleeping, but I stayed awake. I studied the sweet faces of our children. I studied the sweet face of my former husband. Each face projected an angelic aura. I loved each of them with all my heart. I thought about the future.

What would happen to Marvin when he returned home?

What would happen to him if his mother did not survive?

In the aftermath of still another collapse of our romantic connection, what would happen to Marvin and me?

Could I live without him?

Could I live with him?

Hours went by. The drone of the jet engines kept me awake. The unanswerable questions kept coming, kept haunting me.

The plane landed with a thud.

Our weary group walked through the airport to customs. The bags were retrieved and the vans pulled up to the curb. Before Marvin got into his vehicle, he kissed the kids and turned to me.

"Pray for Mother," he said.

"You know I will," I promised.

"Now that I'm back, I don't know what will happen."

"I don't either."

"Are you afraid, dear?"

"Yes," I answered honestly.

"I am too," he said. "I'm very afraid."

The Beginning of the End

A warm winter in Los Angeles.

Months had passed—months during which both Marvin and I had tried and failed and tried again to reconcile the irreconcilable.

It broke my heart when, instead of me, he asked Anna to accompany him to the shooting of the "Sexual Healing" video. I didn't expect to be invited, but neither did I envision any kind of reconciliation between Marvin and his first wife.

I was back in Hermosa with the kids and my mom. Marvin was living between the apartment of his manager Marilyn Freeman, the apartment of his sister Zeola, and the Mid-City Gramercy Place home he had bought for his parents. His mother's operation proved successful. She was recovering nicely. During this period of her operation and aftercare, her husband was in Washington, DC, while her children helped her through her recovery.

It was January 1983 when Marvin called me with alarming news.

"Father has moved back to the house," he said.

"Why would be leave DC?" I asked.

"And where was he when Mother needed him by her side?" asked Marvin.

"Did you ask him?'

"No," said Marvin. "The less I say to him, the less I see him, the better. The fact is, I don't want him back. I don't want him living in the house."

"Have Mother keep him out."

"She won't. I tried to convince her. Tried to show her that he doesn't give a damn about her. But she keeps saying she's the only one who understands him."

"I think she's afraid of him."

"Maybe to a point. She's a good Christian woman. She's quick to forgive."

"And that's a good thing," I said.

"Not when the man is unworthy of forgiveness."

I didn't disagree. The mere thought of Marvin's father made me cringe.

"I want nothing to do with him," Marvin asserted. "I don't want to see him. I don't want to go over there."

"Then don't. Have Mother come to you."

"I'm trying. I've been trying for years to get her to leave him once and for all. I'll not stop trying. Just like I'll never stop trying to make it work for us."

I sighed. It was hard for me to hear this. Hard for me not to buy in to his sentiment. Especially since I shared that sentiment. And yet history and reason argued otherwise. History and reason said that now, ten years after we'd first met, Marvin and I would not and could not find a way to work through the past issues. The pain was too great. We were both too willing to escape that pain, both too dependent on mind-bending drugs that blurred our vision and blinded us from clarity.

We were both overwhelmed with financial fears. I had a hell of a time getting money out of Marvin for basic essentials for me and the kids; Marvin still had the IRS at his throat and had been forced to agree to a long spring and summer tour. Promoter Don Jo Medlevine promised to help with the IRS if Marvin allowed him to book his tour. But a tour excited Marvin's worst fears—fears of performing, fears of flying, fears of facing fans who he felt had lost their love for him.

The freebase pipe numbed Marvin's fear. He agreed to tour.

The freebase pipe destroyed my judgment. I convinced myself that somehow Marvin would care for me and the children. I felt he spoke the truth when he came to Hermosa with words of apology and regret.

In the moment when he spoke those words, when he said, "I love you, Jan, I'll always love you, I love my children more than life itself," he meant it.

But then he was gone, drawn back to the madness of the Hollywood scene he swore he would avoid, drawn back into the life of mayhem. Yet in that life, he was viewed as a conquering hero. Endless articles trumpeted his comeback. "Sexual Healing" was an international hit, one of the biggest of his career. *Midnight Love* was being called a masterpiece.

"To be adored is not good for me," he told me. "It injures my spirit. They are welcoming me as a sex god, but snorting and smoking this shit is killing me. If only they knew . . ."

"They don't love you for your sex," I argued. "They love you for your soul."

He gave me a funny expression.

"Well, maybe some do care about the sex . . ." I said.

We both laughed. But the humor didn't last. Marvin's eyes narrowed and, out of nowhere, he turned paranoid.

"There are plots against me," he said. "I know they exist. I know they involve your mother and dad. Your people want to see me dead."

"No one wants to see you dead."

"I need rest. I need prayer. I need you to tell me that you won't hurt me."

"Never. Not for a moment, Marvin. I've tried to stop loving you, but I can't."

"That's comforting to hear. My heart believes you, but my mind does not."

"Don't listen to your mind."

"I can't listen to you anymore, Jan. I have to run."

Marvin came to Hermosa Beach to see the kids. He took us for a ride in his car and said he wanted to play us a song he'd been working on. He was calling it "Sanctified Pussy." I didn't want to hear it. I didn't want the kids to hear it. I told him that if he put it on, I was taking the children and getting out of the car. He backed off but started driving erratically, frightening Nona and Bubs. When he finally calmed down, he said, "I'm singing at the NBA All-Star Game tomorrow night at the Forum."

"Great."

"Not so great. I said yes, but now I'm saying no. I'm not ready. I don't want to do it."

"You will be great," I assured him.

"I've worked up a funky rendition of the national anthem that will be special, but I'm in no shape to perform. I'm backing out."

"I wish you wouldn't."

"I'm asking Luther Vandross to sing it for me."

When Luther refused, Marvin changed his mind again and turned up at the game. As I predicted, his performance was flawless. He suavely and soulfully resculpted "The Star Spangled Banner" in a manner that was distinctly Marvin. I was proud of him. There was controversy about the liberties he had taken with the rhythm and melody—he sang the song as a gospel blues—but his version would not soon be forgotten and would eventually be considered a classic.

Ten days later, Marvin was also saying that he would skip the Grammys—he had been nominated for "Sexual Healing"—because he was certain that the forces conspiring against him would deny his victory.

"They want me to sing 'Sexual Healing,' but why should I do anything for the Grammys? They didn't give me a Grammy for 'Heard It Through the Grapevine,'" he told me. "Didn't get one for 'What's Going On.' Didn't get one for 'Let's Get It On' or 'I Want You.' I've been turning out records for over twenty years and still haven't gotten one of those little statues. Why should I believe it's gonna be any different this time?"

"Because it *is* different," I said. "This is your time."

"I'm not sure about that."

"I am. Besides, Pie and Bubby want to go to the Grammys. You owe it to your kids to take them."

"And let them watch me lose?"

"In their eyes, you're a winner. To us you'll always be a winner."

At the last minute, Marvin did get it together and took his children to the Grammys. I was not invited and didn't expect to be. We were in the middle of another nasty fight.

I watched the ceremony on television. Despite Marvin's misgivings about his live performances, he sang "Sexual Healing" superbly. Not long afterward, it was time to announce the winner for Best Male Vocal Performance, Rhythm and Blues. The presenters were Grace Jones and Rick James. Marvin had not believed my explanation that Rick and I had remained close friends and nothing more. He spoke of Rick with contempt. I wondered what would happen if Marvin won and was called to the podium.

When he did win, I was ecstatic but also apprehensive about this televised meeting between Marvin and Rick. All I could think was, *Holy shit!*

As it turned out, the men exhibited nothing but love. Rick was charming. Marvin was charming. They greeted each other like old friends. Marvin spoke briefly about how long he'd been waiting "for an award such as this." He waved to Nona and Frankie, who were shown on television. I wept with joy.

Later Rick told me the words that Marvin whispered in his ear: "Take care of her."

A month later, it was the same song and dance.

"They want me to appear on this TV special, *Motown 25*," said Marvin, "celebrating a label I left two years ago. Why should I?"

"Because you're one of the most important Motown artists," I said.

"But I don't want to sing my old stuff. I want to move on to the new."

"Then why don't you?"

"They're saying it's a look back at past achievements. It's really a tribute to Berry."

"Oh, boy. Can you do that?" I asked.

"I'm not sure. Motown released *In Our Lifetime?* without my permission. That was unforgiveable. On the other hand, Berry was the man who signed me. I hate to say it, but without Berry—and Anna—who knows what kind of career I'd have."

"Then express your appreciation by singing a song. Sing 'What's Going On.' Most people think that's the best song in the history of Motown. It'd be beautiful to hear you sing it again on national television."

"If I do agree, Berry is going to have to ask me personally."

"I'm sure he will."

He did. And Marvin accepted. His seamless performance of "What's Going On" would have been the evening's highlight had it not been for Michael Jackson. Michael had agreed to sing a medley of old hits with his brothers, but insisted on also singing his current smash from *Thriller. Motown 25* was the night Michael sang "Billie Jean" and, for the first time, performed the moonwalk. Like the Beatles' appearance on *The Ed Sullivan Show* two decades earlier, Michael's rendition of "Billie Jean" became one of the most electric moments in the history of American television.

Afterward, Marvin was crushed.

"Berry let Michael have his way," Marvin told me. "And Michael killed. He couldn't have been better. But if he got to sing his current material, why couldn't I? Why did I cave? Why did I let Motown dictate to me? They've made a fool of me."

"You were wonderful," I assured him. "You've never done 'What's Going On' better. Everyone adored you."

"No one will remember my performance. All that will be remembered from that night is Michael's singing, Michael's dancing. Michael is about to become the biggest star in the world."

"Your star is just fine, Grammy winner," I said. "Your tour is going to blow up your new album even bigger."

"The tour will drive me mad."

"If that's true, then don't go."

"And who will pay the bills? Who will keep the IRS from throwing me in prison? Who will feed my mother and my children?"

"There are ways to earn money without killing yourself with a five-month tour."

"Please, Jan. Don't pretend you care about my welfare."

"I do. You know I do."

"All I know is that I love you," he said. "But what I don't know is whether the love you have for me is still there."

"It is. It will always be."

"Promise me."

"I do."

"In spite of everything."

"Yes, in spite of everything."

"And if I need you to come on this tour to ease my mind, you'll come?" he asked.

"I will."

"And if I tell you that I need your presence, body, and soul, you won't resist?"

"I won't," I said. "I can't."

The End

I wish this had been not the ending but the beginning—the beginning of Marvin's recovery and rehabilitation; the beginning of his return to sanity, his family, and the God whom he deeply loved; the beginning of a new stage in which he finally learned to harmonize his personal life as beautifully as he harmonized his music; the beginning of renewed beauty, renewed strength, renewed hope.

Yet in April 1983, exactly a year after the composition of "Sexual Healing"—an anthem of hope—hope was hard to come by.

Before Marvin left to go on tour, he drove down to Hermosa to tell me and our kids good-bye. He did not look well.

"I know the tour is a mistake," he said, "but it's a mistake that's already been made."

"You can postpone it until you feel better about it," I said, "until you build up your strength."

"God is my strength. God will not abandon me."

"I know that. I'm glad you're talking about God."

"I know God led me to you, Jan, but the devil led me away. The devil also got into you. But if we pray, if we believe, God will prevail."

"I want to believe that."

"You need to believe that," he said.

"I want you to come along. I want us to be a family."

For thirty minutes we were a family. For thirty minutes there was a sense of calm. We went to the park. We sang songs. We made jokes. We treated each other with patience and love.

Before he left, he invited me out to his car.

"We shouldn't," he said, "but I know you want to. I want to as well. This stuff is primo."

He offered me a vial. I accepted.

"At least we aren't smoking it," he said.

But by evening time we were doing just that.

"Think of it as the peace pipe," said Marvin.

After the high hit, there was peace.

The tour started in San Diego, snaked up the coast to San Carlos, and then turned eastward to Baton Rouge. Houston, Mobile, Atlanta, New Orleans, Dallas, Shreveport—city after city, night after night, the *Midnight Love* tour took its toll on Marvin's frayed nerves.

Alarming reports came back to me. Crazy phone calls.

Marvin was in a perpetual state of fear. Afraid of flying. Afraid of performing. Afraid of facing less-than-capacity crowds. The fact that there were a number of sell-outs did not calm his fears.

"Remember what I told you," he said when he called back to California. " 'A perfect love casts out all fear.' That's scripture. I have a preacher traveling with me who's administering prayer night and day. Only prayer can protect me."

"Protect you from what?"

"You know better than I do, Jan. Long ago you conspired with my enemies. You slept with my enemies. You inspired them to seek my ruin. I can no longer speak with you. Just put the children on the line."

A week later I learned that, although Marvin had employed a clergyman to accompany him, drug dealers were also part of the entourage. Marvin had a three-bedroom hotel suite: he was in one room, the preacher in another, and the drug dealer in the third. Marvin was running between rooms, repentant one moment, sky-high the next.

Reports from the road grew more alarming.

At the finale of the show, Marvin would come out in a robe to perform "Sexual Healing." At some point he'd disrobe, covered only by black briefs.

"I expose myself because the fans demand it," he told me in New York, where I'd arrived to see him play Radio City Music Hall. "I offer myself up for slaughter. I am the sacrificial lamb. If their pleasure requires my destruction, so be it."

"You don't need to do that," I said. "You don't need to strip. You have a beautiful body, but it isn't about your body. It's about your voice, Marvin. Your fans love you because of your voice and the soul it expresses."

"You speak in platitudes, dear, not in truth. The truth is that you have a vested interest in my destruction. And not only you. You and your dad Earl. There are others out here who are plotting. I've caught wind of those plots and have been forced to employ extreme security measures."

Those measures included hiring his friend Dave Simmons as well as his brother Frankie to walk with him through the airports, hotels, and concert venues. Because both men resembled Marvin, Marvin felt that a potential assassin—and he was seeing assassins everywhere—would be unable to identify the real Marvin and consequently hold fire.

"There's no one who wants to harm you," I said. "You're not thinking right."

"And you are?" asked Marvin. "Are you speaking out of sound reason? Can you really set me on the straight and narrow? Have you really put down the pipe?"

I had no answer. Although my level of paranoia was nowhere near Marvin's, I had not put down the pipe.

It was at Radio City when Columbia Records label head Walter Yetnikoff, a man Marvin liked enormously, came backstage before the show and got blasted with Marvin on coke. High as a kite, Walter put on Marvin's red sequined stage jacket and went wandering off. When it was time to perform, Marvin had to find another jacket.

After the show, Jesse Jackson and Al Sharpton met with Marvin and pressed their case that he should be using a black promoter. Marvin argued that he often did just that, but on this tour he was using Don Jo Medlevine, who had been a longtime loyal supporter, especially during the dark days of Marvin's tax problems. Despite the sharp protests coming from Jackson and Sharpton, Marvin held his ground.

My New York trip was reasonably calm. Maybe that's the reason I agreed to join Marvin again on the road, this time in Miami. Big mistake.

I traveled there with my drug dealer and his wife.

When I arrived, Marvin looked dreadful. His eyes were bloodshot, his nose was leaking. He seemed lost. An aura of madness surrounded us.

"You're fucking my bass player!" Marvin screamed the minute he saw me.

The accusation was unfounded.

"No, I'm not," I insisted.

"You've come here to torture me!" Marvin insisted.

"You're talking crazy!" I yelled.

That night I slept on his couch. Given Marvin's volatility, I was afraid.

The next morning I was able to escape to the room of my drug dealer and his wife. I got high. The high deepened my confusion. How could I cope with the insanity surrounding Marvin and the tour?

"He probably just smoked some bad shit," the dealer speculated. "Smoke some of this good shit and you'll feel better."

The good shit did make me feel better, and then worse, and then better again.

That night Marvin's bodyguards called me to say Marvin wanted to see me. I knew I shouldn't go there. For years I'd known that I had to get away. And yet I answered his call. I went to his room.

"I love you and I'll always love you," Marvin told me, "but you're fucking my bass player." Without warning, he threw a hot, steamy towel that hit me in the face.

"You're fucking up my life!" he screamed.

Then he took a pot of hot water and threw it at me. I moved out of the way, but his violence stunned me.

I ran from his room. Ran down a long exterior hallway that stretched the length of the motel. I was on a high floor. I was sure Marvin or his men would catch me and throw me over the side. I ran faster and faster until I reached the room of my drug dealer.

"Get me out of here before something happens," I said.

He gave me money to switch hotels.

The next morning I was on a plane heading to LA.

The next evening I was back in Hermosa Beach, where Mom was caring for the children.

I vacillated between sweet dreams where I was united with Marvin and nightmares in which he expressed murderous rage.

The dreams and nightmares were reflected in reality.

He called to say he was sorry.

He called to say that he knew I'd hired the Crips to murder him. When I called the accusation ridiculous, he hung up on me. I had never felt such frustration, such hopelessness. With all my heart I wanted to help Marvin, but I didn't know how.

In August the *Midnight Love* tour hobbled back to California. By the time Marvin played the Greek Theatre in LA, he was spent. His voice was gone. He was gaunt. He was so paranoid about assassins that he stationed bodyguards to stand on either side of the stage during his performance.

After months on the road, he was sick—sick of mind, body, and spirit. Marvin couldn't remain still. Because he felt chased, because he was increasingly uncomfortable in his own skin, he had to keep moving.

Dreams, nightmares, and reality collided. I couldn't tell one from the other.

In my dreams, Marvin and I were fully recovered, fully healthy. There were blue skies and puffy white clouds, fields of fragrant wildflowers, green rolling hills. In my nightmares, people around me were lost in the dark, dealing with death by fatal diseases or bullets to the head. In reality, I was struggling for sanity.

I feared that Marvin was losing his sanity. He had no real home, moving from his sister's apartment to Anna's home in the Hollywood Hills.

"I need to stay on the move," he said. "The devil's on my trail. The devil can't know my plan. No one can. I have a plan that will shock the world."

His plan was to record a follow-up to "Sexual Healing" with "Sanctified Pussy."

"Some say the song is beneath me," he explained. "And yes, there is humor implicit in the title. But it is no joke. To find a church girl, pure and innocent—as you were once innocent, Jan—"

"I was never innocent," I interrupted. "I lost my innocence when I was a child."

"When I met you—"

"When you met me, you imagined me to be someone I was not. When you met me, I had already been to hell and back. So had you. You forget those things."

"I remember everything," he said. "I remember too much. It's time to forget the past and turn back the hands of time. Time to meet that one woman, untainted and incorruptible—"

"Good luck on that journey," I said.

"I need a woman as flawless as my own mother."

"You'll never find that, Marvin. We only get one mother."

A week later, I was alarmed to learn that Marvin had gone to live with his mother. He had moved back to the rambling house on Gramercy Place.

His father was there, living in a second-floor bedroom next to Mother's bedroom. Down the hallway was the room where Marvin slept.

Back in his parents' home, Marvin grew more distant from reality. From what I heard, his paranoia grew alarmingly worse.

January 1984. February. March.

The winter came and went.

I knew that he couldn't forgive himself for his inability to stop freebasing. For the same reason, I couldn't forgive myself. I was disgusted with myself for staying on the pipe. He was disgusted with himself. He hated himself for turning away from God's path.

Because money from Marvin ceased long ago, I was living on very little. I borrowed money from ex-lovers, friends, and family. I got a job cleaning house for a lady who paid me half in cash and half in cocaine.

Given Marvin's state of mind, I couldn't ask for a thing. He needed help, but no one around him—not his siblings, not his friends, not his management team—was able to reach him.

At one point he jumped out of the backseat of a moving car. He just wanted the pain to stop.

I knew he was desperate. Everyone around Marvin knew. But everyone, including me, was trapped in our emotional prison.

I was told that there was a gun. Supposedly Marvin bought it months earlier and gave it to his father.

"You need to protect me," he told the man who had never protected him, the man who had tortured him. "They are after me. You must stop them. I am afraid."

"I've never seen Marvin so afraid," his brother Frankie told me. "He's afraid of everything and everyone. Everyone except Mother. He clings to Mother."

Mother was protection. But why had he appointed Father as his chief protector? Why had he handed a gun to Father? Or had he? Only God knows.

I was afraid to go over there. I stayed away. I didn't really know the full extent of the madness.

On April 1, April's Fools Day, the day before Marvin's forty-fifth birthday, Father was screaming at Mother, accusing her of misplacing an insurance form. From what I was told, Marvin took up the role of protector. He felt compelled to protect Mother against the man verbally assaulting her, the man he had assigned to protect him, the man with the gun.

He felt compelled to do more than simply assault the man verbally; he had to assault him physically. I don't know the severity of that assault, but I do know that Marvin harbored a lifetime of hatred for the man who had beat him unmercifully, as a boy.

I was home with the children when the calls started coming in. At first I didn't believe any of them, but there were too many to ignore. I wanted to rip the phone from the wall. I didn't want to hear the words. I wanted to run from the reality of what I was being told by a plainspoken detective:

It was true. Marvin Gaye was dead.

I dropped the phone and collapsed on the floor. When I picked myself up, I was still struggling to comprehend the incomprehensible.

Marvin had beaten his father.

His father had responded by fulfilling Marvin's darkest and deepest hope.

His father had taken the gun Marvin had given him and shot his son dead.

Marvin was set free from his human form.

His father had punished him one last time, showing no mercy.

Marvin had punished his father by, according to the teachings of his church, insuring his father's eternal damnation.

This was the last chapter of their poisonous story.

All these were ideas reeling through my brain. None of them made sense. All of them made sense. All I knew was that I was going to have to sit down with our children and tell them the most horrible thing they would ever hear.

"Daddy is gone."

The Beginning

I cannot tell you that Marvin's death led me to the realization that drugs were ruining my life and caused me to put them down. It did no such thing. The sad fact was that in the immediate aftermath of his death, I used drugs to block the pain, only delaying it and ultimately increasing my usage. Like a dark cloud, my drug addiction hung over me for a year after Marvin's passing. Finally, with the support of Rick James—who himself was plagued by a series of relapses—I ultimately did stop and am glad to report that for many decades I have lived a life free of the madness brought on by drugs.

In the years following his death, I went through every emotional phase known to man and woman. I was furious with Marvin for leaving us; for not being there to watch his children grow up; for missing the joy of his grandson.

Mostly, though, I was furious and angry with myself. I had fallen for Marvin. I had followed him. Even after following him proved to be a senseless thing to do, I kept exhibiting the same behavior.

How could I ever forgive myself for fucking up on such a massive scale?

For years I couldn't. For years I was driven by a bitterness fueled by rage. Marvin had abandoned us. I had abandoned myself. Marvin had manipulated and used me. I had manipulated and used him.

The more I thought about those eleven-plus years that we were together, the more potent my self-disgust.

And yet . . .

I put on a record. I close my eyes and listen to Marvin sing "What's Going On." I close my eyes and listen to Marvin sing "God Is Love" and "Save the Children." I close my eyes and listen to Marvin sing "Let's Get It On" and "I Want You." I close my eyes and listen to the sublime ballads from *Vulnerable*.

The softness, the sweetness, the engaging harmonies, the heart-healing soulfulness, the sound of a man in pain and joy and hurt and hope and love, the expression of someone who reflects divinity even as the weight of his human frailties brings him back to earth, back to my arms, back to my life, a life that he has never left and never will. A musical life of love.

It has taken me a long time to learn, but I know now that love is not diminished by the opposing emotions that accompany it. I'm talking about jealousy, insecurity, distrust, even hate. Those emotions pass, but love lasts. It lasts because it contains the one ingredient that ensures its everlasting endurance: compassion.

After the dance of our romance—after all the senseless crazy changes we went through—I've learned to feel more deeply for Marvin than ever before.

In that same poem that Marvin loved, "The Four Quartets," T. S. Eliot wrote:

> *We shall not cease from exploration*
> *And the end of all our exploring*

Will be to arrive where we started
And know the place for the first time.

The love I shared with Marvin was excruciatingly difficult and exceedingly easy. Yet in its difficulty was a gift: it has forced me to do a great deal of introspective work. "Work," wrote Kahlil Gibran in *The Prophet*, is "love made visible." Beyond helping me find compassion for Marvin, that work has led me to find compassion for myself. That I lost myself in someone else—someone as remarkable as Marvin Gaye—is no longer cause for self-condemnation. It is cause for sublime celebration.

I was who I was and I did what I did. In spite of my history, I have survived. Marvin's history, with all its brutal complexities, cut short his survival. He was who he was and he did what he did. I no longer have to judge him or judge myself. Compassion overwhelms judgment.

Night and day, Marvin's voice becalms our hearts and nourishes our souls. And so he lives inside me, he lives inside all of us, as a spirit of harmony, a soaring spirit that connects us to the power of inextinguishable love.

My children and I do our best to move forward. We strive to conduct ourselves with self-respect while honoring the great artistic legacy Marvin has left. Difficult as these past thirty years have been, we remain grateful for his presence in our lives. He is a gift.

Our gratitude is boundless—for all the challenges and strife, all the victories and harmony, for all we enjoyed, all we suffered, all we endured, all we lost, all we gained, all we learned, there is deep and abiding appreciation.

The final words are not "the end." The final words are . . .

THANK YOU.

Gratitude

To say that life has not been a serious and painful challenge in many ways since Marvin's death would be a tremendous understatement. I believe that he left me with enough life lessons and guidelines, though, to survive it all. For years after his death it was just us three . . . me and the kids . . . and now with my grandson we are four. I am amazed that I am now fifteen years older than Marvin will ever be. It's taken me thirty years to feel safe enough to tell my story. Doing so has brought joy, pain, fear, satisfaction, and a sense of freedom.

Marvin was my friend, my lover, my teacher, my mother, my father, my husband; the father to our two beautiful children and grandfather to my incredible grandson; my partner in crime, my advocate, my opponent, my conscience, and my subconscious. He made me laugh, cry, and brought me some of the most wonderful moments of my life. His spirit is so strong that I feel him every day. He walked me through many a long, dark hour after his death. I thank God for the time that he gave us together, good and bad, for without both I would have had none. We were hippies when we met, and I will remain that way.

Marvin was a prophet, who sang of issues decades ago that are sadly still relevant today. Frightening things that should inspire us to wake up, protect our planet, and "save our children." If he had lived, I believe he would be doing just that. "What's Going On" will forever represent the profound need for love, peace, awareness, understanding, and healing that we all need to survive the negative and deadly repercussions of our actions, which threaten to destroy us all. "Time to Get It Together" . . . now. I believe there is a part of him that is at peace. The physical. I believe his spirit is restless, and I believe many of us that knew him, and many who didn't, might agree and know the reasons why. "Someday we'll all be free. . . ."

To my family: My daughter, my sweet Nona Marvisa, who was born with her eyes open and who is a survivor. I am so proud to call her my girl. My son, gentle and generous, never hurtful and always loving, my baby boy, Frankie Christian aka Bubbie, who was born with a broken arm and a beautiful soul and named for his Uncle Frankie and his Uncle Mark. To my grandson, my heart. God blessed me with a thoughtful, funny, and wise one, Nolan Pentz Gaye. I only wish that he and his grandfather could have known each other in this life. My big brother, Mark, my protector; my nieces, Jennifer Elizabeth and Christina Suzanne, and their mom, sweet Mary; my loving younger brother Michael, my sister Felicia, and my nieces Tenesha, Tierra, and Liz; Earl 2, Gwen, Shannon, Brianna, and Robbie; Lynda, Janay, Janessa, Christian, and Pia; Jada and Alysia, Tamiko, and Tevin; William and Lori and the girls; Stephanie, Victoria, Sasha Marie, and clan; Angela and Cle, Celina; my sister Judy, who cared for me when I was unable, and her daughters, Christy and Denise, and their children; to my Asa and her children; to April, Frankie M., and Fiona; Barbara Brooks, Beatrice Willis, Wilson Gaillard, Andre, Mary P., Karen S'mylez, Bonnie Gay, and Mark Gay; and to Antwaun Gay, Marvin's baby brother and a true blessing to our family, and his amazing wife, Carolyn, the rock. I love you all.

Thank you to my friends, still here, old and new: Craig McKay, Dazz, Michelle LeClair, Karen Mandel, Kim Wilson, Deboragh, Rain, Richard Jr., and Elizabeth Stordeur-Pryor; Lem, Martha, Trece and Lem Barney, Laura Brown and her beautiful family, Leigh Blake and India, Earle Sebastian, Alia Rose, Penny and Melia, John

Altman, Ramon, Big Dad, Jon Nettlesbey, Faith N., Larry Fleming, the best babysitter; Ladybug, Nicholas Payton, Robin Harrison Stoker, Sheldon Scott, Preston Wilcox, Bill, Stacy, Cam and Nicole Snelson; Bill, Jonna, and Denim; Jonathan and Nathalie Stroum, the Saunders family, J. Kevin Swain, Angie Osborn, Woody J., Lynn Stuart, Stephen Ferrone, Azizi Johari, Mary Anderson, Patty Allison Fairweather, the Evans family, Mike Ladd, Miss Kitty, Lynne Bell and Maya; Gino and Gino, Harry W., Brian S., Ken C., Richard R., Diana and Elizabeth Z., Terri Walters and family, Jason Logan, Candice Ghant, Amy Rogers and Maddie, Princess Bomba and family, Rachel Goldstein, James W., Leon and Carol Ware, Melvin Ragin, Jabali Hicks, Eric Farrell, Satie Gossett and his beautiful family (thanks for the visit), Gordon Banks, Doni Hagan, Duane and Rashgene Gazi-White and Lola; Freda Mays, the ever fabulous Odell 'Gorgeous' George, Art and Dean Stewart, Richard L., Dominique Batt, Eric Johnson, Yvonne A., Joshua Evans, Barsheem Fowler and Tauros Essex, Gamel Moore and Miss Pat, the Estelle family, Megan, AlBabe, CC; and to Michael A. I love you all.

Many thanks to the incredibly talented musicians, arrangers, and producers who worked with Marvin throughout his career. The very best always.

Many, many thanks to John McClain for endlessly encouraging me to tell what he has always described as a "cautionary tale." He believed when I could not. To Regina Jones for her unending compassion and understanding and for her time and energy. She is an angel. When I grow up I want to be just like her. I am eternally grateful to David Vigliano, our agent, who never gave up on me. He has a staff that always made me as welcome as he did. He is so special and a beautiful and gentle human being. I thank my God and the universe for allowing David Ritz and I to reconcile our differences and to get down to the business of telling my story. I never thought that would happen. Thank you, Roberta, for sharing his talent.

Thank you to those at HarperCollins/Amistad: To Ms. Tracy

Sherrod and her soothing ways and calming voice and her team who tolerated my procrastination and fears.

To those who have cared for us emotionally and physically: Dr. Alan Gordon, Dr. Caron Zlotnick, Dr. David Carpentier, Dr. David Dove, and a very special thank you to Dr. Joshua Kane, who guided me to the right surgeon and hospital—Massachusetts General, whose staff and doctors kept me alive through my experience with breast cancer. I would not be writing this without him and them.

Rest in peace and love: To my mother, Barbara Frances Hunter, and my father, Bulee "Slim" Gaillard. To my dad, Earl Hunter, who raised me as his own. To Alberta Cooper Gay, a warm and loving mother and grandmother to many, and her sisters, Aunt Tolie May, Aunt Zeola, and Aunt Pearl. To Uncle Earl. To Marvin's brother and my son's namesake, Frankie Timothy, we miss you. To Uncle Micheal Cooper, silent and dear. To my older brother Michael and my sister Casonna; to my darlings, Barbara Stroum, who could always make me laugh, and Dianne Ogden-Halder, my sweet sister. To Edward Benjamin Townsend and David, his son; to Odell Brown. My love, Teena, words cannot express how you are missed. To RJ and TP, your families continue to honor you and your legacies. To MJ and Richard Pryor, simply the best. To Whitney, who helped my baby, and Andrew Brown and Marjorie "Mama" Fontenette, forever loved. Frances Miller and Mr. Errol Augustus, so dear. I miss you all deeply. We will meet again. . . . I love you all.

I thank my God for allowing me to have lived this incredible life. I give thanks every day. It has been the stuff of dreams, yet sometimes nightmares. I choose to focus on the dreams that came true thanks to Marvin. The beauty, the love, our children, and the music and the legacy that we hold dear and close to our hearts and souls. . . . I am thankful for all because therein lie the lessons I've learned. We never stop learning. We move forward. We do our best. We trip, we stumble, but we go on. We survive. PEACE.

Acknowledgments

Much love and many thanks to Jan, a strong and courageous woman; David Vigliano, Jonathan Burnham, Tracy Sherrod, and Laura Brown; my wife, Roberta, and my family—Alison, Jessica, Jim, Henry, Charlotte, Alden, James, and Isaac; and my ever-loyal friends Alan Eisenstock, Harry Weinger, Herb Powell, John Bryant, and John Tayloe.

—David Ritz

About the Author

Jan Gaye is the second wife of the legendary recording artist Marvin Gaye and the mother of his children, Nona and Frankie Gaye. Born in Los Angeles, she currently resides in Rhode Island.